Another Pair of Eyes

'No blind man, no matter how clever he is, can cover the ground with the ease and speed that I can, with Bella's help. Now do you see what I mean by saying that I have regained my freedom? The fact is I have another pair of eyes.'

(Alfred Morgan in *The "Tail-Wagger" Magazine* – June 1933)

ANOTHER PAIR OF EYES

The Story of Guide Dogs in Britain

PETER IRESON

Foreword by

HRH Princess Alexandra, the Hon. Lady Ogilvy, GCVO

PELHAM BOOKS

PELHAM BOOKS

Published by the Penguin Group
27 Wrights Lane, London W8 5TZ, England
Viking Penguin, a division of Penguin Books USA Inc
375 Hudson Street, New York, NY 10014, USA
Penguin Books Australia Ltd, Ringwood, Victoria, Australia
Penguin Books Canada Ltd, 2801 John Street, Markham, Ontario, Canada L3R 1B4
Penguin Books (NZ) Ltd, 182–190 Wairau Road, Auckland 10, New Zealand

Penguin Books Ltd, Registered Offices: Harmondsworth, Middlesex, England

First Published 1991
1 3 5 7 9 10 8 6 4 2

Typeset in Linotron 11/13 pt. Raleigh Medium by
Goodfellow and Egan Ltd, Cambridge

Printed and bound in Great Britain by Butler and Tanner, Frome, Somerset

A CIP catalogue record for this book is available from the British Library.

ISBN 0 7207 1920 8

The author and publishers are grateful to the estate of the late Norman Parkinson, OBE for permission to reproduce the portrait of HRH Princess Alexandra in this book.

Contents

Foreword

by HRH Princess Alexandra, the Hon. Lady Ogilvy, GCVO

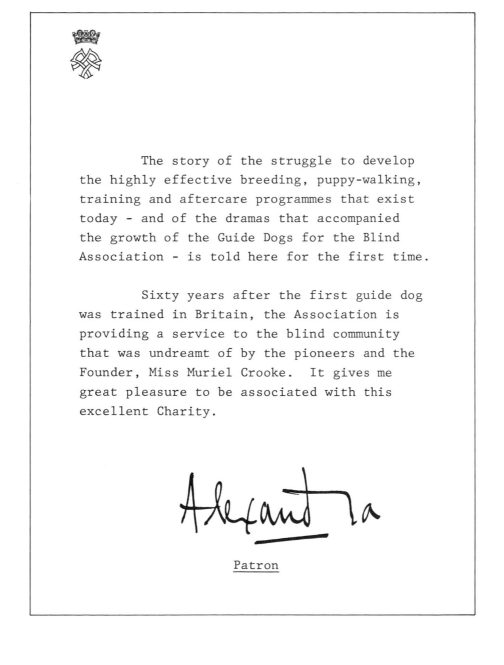

The story of the struggle to develop the highly effective breeding, puppy-walking, training and aftercare programmes that exist today - and of the dramas that accompanied the growth of the Guide Dogs for the Blind Association - is told here for the first time.

Sixty years after the first guide dog was trained in Britain, the Association is providing a service to the blind community that was undreamt of by the pioneers and the Founder, Miss Muriel Crooke. It gives me great pleasure to be associated with this excellent Charity.

Patron

Acknowledgements

It is not possible to name all the people to whom I am indebted for their help with this book, but my thanks go, firstly, to the many past and present staff of The Guide Dogs for the Blind Association who responded to my calls on their time with great generosity and patience. John Weeks, in particular, spent many hours talking to me and reading the manuscript.

I am grateful to the RNIB and St Dunstan's for allowing me access to their archives, which yielded important detail without which the chronicle would have suffered. The staff of both these charities were always willing to help and I thank them.

In the early research for the book I was helped for a period by Melanie Hallam. My assistant for most of the time, however, was Cheryl Laughlin, whose help has been invaluable. She not only managed the word processing with great skill, but also made a far greater contribution by her perceptive and detailed comments on the manuscript. For the very special part that she has played in the preparation of this book I am particularly grateful.

My thanks are also due to Richard Wilson for his wise counsel and for his great help in reading and commenting on the manuscript.

Finally, I should like to record my appreciation of the welcome given by the chairman and director general of The Guide Dogs for the Blind Association to a manuscript that did not gloss over the difficulties and setbacks that inevitably occurred among the Association's many achievements. Without that balance the book would not only have been less interesting, but it would have given a less credible picture of the Association's struggle to reach its present very high standard of service to the blind.

1

Leading the Way

$\mathbf{A}$ visitor to Nashville, Tennessee, in the early years of this century might have seen a blind man using one of the most astonishing techniques ever devised for crossing the road with the help of a guide dog. The man would stand at the kerb and send the dog across on its own, allowing a long leash that he held in his hand to unwind until his guide halted on the pavement opposite. After taking up any slack in the lead, so that he could feel anything that touched it, he would then set off himself for the other side.

This extraordinary scene was witnessed by Elliott S. Humphrey, who played a leading part in the development of rather more formal and reliable guide dog techniques in the 1920s and '30s. He also described other dogs that he had seen working with blind people, but the Nashville example was the only one in which they crossed the street unaided. In Basle, he saw a dog that took its owner to the kerb and waited until help came along. Another, in Paris, showed greater initiative and after reaching the kerb barked to attract attention.

According to Humphrey, all the dogs that he saw were reasonably skilful at avoiding obstacles and pedestrians on the pavement. They were safe within certain limits, outside of which the help of passers-by would be sought.

The blind man and his dog were familiar figures long before this century, of course, although one can only guess the extent to which the dogs were used as guides or how effective they were. Pictures invariably show the dog leading rather than walking to heel, suggesting that it was used as some sort of guide. A very early wall-painting of a blind man apparently being led by his dog was discovered during excavations at Pompeii, which was buried under ash and volcanic mud when Vesuvius erupted in 79AD. The Metropolitan Museum in New York possesses a 13th century Chinese scroll painting which shows a blind man being led

Medieval 'guide dog', from an unnamed manuscript. (Mary Evans Picture Library)

by a dog. Similar scenes occur more frequently from the 16th century onwards in woodcuts, engravings and paintings. Gainsborough (1727–1788) in his *Blind Man on the Bridge* shows a dog leading its master. William Bigg (1755–1828) depicts *The Blind Sailor* crossing a narrow wooden bridge with the help of his dog and Thomas Bewick (1753–1828) illustrates a comparable scene in one of his woodcuts.

Bewick confirms that the dog in his picture really is leading its master when he writes about 'some of the more common instances of this creature's sagacity . . . amongst these, its care in directing the steps of the blind man . . .' Other writers also leave little doubt that the blind man's dog was more than a companion. In Trollope's novel *Can You Forgive Her*, published in 1864, Lady Glencora tells the Duke of St Bungay that she will lead him 'as the little dogs lead the blind men'.

By the latter part of the 19th century the value of a dog as a guide for blind people was clearly well recognised because in 1878 exemption from the excise licence was granted by the British Parliament to 'shepherds' dogs and those kept by the blind as guides'.

The earliest surviving description of a systematic method of training guide dogs was published by Johann Wilhelm Klein in Vienna in 1819,

*The Blind Beggar of
Bethnal Green was the
story of a knight who
lost his sight in battle
and subsequently
became a beggar. His
friends gave him a dog
and a bell, and the dog
was 'trained to the
business and had
before been the
companion of an
eyeless beggar
deceased . . . he
trudged home with his
tractable guide, which
ever after proved
serviceable to him.'
The ballad was
published many times,
with different
illustrations, this one
appearing in the 1715
edition.* (Pat Hodgson
Library)

although a Viennese oculist, Georg Joseph Beer, refers, in a book published in 1813, to well-trained dogs that were used prior to 1780 by the blind of the 'Quinze-Vingts' hospital in Paris. In fact, they must have been in use by patients of the hospital some 30 years earlier, because they feature in a painting by Chardin which was hung in the Louvre in 1752.

There was also a blind Viennese journeyman sieve-maker, Joseph Reisinger, who at the end of the 18th century trained a spitz to guide him so well that he was suspected of simulating blindness. He subsequently trained two more dogs for himself, one of them being a poodle.

Klein, who was director of the Institute for the Blind in Vienna, believed that the poodle and the shepherd dog made the best guides and described a method of using them in which a stick attached to the dog's collar was held in the left hand.

'The rigid stick must run through a loose brace around the body of the dog, so that a side movement of the animal is fully felt in the hands of the blind person. The guiding stick is arranged with a crossbar in such a manner that it can easily be fastened to the collar of the dog; and it also has, near the top, a loop, so that the hand of the blind person will not easily lose its grip.

'This use of a guiding stick has the advantage that the blind person notices at once when the dog is standing still, which is not true when he is led by a strap.

'The training of the dogs, at least in the beginning, must be done by a sighted person. One leads him, many times, on the same road and drills him, particular attention being paid to places where through turning, through slow pace, through standing still, or through other movements which might be useful to the blind in situations such as the turning of the street and in the avoidance of obstacles that lie ahead – through all this the dog will be made alert to various kinds of dangerous situations.

'Then the blind person takes the dog in hand himself and goes with him, at first on the same road with which he is already acquainted, in order to become accustomed to the movements and signals of the animal.

Engraving by Thomas Bewick from A General History of Quadrupeds *(1790). In the chapter on dogs, Bewick says that among 'the more common instances of this creature's sagacity . . . its care in directing the steps of the blind man is not the least worthy of notice.'*(By permission of the British Library)

The Blind Sailor, *an engraving after the picture by William Bigg (1755–1828). Although he is accompanied by a dog, the man is clearly relying on a sighted guide to lead him across the narrow bridge – unlike the subject of Bewick's picture.* (Ann Ronan Picture Library)

'It is obvious that from now on the dog will be fed and cared for by the blind person himself, in order to arrive at a mutual understanding and to establish a true and faithful attachment with the leader dog.'

Klein's method would clearly have worked, but there is no evidence of the extent to which it was used, if at all. One of its interesting features was the use of a 'guiding stick', which, as he pointed out, gives a more positive signal to the blind person than a leash. A very similar arrangement was apparently in use in the United States in the early years of this century. Leon Whitney, an American vet and author of books on dogs, recalled

This engraving was published in 1813 in Das Auge (The Eye) by Georg Joseph Beer, a leading Viennese eye specialist. Beer obviously intended to draw attention to the figure in the foreground wearing spectacles, but the picture is also interesting for the blind man and his dog making their way through the crowd, apparently with great confidence.

seeing, as a child, three blind men who were led around the neighbourhood in which he lived by American fox terriers at the end of a cane. In
his view 'the small dog on a cane was far more effective than the large dog
at the side . . . Nobody tripped over the cane. Everyone saw the little white
dog.'

Like most of the dogs associated with the blind up to the early years of
this century, Whitney's fox terriers, which were also known as feists or
feices in some parts of the United States, were small animals. When the
systematic training of guide dogs on a large scale started at the end of the
First World War bigger dogs were used, but the choice then must have
been influenced as much as anything by what breeds were available in
sufficient numbers.

Klein's book of 1819 was followed, in 1847, by a work in which a blind
Swiss, Jacob Birrer, recorded the technique he had used to train a spitz for

*A guide dog on the end
of a rigid stick, an
illustration from the
textbook by Johann
Wilhelm Klein
published in Vienna in
1819.*

Jacob Birrer with the guide dog that he trained for himself. The illustration is taken from the book, published in 1845, in which he described his method for the benefit of his 'blind colleagues who want to be guided by dogs'.

himself. It seems to have been an improvement on Klein's method in some respects, but it suffered the same fate. No-one was interested. When the idea surfaced again in 1916, two years of war had already produced large numbers of men blinded in action, and a Viennese doctor, Dr Senfelder, apparently suggested that dogs might be trained to guide them. There was no response to his proposal in Austria-Hungary, but it was taken up by the German Red Cross Ambulance Dogs Association, whose president was Geheimrat (Privy Councillor) Dr Gerhard Stalling.

The Association had been founded in 1893 to train dogs for tracking down casualties, and initially collies were the preferred breed. They soon proved their value during manoeuvres with the German army and in 1904 were being used on the battlefields of the Russo-Japanese war. By the time the First World War broke out in 1914 the Association was under the patronage of the Grand Duke von Oldenburg and was co-operating with other organisations to train dogs that could be used in either ambulance or police work. By the end of the war in 1918, Germany and her allies had about 4,000 dogs serving with their armed forces.

Taking up Senfelder's idea, Stalling started training some of his

A drawing from The Graphic *in 1899 showing how dogs trained by the German Red Cross Ambulance Dogs Association were used to help find the wounded on a battlefield. The Association started training some of its dogs to lead blinded veterans during the First World War, and the work developed rapidly thereafter.* (Mary Evans Picture Library)

Association's ambulance dogs as guides for the blind and the first was handed over to a blind war veteran, Paul Feyen, in October 1916. A year later the Association was able to claim that 100 guide dogs were in service, and in 1919 that 539 war-blinded men had been provided with guides. Supported by funds from the State, the work developed quickly. At Oldenburg, the training school had accommodation for over 200 dogs and could train up to 600 units every year. At first their guide dogs were trained exclusively for men blinded in the war, but classes for blind civilians started at the beginning of 1922.

Inevitably, perhaps, the pressure of demand and the pace of development led to problems. Veterans began to complain about the quality of their dogs, which had fallen from the high standard of the early years. The decline was probably caused by a change from a method of training based on kindness and firmness to one that employed much harsher techniques. The result was greater nervousness in the dogs and a reluctance to work. There were also difficulties in acquiring suitable dogs and training staff. Eventually the Association decided to withdraw from the provision of guide dogs for the war-blinded because 'the constant dissatisfaction of veterans with the Association's work had taken away any desire to collaborate with them'.

The Oldenburg school continued to serve the civilian blind population for a few more years, and the task of catering for blind war veterans was given by the Ministry of Labour to the German Shepherd Dog Association, which opened its guide dog school in Potsdam on 15 September 1923. It was an impressive establishment, with kennelling for about 100 dogs, 50 dogs at various stages of their three to four months' training and a maximum output of 12 units each month. The methods used by the school were similar to those employed today in dozens of guide dog schools around the world: initial training in the school grounds, further instruction around the streets of Potsdam and testing by an instructor wearing a blindfold. Within the grounds there was an obstacle course and a variety of hazards such as steps, bridges, ladders and letter boxes. Teaching the dog to walk round an obstacle such as a ladder, rather than under it, was apparently achieved by causing a sackful of sand to fall on the animal if it attempted to take the wrong route (not approved practice today!).

The controller of the school, Eric Liese, identified three key factors in guide dog work: the selection of good dogs; matching the dog to the future owner; and continuing aftercare in the unit's home town. Over 60 years later these fundamental principles have not changed.

The movement progressed rapidly and by the early 1930s there were 4,000 or more guide dogs in Germany. Their reputation, and the achievements of the Potsdam school in particular, had by then started to arouse interest in other countries, although it is perhaps surprising that it took so long. There was, however, a good deal of prejudice to overcome, as these words by Sir Arthur Pearson, the founder of St Dunstan's, written in 1919, make clear.

'In the early part of 1918 I read an account of arrangements that were being made in France for the special training of dogs to be used as guides for blinded soldiers. Very interesting particulars were afforded of the special training given to these dogs with the object of teaching them to keep exactly in front of the man whom they were taking along, to give him warning of steps, to keep him from hitting against obstacles and to note the approach of motors and other vehicles. As I read the article it seemed to me that it would need a very special brand of dog intelligence if the canine guide were to be brought up to the point that would make him really trustworthy. Besides this, I had a feeling – which I had no doubt the men of St Dunstan's fully shared with me — that a dog at the end of a string was apt to remind one a little too much of the blind beggar with his tapping stick and shuffling gait. However, I sent over to France for further particulars, but was not surprised to receive a reply telling me that the idea had not proved as practical as was expected and had been abandoned.'

*   *   *

By the mid-1920s the popularity of German shepherd dogs had spread and it was their breeders, and other enthusiasts, who were largely responsible for getting guide dog training started outside Germany.

One of these enthusiasts was an American, Mrs Dorothy Harrison Eustis. She had come to admire the breed through owning a fine working dog called Hans, and in the early 1920s at her home at Mont Pelerin, in the mountains above Vevey in Switzerland, she and her husband, George, set out to breed dogs with similar qualities: sound in temperament, intelligent, sturdy and willing, rather than the nervous, shy and often aggressive specimens that were widely bred for the show rings or police work. Early on, she managed to attract to her Fortunate Fields kennels (as the growing concern was later called) a remarkable man, Elliott Humphrey, who was also to play a major role in spreading guide dog training internationally. Jack Humphrey, as he was better known, had done a variety of jobs as a young man, including animal training. It was said that he achieved a remarkable feat in teaching a camel to walk backwards. During the First World War he worked with the US army remount service and when the war ended bred and trained horses as manager of a large stable of Arab horses in New England. He was also engaged in some interesting studies on German shepherd dogs which were published as a

Waiting with Mrs Dorothy Eustis for the cable car from Vevey to Mont Pelerin, where her Fortunate Fields kennels were situated in Switzerland, are Jack Humphrey, on the left, who as manager of the kennels played a leading part in the development of guide dog work, and Georges Gabriel, the instructor loaned by Mrs Eustis to run the second and third classes in Britain in 1932 and '33.

series of articles in the *Shepherd Dog Review*. It was these articles that caught Mrs Eustis's eye and led to his appointment as her manager in Switzerland.

The principal purpose of Fortunate Fields was to develop a selective breeding programme that would produce dogs suitable for a wide range of work. Allied to this was the search for better teaching methods and for new ways in which the dogs could serve man. Dorothy Eustis and Jack Humphrey obviously understood the importance of upbringing, as well as

exercises. I have been told an article is appearing in Country Life on my dogs, or rather a letter, and an article in the Sept. the World's To-Day. Looking forward to seeing you, sincerely,
A. H. Eustis

selective breeding, in forming the character and temperament of a dog because Fortunate Fields' puppies were not brought up in kennels. As soon as they could fend for themselves they were boarded out with local farmers who were paid a small amount to raise the pups in their homes so that they grew up to be thoroughly domesticated, sociable animals.

Fortunate Fields trained dogs for work with the army, the police and the customs service, and it was while George Eustis was visiting the renowned police training school at Gruenheide in Germany in 1927 that he came across the guide dog school at Potsdam. He was so impressed by the school's achievements that he sent for his wife to join him. She was equally struck by what she saw and returned to her home in Switzerland to write an article for an American magazine, *Saturday Evening Post*, that proved to be a turning point for her and blind people in many countries.

The article, published on 5 November 1927, was called *The Seeing Eye* (from *Proverbs* ch. xx verse 12 'The hearing ear, and the seeing eye, the Lord hath made even both of them') and in it she described how she had watched the blind men gathering with their harnesses and canes for an afternoon training walk (the German practice of using a cane in the right hand as well as a dog in the left was not followed later in Britain).

Before she became interested in guide dogs, Mrs Eustis was breeding and training German shepherd dogs for work with the army, the customs service and the police at her Fortunate Fields kennels. On this postcard, dated 29 July 1930, which shows some of the police dogs, she reassures Miss Crooke that 'no blind-leading dog is ever taught any police work.'

'I shall never forget the change that came over one man as he turned away from the gate,' she wrote. 'It was as though a complete transformation had taken place before my eyes. One moment it was an uncertain, shuffling blind man, tapping with a cane, the next it was an assured person, with his dog firmly in hand and his head up, who walked towards us quickly and firmly, giving his orders in a low confident voice. That one quick glimpse of the crying need for guidance and companionship in the lonely, all-enveloping darkness stood out clearly before my swimming eyes. To think that one small dog could stand for so much in the life of a human being, not only in his usual role of companion but as his eyes, sword, shield and buckler! How many humans could fill those roles with the same uncomplaining devotion and untiring fidelity? Darned few, I think.

'I quickly asked permission to follow him on his walk, first getting a few details about him. He had never before owned a dog, and since his blindness had been led everywhere by a member of his family; on arriving at the school he had been particularly nervous, helpless and lacking confidence. He was a man of about forty-five, thickset and husky, who had evidently been accustomed to lots of exercise and had become overfat through lack of it. He passed us whistling through his teeth and feeling for a cigarette, his dog looking us over with an appraising eye. I turned quietly and followed. Walking at a good pace, the pair went down the street to the first crossing, where the dog pulled back to indicate the curb. The man's cigarette was apparently his last, as he gave orders to be led to the tobacco shop, went in, made his purchases and then continued his walk.

'As I followed him it seemed impossible to believe that the man wasn't taking the dog for a walk and stopping for traffic of his own accord, so quietly and evenly did they work together. I had to pull myself up pretty sharply once or twice to realize that the man was blind and that the only thing that kept him from pitching off the curb into the street was the intelligence and faithfulness of his dog. For not once through the whole hour that I followed them did that dog's attention wander.

'The walk lay through the crowded shopping street with all the traffic of a big city, its noises and distractions, its scents and stray dogs on mischief or business bent. Understanding responsibility and never-failing protection radiated from that blind leader as he went about his work. His attitude was, "You mind your business and I'll mind mine", as he threaded his way along the street, and the pair went much more quickly without interference than I, who continually bumped into people in my efforts to keep up. I was amazed at the pace; I had started by walking briskly, but found the distance ever widening between us and the need to make it up every so often on a jog trot.

'The streets in German cities are wide and in many places lined with two or three rows of trees and paths. To keep cyclists from riding along these paths barriers have been put up at intervals with narrow openings for pedestrians. The barriers are of one bar each and about the height of a man's waist. I had been told at the school that one of the hardest things to teach a dog was to pass between these barriers and not under them, the way being clear for the dog but not for the man, who would receive the full force of the bar across his middle without warning, so I was interested to follow the pair into one of these wide, shady lanes on the homeward leg.

'A couple strolling ahead had dropped a coat directly in the path but man and dog skirted it and the dog immediately came back to a line that would lead him between the barriers, although for him it would have been simpler and shorter to go under. There was a big catch in my throat as I saw them turn into the school grounds together with other pairs coming from different directions and knew that I was converted. It had not been a particular exhibition staged for my special benefit, but just one of the many dogs turned out every month with his blind master. There were no fireworks, no display, no excuses, no muddling, but honest work done by honest dogs, and my hat was off to those who had worked out and perfected such a method of sympathetic training.

'As always happens when you are interested in some one thing, you find examples all around you, and the day after my visit to Potsdam I was taking a respite from a big dog show and quenching my thirst with a lovely long, cool glass of beer in a public garden across the way, when along came a blind man and his dog, threading their way between the tables. The man had apparently told his dog to take him to a table, as she stopped beside one with her master next to the chair.

'I watched them for some time. The waitress could come and go as she pleased, and people could pass close by in all directions as long as they did not show any interest, but let someone stop and look curiously at them and a low warning growl issued forth immediately.

'Captain Schoenherr, of the Instruction School for Police Dogs at Gruenheide, was with me and he invited the man to take a glass of beer with us, which he accepted very pleasantly. Picking up his harness handle and his cane, he gave the dog the order to follow Captain Schoenherr, who, to test him, took a curving course between the tables. Step for step and curve for curve, the dog followed him, saw her master safely into his chair and lay down quietly beside him. The man told us that he had had her for three years and only once in all that time had she run him into anything, and then he said it was largely his own fault.

Man and dog had such understanding that they worked as one. Once, while the man was talking, Captain Schoenherr got up and crossed in front of the dog so close as almost to step on her paws without bringing forth a complaint, but when he stopped back of her master and stood there without speaking, the grievance came swiftly into her throat – just a quick warning "Hands off!"

'Her master laughed, patted the head always ready for his hand and said, "I never have a moment's anxiety." That from a blind man! Later he went with us to the entrance to show us how beautifully she worked, and after he'd said goodbye gave the order to take him back to his table. She took him quietly and without question back to the same table and the same chair, although the way led across the whole garden, up some steps, through a pergola and between tables crowded with people.

'The future for all blind men can be the same, however blinded. No longer dependent on a member of the family, a friend or a paid attendant, the blind can once more take up their normal lives as nearly possible where they left them off, and each can begin or go back to a wage-earning occupation, secure in the knowledge that he can get to and from his work safely and without cost; that crowds and traffic have no longer any terrors for him and that his evenings can be spent among friends without responsibility or burden to them; and last, but far from least, that long, healthful walks are now possible to exercise off the unhealthy fat of inactivity and so keep the body strong and fit.'

Mrs Eustis finished her article with a toast: 'Gentlemen . . . I give you the shepherd dog.'

Proud though she was of this new, spectacular achievement of the breed she admired so much there is no suggestion at this point that she was contemplating taking up the work herself. It was enthusiastic letters from a number of blind Americans – and of one, Morris Frank, a 19-year-old insurance salesman from Nashville, Tennessee, in particular – that led to the next step.

Frank's letter differed from others she received in that it expressed his wish to test a dog for himself in America and if it was a success to start a non-profit-making school in that country to make similar dogs available to more blind people. His combination of enthusiasm and concern for others impressed Mrs Eustis and so she arranged for him to travel to Switzerland to be trained with a suitable dog. In the meantime, the Potsdam school helped George Eustis and Jack Humphrey to prepare two dogs, Gala and Kiss, for the American trial. When Frank arrived at Fortunate Fields in April 1928 and the training team were able to assess which dog would suit him best, Kiss was chosen. Not surprisingly, Frank

Morris Frank, the young American whose enthusiasm inspired Mrs Dorothy Eustis, with Buddy, the guide dog she trained for him in Switzerland in 1928. In 1929 Frank and Mrs Eustis launched The Seeing Eye in the United States.

did not think much of the name and changed it to the one that would soon become famous – Buddy.

Morris Frank travelled back to the United States with Buddy in June on board the liner *Tuscania*. Before leaving Switzerland he talked with Mrs Eustis and Jack Humphrey about his intention to start a guide dog school which he wanted to call The Seeing Eye – the title of the article that had brought them all together. He was warned of the problems he would encounter, not least the different conditions in the United States and public ignorance and prejudice. But, promised Mrs Eustis, if he and Buddy proved equal to the test she would guarantee $10,000 and send staff to help start the school.

Frank's first real challenge was when one of the crowd of reporters that met the boat in New York dared him to cross West Street. He had never heard of West Street, which was wider than Fifth Avenue and full of heavy traffic, and so in blissful ignorance he accepted the challenge and set off. Later, he described the experience.

> 'We entered a street so noisy it was almost like entering a wall of sound. She went about four paces and halted. A deafening roar and a rush of hot air told me a tremendous truck was swooshing past so near that Buddy could have lifted her nose and touched it. She moved forward again into the ear-splitting clangor, stopped, backed up and started again. I lost all sense of direction and surrendered myself entirely to the dog. I shall never forget the next three minutes. Ten-ton trucks rocketing past, cabs blowing their horns in our ears, drivers shouting at us. One fellow yelled, "You damned fool, do you want to get killed?"
>
> 'When we finally got to the other side and I realized what a really magnificent job she had done, I leaned over and gave Buddy a great big hug and told her what a good, good girl she was. "She sure is a good girl," exclaimed a voice at my elbow – one of the photographers. "I had to come over in a cab, and some of the fellows who tried to cross with you are still back on the other side!"'

After reading an account of this incident some 25 years later, Britain's leading authority on guide dog training at the time, Captain Liakhoff, who was himself a product of Mrs Eustis's school in Switzerland, commented that Morris Frank and Buddy had had a narrow escape and that their safe crossing had very little to do with the dog's skill, except that she had kept a straight line. The competence of the drivers, the quality of their brakes and good luck had done more than anything to ensure their survival.

Nevertheless, the ordeal was a tribute to Frank's courage and determination, and he rapidly went on to gain the public confidence and recognition that he needed to get the guide dog movement started in

America. Articles and pictures started appearing in the press throughout the country and he was soon receiving letters from other blind people who wanted a guide dog. Determined to press ahead with his plans as soon as possible, he persuaded Mrs Eustis that the first class should be held early in 1929. With this class The Seeing Eye was established.

*   *   *

Frank and Buddy are usually credited with being the first properly-trained guide dog partnership in America, but the distinction really belongs to another pair. A partly-trained German shepherd dog, Lux of La Salle, was imported, presumably from Germany, by John Sinykin, trained further under his direction and given in 1926 to a blind senator, Thomas D. Schall, who used the dog as a guide until its death in 1933. Sinykin was a Minnesota businessman who initially trained German shepherds as a hobby, but after the success of Lux and Senator Schall he went on to develop a guide dog training school under the name of His Master's Eyes Institute. His home and kennels were destroyed in a disastrous fire in 1935 and although he continued guide dog training using the 'Master Eye' name his pioneering achievement was eclipsed by the growing influence and reputation of The Seeing Eye.

One of the first problems Mrs Eustis encountered in helping to promote guide dog work in the United States was the difficulty of getting good trainers. There was no shortage of people keen to do the job, but few of them turned out to have the qualities that were really needed. As she pointed out to a conference on work for the blind in May 1931, the dogs needed to be *educated* rather than trained, so that they would obey only those orders that were safe to obey. The difference between training a dog and educating it so that 'of its own volition' it would ignore an unsafe command was not understood by many aspiring instructors.

She also observed that many trainers who might be capable of understanding the psychology of the dog and educating it successfully failed when it came to understanding and instructing their human trainees. A third group failed to qualify because their nerves could not stand the strain that the work imposed.

The end result, she reported, had been that in Germany, 'a nation of dog lovers, dog trainers and dog education', no more than eight per cent of apprentices stayed on to become competent instructors. This experience, together with language and immigration problems if the work were to spread, led Mrs Eustis to conclude that there was an acute need for a school to train instructors for the various countries that were becoming interested in guide dogs. And so, using a translation of the name of the American organisation she had helped to found, she established L'Oeil qui

Mrs Eustis soon discovered that few dog trainers were suited to guide dog work, and with more countries asking for help she therefore established L'Oeil qui Voit as a school for instructors. The school also trained guide dogs for countries that wanted to try them before setting up their own schools.

Voit at Vevey in Switzerland, not far from her Fortunate Fields home and kennels.

L'Oeil qui Voit had another purpose besides training instructors. A number of countries were enquiring about guide dogs, but before going any further they wanted some trained dogs that they could study under their own conditions. L'Oeil qui Voit therefore undertook the training of these trial dogs, and by 1931 had supplied 10 to Italy, 11 to France and three to Switzerland.

Quarantine regulations were an obstacle to the use of Swiss-trained dogs when interest in guide dogs started to grow in Britain, but without the support of Mrs Eustis and her school the British pioneers would have had a much harder time than they did in getting the work established.

2

The British Pioneers

The success of guide dogs in Germany was well known in blind welfare circles in Britain during the 1920s, but it was left to the German shepherd dog enthusiasts to get the work started in this country. An article in *The Beacon*, the journal of the National Institute for the Blind, in February 1921 gave a detailed account, taken from the *Swiss Messenger for the Blind*, of developments in Germany. It pointed out that guides were an important consideration in getting employment for blind people and then went on to say that in Germany 'the problem has been very largely overcome by the employment of dog guides'. The article described the training, without minimising the difficulties, and concluded that 'war-blinded men have just begun to enjoy the advantages of dog guides ...' Despite this testimonial, no interest or enthusiasm seems to have been generated in Britain.

It is difficult to know how accurate the article was, but British readers may have had reservations about the author's description of the 'severe and often cruel training' which the dog had to undergo. 'Amongst other things he is led past deep ditches, into which the trainer throws him without compunction, until he learns to avoid them by making a wide detour.' Whatever the reason for the lack of interest, eight years were to pass before *The Beacon* published anything else about guide dogs.

In the meantime, the German shepherd dog had become popular in Britain. During the 1914–1918 war, soldiers had seen the remarkable work being done by these animals in the German army and many were captured and brought back to Britain, where their qualities soon won them a growing following. Dogs had not been used to the same extent in the British army, a fact that led the War Office to conclude, in a report on the training of war dogs published in 1952, that Britain 'lagged lamentably behind' in the First World War.

In 1919 a few enthusiasts, headed by Lieutenant-Colonel Moore

Brabazon (later Lord Brabazon of Tara) decided to form a breed club for the German dogs, but had some difficulty choosing a suitable name. Anti-German feeling was strong and to have called it the German shepherd dog would have invited hostility and prejudice. In the end, alsatian wolf dog was chosen, an unfortunate choice because it probably helped to encourage the belief that the breed was fierce. In fact, there is no evidence of any wolf blood in its ancestry and the name was given purely on account of the wolf-like grey colour of many of the early specimens. Alsatian was a logical enough name because Alsace-Lorraine had been one source of the first dogs to come to Britain.

One man who was fiercely opposed to the rise in popularity of the alsatian was Lieutenant-Colonel E.H. Richardson, who had been commandant of the British War Dog School during the war. In a fiercely chauvinistic book published in 1923 he maintained that 'to all statements that German dogs helped our soldiers in the war (a lie very frequently met with), or that they are capable of far higher skill under training, a deaf ear should be turned. For intelligence, reliability of character, courage, humour, and fidelity, there are no dogs in the world which can touch the British native breeds, and the position of anyone who claims that German dogs can attempt to replace these, is not one to be admired by lovers of our own land and race.' The service performed by British breeds 'breathing ardent British characteristics all over the world' could not be lightly held, in Richardson's view, because of the immensely important work many of their masters were doing. 'To keep up the prestige of the British Empire all over the world, is one of the great props on which the whole fabric of civilisation is based. Amalgamation with alien ideals, which are immensely lower than ours, will never accomplish this, and, not understanding this fact, is one of the dangers with which this country is faced at present.'

One hopes that Richardson's view of the world was not shared by many of his countrymen, even at that time, and it will seem even more outrageous now. Fortunately it did not interfere with the rise in popularity of the alsatian. In 1923, the year Richardson's book was published, the Alsatian, Sheep, Police and Army Dog Society (ASPADS) was formed to encourage the working qualities of the breed and hold trials. The following year the Alsatian League of Great Britain was established and later merged with the Alsatian Wolf Dog Club.

This rapid progress had its darker side, however, because the high prices that people were prepared to pay for puppies encouraged a good deal of irresponsible breeding, resulting in many shy and nervous animals. The image of the breed suffers to this day from the bad reputation acquired in the 1920s. The dogs' appearance and their use as police and guard dogs may also encourage the apprehension with which they are still viewed by some people, although well-bred and carefully-reared German shepherd dogs (as they are now correctly called in Britain) are gentle, reliable and intelligent animals that make good family pets provided they are looked after properly. They are not as gregarious and friendly as some other breeds, but handled correctly they are not aggressive. They formed the vanguard of the guide dog movement in this country, as in Germany and the USA, and although they are a minority among guide dogs in Britain today – about one in 10 is a German shepherd – there are many who think that they still make the finest guides when matched with a partner who can get the best out of them.

Throughout the 1920s Britain's leading alsatian enthusiasts followed the activities of their counterparts in Germany closely and among the breeders who attended the German championships in September 1928 were Lady Kitty Ritson, Captain Alan Sington, Miss J.M.A. Workman and probably Mrs Lucy Schuster. During this visit Lady Kitty, and perhaps the others, went to the Potsdam school, where she was given a former guide dog called Lona whose owner had died. She brought the bitch back to England and when it came out of quarantine, presumably about March 1929, gave it to Mrs Rosamund Bond, another alsatian breeder who lived at Arncliffe-in-Craven, Yorkshire, apparently because Lady Kitty could not stand a dog that was so devoted that it never left her.

At about the same time she seems to have joined with Mrs Schuster and Captain Sington in an attempt to get guide dog training started in Britain. According to Miss Muriel Crooke, who was soon to take the lead in pioneering the work, Lady Kitty and her two companions approached St Dunstan's, the British charity for blinded servicemen, with a plan to train 12 dogs. Although the proposal was turned down, British blind welfare organisations were following events in the guide dog movement elsewhere with interest. In September 1929 there was a meeting between W.M. Eagar, secretary general of the National Institute for the Blind, and Mrs Eustis. A few months later Captain Ian Fraser (subsequently Sir Ian and then Lord Fraser), who had succeeded Sir Arthur Pearson as chairman of St Dunstan's, visited L'Oeil qui Voit in Switzerland and another guide dog school in Berlin.

Fraser confessed, in an article in *St Dunstan's Review* (February 1930), that before his visit he had been sceptical, but he returned 'greatly influenced in favour of the guide dog by what I have heard and experienced'.

'I am of opinion that an experiment should be tried in England,' he continued. 'There is one factor which is unknown at present and in regard to which continental experience gives us no clue – namely, the attitude of the English blinded soldier towards the proposition that he should have a dog guide. He may not receive the idea with an open unprejudiced mind. The desire to disassociate himself in his independent outlook upon life, from the traditional idea of a blind man and his dog, may be very strong. I should have taken this view myself soon after I was blinded, for I can well remember the immense trouble I would take in those early days to try to avoid people noticing that I could not see. This was, I think, partly the desire to behave as normally as possible, and partly a measure of self-defence against the awkwardness caused by the excessive sentimentality of a few of the people whom one used to meet. The passage of time, however, alters one's attitude in these matters a little – at least it has altered mine – and I have long ago become accustomed to the fact that I am blind. While I may still strive to do things normally it does not upset me to be recognised as a blinded soldier, as it used to do. I think perhaps this change of attitude may have been experienced by many of my comrades throughout the country, and now that they have become known and respected in the neighbourhoods in which they live, there will perhaps not be the same objection in their minds to the association with the dog as might have been the case earlier. I picture the blinded soldier walking, upright and confident, with his dog by his side, and his friends who meet him being interested and full of admiration for his and the animal's skill in getting over their very great difficulties.'

On 15 March 1930 the NIB's journal, now called *The New Beacon*, published an article by Mrs Eustis, followed by a long extract from Captain Fraser's *St Dunstan's Review* article. An editorial footnote suggested that Fraser's remarks applied equally to progressive civilian blind people. 'We see no reason why the splendid friendship that so often exists between dog and man should not be fostered for the benefit of blind people who love dogs and dogs who love them.'

In February 1930, after hearing Fraser's account of his visit to Switzerland and Germany, the council of St Dunstan's asked him to prepare proposals for a small experimental scheme in Britain. The following month, however, they decided not to proceed with it. They recognised the great advantage that blind servicemen on the Continent had gained from guide dogs but considered 'that these advantages did not apply to quite the same extent to British blinded soldiers, who are fortunately better provided for and less in need of a guide than other European blinded men.' The council also thought there could be problems because there was not the same tradition in Britain as in Germany of using the dog as a working animal. There was the possibility of adverse 'though probably unenlightened' public criticism, and of course considerable cost.

In short, 'the Council felt that they should be much more certain of the scheme', particularly as there had been little response to Fraser's article in the previous month's issue of their *Review*. However, they did decide to publish extracts from letters that had been received for and against the scheme in the next issue of the magazine in order to encourage more response.

The letters were duly published in the April 1930 issue of the *Review* and were perhaps most interesting for their agreement with Fraser's view that there was no need to be over-sensitive about the idea of being led by a dog. 'It does not advertise the fact that one is blind', one man wrote, 'but merely suggests a man taking a stroll.' Others agreed, and 'T.A.C' made an additional point: 'My great difficulty is getting enough exercise . . . I should not be in the least bit sensitive about being led by a dog.'

Eight days before the St Dunstan's council decided not to go ahead with a trial project Fraser had written a long article in *The Times* (18 March 1930) about guide dogs and the possibility of introducing them in Britain. But it was a short piece, only five column inches in length, in the *Liverpool Echo* of 10 April 1930 that helped to bring matters to a head. The report quoted an official of the National Institute for the Blind as saying that they were considering the question of training alsatians as guides and companions for the blind. Shortly after this, on 21 April, a brief letter, only 14 lines long, appeared in the *Echo* from Robert Tissyman, who was a local Liverpool politician. He wrote:

> 'My aid has been sought by a blind man in Edge Hill, who has asked me to write to the *Echo* on the subject of guides for blind people.
> 'It is suggested in the *Echo* of April 10, that with a little training, Alsatian dogs could be most useful companions to blind persons, and protect them from all kinds of dangers. On behalf of those so afflicted, I desire to appeal to such dog owners, to assist the project, by offering their help to the National Institute for the Blind, 51, North John Street.
> – ROBT. TISSYMAN'

Unfortunately, Tissyman had not taken the trouble to consult the Liverpool branch of the NIB before writing his letter. The secretary, Musgrave Frankland, who was blind himself, fearing that a generous response to the appeal might result in a deluge of alsatians, immediately wrote to Tissyman (whom he described later as 'one of our famous, or perhaps notorious would be a better word, politicians . . .') diplomatically trying to dampen his ardour and engage his interest in other work for the blind.

Tissyman's letter did not produce the result that Frankland feared. In fact, there was only one response, a letter from Miss Muriel Crooke, who lived across the Mersey at Wallasey, on the tip of the Wirral, and was secretary of the local Alsatian League. Looking back on events some years later Miss Crooke said that she had had no intention of becoming actively interested in a new venture. She was fully occupied with her own work and interests, which were mainly painting and dogs. 'But fate somehow guided circumstances so that it fell upon me to do things.'

In contacting Musgrave Frankland, Miss Crooke thought that it would be possible to obtain a book on guide dogs written in French, in which she was fluent. Having translated the book, she hoped to encourage 'some willing person in one of the Liverpool Alsatian Training Clubs to do something.' There are differing accounts from the two participants of the meeting that then took place between Miss Crooke and Frankland. According to Miss Crooke he was 'so tremendously enthusiastic that something had to be done.' Frankland reported that 'whilst cooling her interest in guide-dogs, I tried to arouse it for other sections, but this was not to be so easily achieved.' Either way, Miss Crooke left the meeting committed to explore further. She immediately wrote to Captain Alan Sington, the breeder and trainer of alsatians whom she had met a few years earlier when she had started entering her own dogs in working trials. Sington had been very kind to her and had gone to Wallasey on several occasions to teach her and some friends more about the technical details of trial work. He had been with Lady Kitty Ritson in Germany when she was given the guide dog Lona and may have told Miss Crooke about the gift and something of the interest he and some other British breeders had taken in the work.

In his reply to Miss Crooke on 5 May 1930 Sington referred to the decision by St Dunstan's not to press on with a scheme but said that a Mrs Schuster was actively interested and in touch with others. He was therefore passing Miss Crooke's letter on to her. 'Whether the scheme for training these dogs will come off later on or not I cannot yet say. Personally I rather doubt it,' he concluded. However, he did suggest that Mrs Bond might be prepared to give a demonstration with Lona to one or two officials of the NIB.

Mrs Bond had been given a harness for Lona and had, it seems, been trying to work the dog. She was keen to help and issued several pressing invitations to Musgrave Frankland, which he eventually accepted in September 1930. In the meantime, Miss Crooke wrote to Mrs Eustis, still thinking she could get a book on the subject. 'Even if there were literature on the technical questions of this training', replied Mrs Eustis from Fortunate Fields on 9 July, 'you would learn nothing of practical value from them, because it takes the years of experience with different dogs to acquire the sense of what the dog needs to educate him as a blind guide.'

She left Miss Crooke in no doubt about the size of the task. 'I don't think anyone who has not actually done the work can realise the difficulties that are encountered. It is apart from any other kind of training, as the basis must be to form a dog who takes the initiative. The man who is good at training dogs for police work usually fails with dogs for blind work as the whole principle is just the opposite.' She then went on to outline the problem of getting good instructors and made a tentative offer of help and support.

Mrs Bond had also been in touch with Mrs Eustis, who replied with a great deal of sound advice. She warned, in particular, against the danger of the blind man being exploited for the sake of the German shepherd dog. She then offered to send over, at her own expense, one of the instructors from L'Oeil qui Voit, if four blind people could be found who wanted dog guides. At the same time she would be prepared to train a suitable young man from Britain as an instructor. The location for a training centre had to be dictated by the need for the actual training to be done 'in town or village streets with a fair amount of automobile traffic, pavements with kerbs, building operations, scaffoldings, manholes, steps, in short all the things that a person would meet in city life.'

The following month Mrs Eustis confirmed her offer of help in a letter to Miss Crooke, saying that 'it must be clearly understood as a trial'. She sent a number of pamphlets as a guide for producing publications, and suggested a meeting in London in September. At that meeting, on 23 September, at which Mrs Bond was also present, she must have encouraged the British women because they were soon trying to decide on a training spot and thinking about fund-raising. On Mrs Eustis's advice, Wallasey was chosen because the right conditions existed there and it was near Miss Crooke's home, whereas there was nowhere suitable near Mrs Bond's kennels.

The National Institute for the Blind adopted a cautious attitude to developments. They had published articles from time to time in their journal and had talked to Mrs Eustis in September 1929. But nothing seems to have come of that meeting until the following September, when the NIB's secretary general, W.M. Eagar, wrote to Mrs Eustis three days before her meeting with Miss Crooke and Mrs Bond in London, apologizing for the silence ('we have been compelled to wait for St Dunstan's') and hoping that she would attend a meeting with the two English women and others.

Within days of her meeting with Miss Crooke and Mrs Bond, Mrs Eustis went again to see Eagar at the NIB and told him that she would rather work with a national organisation than individuals. His position was that as Fraser of St Dunstan's had the matter in hand he was not prepared to take any action before consulting him, but that as soon as he had done so he would let her know what they thought about starting a scheme in England.

Musgrave Frankland, meanwhile, had made the journey to Mrs Bond's kennels to learn about Lona. A few days later, on 22 September, he reported enthusiastically to the NIB's appeals secretary that he was sure guide dogs would be a great boon to the blind community. Although Lona had not worked as a guide dog for two years and had at first been puzzled by traffic on the left and commands given in Frankland's imperfect German, he had nevertheless had several 'most successful' walks. He foresaw the prospect that 'with a Dog-Guide many occupations could be really profitable that would otherwise be impossible on account of either the cost or the uncertainty of human guidance.'

Some of his other comments on his experience with Lona throw an interesting light on guide dog training in Germany at the time. Guide dogs were taught not to be too friendly, he reported, and so it had taken him some time to win the dog's confidence. From other accounts, it is apparent that in Germany the dogs were expected to guard as well as to guide their masters. It was not uncommon at that time for blind pensioners to be set upon and robbed of their pensions.

Frankland described how Lona 'stopped at all places where her previous training dictated, such as closed doors and tops of flights of stairs, and these she would only commence to descend after I had tapped the top step with my stick.' (In Britain the stick was discarded, the dog's signal to continue being the spoken command 'Forward'.)

As secretary of the NIB's Liverpool branch Musgrave Frankland found himself in a difficult spot. A new and potentially attractive scheme to help blind people was developing on his doorstep and he was being pressed by Miss Crooke and Mrs Bond to participate. He saw its potential, both as a benefit to blind people and as a rival to the NIB for funds, but he was not sure where his duty lay and asked his masters at the head office in London for guidance.

'It is difficult for me to refuse to co-operate with her (Miss Crooke) unless I can say definitely that after consideration of the subject, my Head Office are not prepared to co-operate even in an advisory capacity,' he wrote. There is little doubt about the answer for which he was hoping. 'As a student of "blind people"', he continued, 'I think, and this after much consideration, that the introduction of guide-dogs would be an untold blessing, and would do more than all else to increase the number of blind people who could find profitable employment outside Workshops and Home Workers schemes.'

He left his head office with no illusions about his own view of the money-raising potential of the new venture. A 15 guinea cup had been given for an alsatian competition to help Miss Crooke's fund, which was to be further boosted by the takings of an alsatian show to be held at the Auditorium, Port Sunlight. Evidence of the strong appeal of the fund was that when Lord Leverhulme heard where the proceeds of the show were

The first effort to raise funds to start the training of Guide Dogs

PLEASE READ PAGE 1 and CENTREPIECE.

SCHEDULE

—: OF :—

Open Alsatian Dog Show

To be held under Kennel Club Rules, by the

Alsatian League & Club of Great Britain

(LIVERPOOL SUB-BRANCH)

AT THE

AUDITORIUM, PORT SUNLIGHT,

TO START THE WORK OF

Dog Guides for the Blind

IN ENGLAND.

—: ON :—

Saturday, November 1st, 1930.

Dogs can be carried on the Birkenhead Trams and Buses.

Judge:

MONSIEUR GEORGES BARAIS.

President of "La Société du Chien de Berger Allemand."

GUARANTORS TO THE KENNEL CLUB :

Mr. J. H. SCOTT, Winleigh, Gores Lane, Freshfield.
Mr. J. F. CHARPY, Chardai, Woodhey Road, Rock Ferry.
Mr. J. W. BURRELL, Abbott's Farm, Sutton, St. Helens.
Miss M. E. CROOKE, 3 Warren Drive, Wallasey.

Benching 12-30 p.m.   Judging 1-0 p.m.
Show will close at 6-0 p.m.

ENTRIES CLOSE OCTOBER 27th.

OLD CALABAR Bench and Feed.   JEYES' Disinfectant.

J. F. Doran, Printer, 1a, Cullen Street, Smithdown Road.

THE RING MEASURES 30 × 15 YARDS.

THE JUDGE IS ONE OF THE LEADING AUTHORITIES ON THE BREED IN FRANCE.

'The first effort to raise funds to start the training of guide dogs' noted Miss Crooke on this programme. When he heard where the proceeds were going, Lord Leverhulme offered to forego the usual rent on his auditorium. 'It was a generous gesture', wrote the NIB's Liverpool branch secretary, Musgrave Frankland, 'that I have never yet succeeded in getting him to do for either efforts for our Merseyside Fund or for our national appeal including blind babies.'

going he offered to forego the usual rent for the premises. It was a generous gesture, Frankland pointed out, 'that I have never yet succeeded in getting him to do for either efforts for our Merseyside Fund or for our national appeal including blind babies.'

With no experience of fund-raising Miss Crooke had done things that would have been quite impossible but for the fact that she had 'what is undoubtedly an entirely new and fascinating appeal'. Would it therefore not be in the best interests of the NIB, he asked, to 'watch over and in some slight way to co-operate in the experiment in view of future developments?'

At the head office the force of his arguments was appreciated and a hand-written comment on the bottom of the memorandum accepted that 'the guide-dogs have as good an appeal from a money-raising standpoint as blind babies – the idea is romantic.' The writer, the appeals secretary, suggested that the NIB should 'get in' immediately, before the new appeal was able to stand on its own feet financially and become 'another National Blind Charity'.

Prompted by the urgent representations of his Liverpool branch secretary, and by his meeting at the end of September with Mrs Eustis, the NIB's secretary general, W.M. Eagar, now proposed a meeting between the NIB, St Dunstan's and all the people interested in the guide dog work. He told Fraser that although he recognised the potential cost, he thought it would be quite wrong to obstruct the beginnings and growth of the movement in Britain, and that he attached great importance to co-ordinating any new movement in the world of the blind with the existing agencies. He hoped their appeal could be 'wisely directed' towards dog lovers so as not to interfere with existing appeals.

This concern over fund-raising for guide dogs was to haunt relation-ships between the NIB and The Guide Dogs for the Blind Association in the years to come. Although the founders of the new organisation felt obliged in 1932 to give an undertaking to restrict their fund-raising to 'doggy' circles, it was a constraint that their successors were later not prepared to tolerate, to the considerable frustration and annoyance of the NIB.

3

The Experiment is Launched

At the end of 1930 the NIB was still a long way from obtaining any kind of agreement on fund-raising from the members of the new movement. However, an important source of support from the dog world was already standing in the wings and had been hinted at by Eagar in a letter to Fraser in November. The first reference to the backing on which guide dog work was to rely heavily for many years was in April 1930 when the secretary of the Greater London Fund for the Blind sent Eagar the card of Captain H.E. Hobbs, who was a dog enthusiast and advertisement manager of Spratts, the pet food and accessories supplier. More importantly, this energetic and enterprising man had, through The "Tail-Wagger" Magazine, 'the magazine for everyone who owns and loves a dog', already raised over £30,000 and was looking for some way of helping the blind if a 'doggy context' could be devised.

We shall hear more of the Tail-Waggers later, but in the meantime there was a great deal of uncertainty as to the way events would develop. Frankland told his head office that there were signs of a divergence of views among the enthusiasts and warned that too many 'doggy' people and too few 'blind' people on the committee of the experiment would in the end almost certainly cause it to lose some of its main purpose, which 'would be disastrous'. Miss Crooke, however, was entirely on the 'blind' side. She had by now raised about £90 in cash and two £50 'scholarships' had been promised.

'With this sum in hand', Frankland wrote to his head office, 'and the loan of two trainers, free of cost from Mrs Eustis, the independent running of the experiment in Wallasey is assured, and so, as you will guess, I am watching developments very closely, not only in the interests of the NIB but also of the blind community.' He believed the work could be self-supporting through an appeal to dog-lovers without detriment to other activities, provided that the new publicity was co-ordinated with, and not independent of, their own appeals. This concern to keep control of the emerging threat to the NIB's own fund-raising efforts was echoed by the Institute's appeals secretary, who was perhaps being too optimistic in suggesting that while the guide dog people should be encouraged to raise money for the dog movement, the NIB should still be able to include the dogs as part of its general appeal. 'We do not want St Dunstan's to be able to include it in theirs and still less do we want any other blind charity to be able to use it as a "plank" in their platform,' he wrote.

The 'divergence of views' to which Frankland had referred had also been the subject of correspondence between Miss Crooke and Mrs Eustis. Unfortunately, Miss Crooke very rarely kept copies of her own letters, although she did preserve and pass on many letters from Mrs Eustis as well as other papers covering the period up to 1940, when she dropped out of the movement. One can only guess from Mrs Eustis's replies at some of the issues on which she sought advice. What, for example, prompted Mrs Eustis to write on 10 November, 'I think you and Mrs Bond have got to make a firm decision whether you are starting a piece of work for the blind or a Society for the Prevention of Hurt Feelings – this decision has to be made now or you will gradually wander into a sea of personality and petty jealousy – I should suppose the very fact that the lady in question had not succeeded in her efforts should militate against her being included in the nucleus. Obviously her tactics were wrong so why burden yourself with them?'

Who was 'the lady in question'? Possibly, Mrs Lucy (later Lady) Schuster, who had been interested in the work for some time. She does not seem to have been working with Miss Crooke and Mrs Bond, however, and did not come into the fold until later. When she did, she proved to be a considerable driving force.

Like Musgrave Frankland, Mrs Eustis was clear where the priority must lie. 'Keep always in mind', she wrote, 'that you are working for the BLIND, otherwise your work will be a dismal failure . . . Mr Frankland is the man to refer to *not* dog enthusiasts. I know whereof I speak and am only trying to keep you from falling into a boiling caldron!'

While the conflict between the different interests was being resolved Miss Crooke was pressing ahead with the practical aspects of the work and acquired some second-hand wooden kennels and a netted run which were placed in a disused corner of the yard of a garage in Cardigan Road, New Brighton – a northern suburb of Wallasey at the mouth of the Mersey. A 'lock-up garage' was also hired for storing and preparing food.

Mrs Eustis thought that it would be politic to have in the first class at least two of the old working type of Scotch collie – now known as the border collie. This would, she declared, 'kill the alsatian stories and plant yourself squarely on the work for the blind.' She also had in mind the interest and support of influential people. Mrs Harold Baring, already an enthusiast, had interested Florence Hoare, the Marchioness of Londonderry's sister, who could get dogs from sheep trial collie stock. Through this connection Mrs Baring also hoped to interest the Earl of Lonsdale.

No date was yet fixed for the start of training and Miss Crooke was told by Mrs Eustis that there was no question of a second course until the first dogs had been working for six months or so and there had been an opportunity to decide on their practicality. After that a permanent programme could be discussed. In the meantime, Miss Crooke continued to receive a stream of advice. 'I don't know what the NIB plans are except that Mr Eagar told me that if the trial dogs are a success there would be no difficulty about funds and led me to believe that there was some one person who would finance it' (1 January 1931). This is clearly a reference to Tail-Waggers. Two weeks later (15 January) Mrs Eustis is suggesting that it would be 'a great thing if the NIB recognises you officially', and asks Miss Crooke to make it very plain that L'Oeil qui Voit would help in every way to prepare the *trial dogs* and would only discuss the future after the dogs had been working for a while. Nevertheless, anticipating the future, she warns that 'when the dogs are a success' professional trainers would want to take up the work and they would be under nobody's control. 'The blind should be protected from them,' she insisted.

*   *   *

The 'nucleus' of four enthusiasts who would comprise the first organising committee had now been formed. Apart from Miss Crooke and Mrs Bond there were Lady Kitty Ritson, who had brought Lona back from Germany in 1928, and Captain Alan Sington, the helpful alsatian enthusiast to whom Miss Crooke had written early in 1930 and who had been with Lady Kitty in Germany in 1928. Captain Sington became the chairman.

Early in February 1931 the four were invited to discuss their plans with W.M. Eagar of the NIB, Captain Fraser of St Dunstan's and Jack Humphrey, Mrs Eustis's manager from L'Oeil qui Voit. The experiment had already started, they reported, and sufficient finance was assured. They had obtained four alsatians and two scotch collies and were only awaiting the trainer promised by Mrs Eustis. However, they recognised that they could not extend the movement widely on their own resources and that they needed to be involved with agencies for the blind.

Fraser told them that although he had not been able to persuade his colleagues to share his view, he personally was in favour of guide dogs and hoped the scheme would go forward in association with established charities for the blind. Eagar supported this position and then exploded a bombshell by telling the 'nucleus' that the appeal they had already made for funds was illegal. He thought the NIB should interest itself in the experiment for two reasons: first, to give it the best chance of success; second, to regularise the fund-raising activities.

The main outcome of the discussion was agreement that the 'nucleus' should form themselves into a committee or society under an appropriate name and apply to the NIB for affiliation. This was formally granted on 25 February 1931 to the 'Committee of the Dogs as Guides for the Blind Training Scheme'. The NIB further undertook to give 'general assistance', particularly by enlisting the co-operation of local societies in the area around Wallasey.

The experiment was now gathering momentum, thanks largely to the financial and practical support of Mrs Eustis, who persuaded several of her friends – Mrs Baring, Mrs Hickman Morgan and Mrs Pratt – to give £50 'scholarships' that would each cover the cost of training one guide dog and its owner. A friend of Miss Crooke's, Mr Henry Williams, was connected with the Liverpool Corn Trade, which donated another £50. The alsatian show at Port Sunlight, which had inspired Lord Leverhulme's generosity and Musgrave Frankland's envy, together with other small donations brought the total up to nearly £300: not a lot, even in those days, but sufficient for a pioneering enterprise in which the participants expected to rough it.

A practical start to the work now waited on the trainer that Mrs Eustis had promised. Unfortunately, she was having some difficulty in honouring her undertaking. When it had been given she had five apprentices in Switzerland and three in America, but by early 1931 three Swiss and two American apprentices had dropped out because they were not suitable for the work. While she was trying to resolve this crisis she continued to shower Miss Crooke with advice. 'It will be absolutely necessary that the Society for the protection of animals and the police should be notified of the work and if possible be given their protection as our instructors have orders not to talk to people in the street or to answer questions. If some complaints are made through the public misunderstanding the work that is being done, the instructors have orders to refer the complaints to the nearest policeman, this protects our instructors from the insults which are hurled at them from well-meaning but mistaken dog lovers!!'

Mrs Eustis also wrote to the Duchess of Hamilton to enlist her support for guide dogs in England. The Duchess, who was apparently interested in the humane treatment of animals, had expressed enthusiasm for the work after visiting L'Oeil qui Voit in 1930.

At last, on 3 May, Miss Crooke heard that a Swiss trainer working at The Seeing Eye school in America would be sent over to conduct the first class. William Debetaz had been chosen, according to Jack Humphrey, because he was the only trainer available who combined 'a working

William Debetaz, the instructor sent by Mrs Eustis from The Seeing Eye *in America to train the first four British guide dogs and their owners in 1931. He is seen here with Judy, whose training was interrupted, but only briefly, when she produced a litter of puppies. None was kept, Miss Crooke recorded, 'and she recovered and went on with her training.'*

knowledge of English – or rather American – and the ability to do most of the work without supervision.' It is a measure of Mrs Eustis's generosity and commitment to spreading the benefits of guide dogs internationally that she cancelled classes in America in order to make Debetaz available.

Humphrey proposed to select the dogs himself, because Debetaz had no experience of this aspect of the work, and asked Miss Crooke to arrange for him to see the potential guides at convenient places immediately after his arrival in London at the beginning of July. While Miss Crooke was planning the selection process and arranging the necessary permits and visas that would allow Debetaz to enter and work in the country, Humphrey was assessing a possible permanent trainer named Jowett who had been sent to Switzerland to study the work and to be measured against the standards set by L'Oeil qui Voit for aspiring instructors. Humphrey's initial reservations about him were later confirmed by a detailed 'psycho-technical examination'. A three-page report concluded that 'he is a boy who could work under continual direction, who would take endless pain and trouble but from whom one could never expect much initiative.' He was therefore ruled out and the question of a permanent trainer was left for later consideration.

Humphrey arrived on 1 July, in London, where several dogs were brought to Hyde Park for his inspection. Others were seen during a short stop between trains in Birmingham. Still more were seen in Wallasey. In all he tested 28 dogs of which seven were chosen for training. There is no record of the breeds of the dogs from which Humphrey had to make his choice – were the scotch collies referred to by the 'nucleus' at the meeting on 10 February among them? – but the final seven were all pure-bred alsatian bitches. No doubt this outcome was influenced a good deal by the experience that Humphrey and Debetaz would have had in Switzerland and America and their natural preference to continue working with a breed they knew well and understood. The first time any other breed was used was in 1936 when a cross, which failed, and a golden retriever broke the solid ranks of the alsatians.

Six of the seven chosen dogs were donated. They were Judy (Mrs Fullerton), Flash (Mrs Hemingway), Folly (Mrs Brian Hill), Meta (Miss Workman), Fenella (Mrs Bond) and Peggy (Mr Kaiser). The seventh, Jock, was bought for £2.10s from Mrs Welch.

Training could now start. Humphrey had not stayed long and Debetaz, who had been found lodgings near the kennels with a Mrs Austin, was left to get the dogs ready. In addition to the training he also had to do all the kennel work, although a boy, Leslie Green, came in to feed the dogs on Sunday. The work load did not prevent him having a flutter on the horses, however, an indulgence that might have had disastrous consequences. William Austin, his landlady's son, recalled that one day the trainer narrowly missed being knocked down by a car in his haste to buy a newspaper containing the race results.

The problems with which Debetaz had to contend in 1931 were vividly described by Miss Crooke some years later. 'The British public were completely against the idea of making a dog work, which they thought cruel. In general they had never seen such a thing. There were no dogs working for the police, army, RAF in those days, even obedience tests were comparatively rarely seen and then only at dog shows ... Some people tried to stop the work. Often, and always in certain streets, Debetaz used to ask me to follow him in order to ward off these people who were such a nuisance so that he could carry on his training at all. There was one old man, the father of one of the men at the garage, who was a complete nuisance owing to his sentimental objection to dogs having to work.'

Conditions may not in fact have been quite as severe as Miss Crooke recalled them in the mid 1950s. At the time she recorded that the attitude of the public seemed all right 'and on the whole kindly'. A few 'fussy' types who liked to hear their own voices had tried to say the training was cruel but most of them lacked the courage to complain to the police. The only complaint she had heard of had been answered 'most satisfactorily' by the policemen – no doubt due to her sensible precaution of going to see the chief constable, Mr J. Ormerod, to explain what was happening. As a result they could always count on the help and understanding of the police.

When a complaint was brought before the local magistrate in 1932 by one or two people protesting about the noise from dogs being prepared for the second class, the case was dismissed. The training establishment was not even required to defend itself, because the summons was taken out against the wrong person. But there was never much doubt about the outcome, Miss Crooke reported, 'as we had a dozen people in court from houses near, in the road and the road behind and papers signed by 98 people in the road and the other three roads around, to say that the Guide Dogs were not a nuisance. No-one in those roads refused to sign.'

One unfortunate incident which occurred while the dogs were being trained for the first class was that Judy had puppies. It was not entirely unforeseen, because she had escaped at a vulnerable time while with her former owner, but the pups arrived rather sooner than expected, on one of Debetaz's days off, and Leslie Green, the kennel boy, went running to Miss Crooke to tell her that 'a big rat' was in with Judy.

'No puppies were kept', Miss Crooke recorded tersely, 'and she recovered and went on with her training.' Anticipating the event, Humphrey had told Miss Crooke what to do: ' ... have them knocked on the head as they are born and then dry up the milk at once. Use vinegar and water or have your dad (who was a doctor) tell you what to do or rather what to have done. The having of pups should not throw her out of work for more than three or four days, though her routes will have to be shortened for a few days after having the pups.'

Humphrey's matter-of-fact approach to the incident was the product of many similar experiences. 'The bitches we buy almost always seem to be in whelp', he wrote, 'but it does not bother our training schedule.'

By the last week of August, with the training proceeding well, Mrs Eustis was planning to send Humphrey and her son, Harrison, over towards the end of September to assess the dogs and help select the ones that would be given to the first blind applicants. She was hoping to accompany them for a day or two but her plans were so changeable that she had 'given up depending on such foolish things as calendar days!! The Seeing Eye is my lord and master', she declared, 'and I act accordingly.'

Five men had been asked to turn up at Wallasey on 3 October for the first class, but one turned out to be physically unsuitable. Rooms were taken for the remaining four in a boarding house in Victoria Road and they embarked on the training programme from which they would emerge three weeks later as Britain's first guide dog owners.

The obvious benefit that the dogs were bringing to these pioneer guide dog owners was quickly recognised by the local community. After about a fortnight, Miss Crooke recalled, 'we saw a change in the attitude of the people that we met daily on the roads and the shopkeepers along them. They began to see what it was all about and they were delighted. From then on these people would take a pride in explaining to strangers about our work and in preventing them from hindering us . . .'

Like most of the early guide dog owners, the first four were people of some courage. They had to be to overcome all the inadequacies of the new movement and the public ignorance of the work. Among them was Musgrave Frankland, whose early and continuing enthusiasm had helped to get the experiment launched. He was given Judy, the bitch who had had pups a few weeks earlier. Folly went to Thomas ap Rhys, from Bangor, who went on to use guide dogs for 48 years and died in 1979 at the age of 82 while training with his sixth dog. Ap Rhys had been studying electrical engineering at Bangor University College before the 1914–1918 war in which he lost his sight. He worked as a masseur for a while but had to give it up in 1920 due to the effects of mustard gas and then re-entered Bangor University and graduated with first class honours in philosophy and history. In the 1929 general election he stood unsuccessfully as a Labour candidate against Lloyd George. After the 1939–1945 war he re-trained in massage and physiotherapy and continued working until he was over 70. He was an outstanding competition walker and used to train with Folly up and down Bangor pier.

The last two members of the course were Allen Caldwell, who was given Flash, and G.W. Lamb who had Meta. Three of the four were St. Dunstaners, a fact which did little to bring about any immediate change of view among the council of St Dunstan's, although they did gradually

recognise the enormous benefit the dogs were bringing to the lives of blind people and eventually became firm supporters of the work.

Frankland had undertaken to find suitable people for the class, but the task had not been easy. Although there was considerable interest among members of the blind community, few were willing to participate in the experiment. Frankland pointed out that there were three St Dunstan's men on the first class, not because preference was given to ex-servicemen, but because with their pensions they were less dependent on actual earnings and could therefore spare the time for three weeks training more easily than civilian blind workers.

Miss Crooke made the same point to Eagar a few weeks later and he responded, unofficially, by assuring her that he was sure the NIB would be

Britain's first four guide dog owners completed their training in Wallasey, in October 1931. From the left, Allen Caldwell with Flash, G.W. Lamb with Meta, Musgrave Frankland with Judy and Thomas ap Rhys with Folly.

prepared to help men who were deterred from taking the course by the prospect of losing their wages – 'failing, of course, a sufficiency of funds in the coffers of your Fund'.

From the evidence of record books and a letter from Jack Humphrey written in Switzerland on 19 October 1931, the first class probably finished on 20 October or a day or two later. The occasion moved him to write with a message for the men and praise for Miss Crooke. 'Tell them for me to remember that when they leave they are like the boy leaving university, i.e. they are not fully-fledged business men but they have the basic knowledge so that they can be turned loose in the world without danger to others. Their real schooling will commence when they get home. If they will use the same care in work the first three weeks at home that I am sure Mr Debetaz has insisted on during the course, there will be no question of their success.'

The essence of this headmasterly, end-of-term address remains true. To use another analogy, newly-qualified guide dog owners are rather like drivers who have just passed their test: they know the techniques and they are probably safe, but they need a good deal of practical experience before they become really proficient and can use their mobility aids to the fullest advantage. An experienced guide dog owner who knows how to handle a dog, who has the ability to motivate it to realise its full potential, can achieve a degree of mobility and independence that is quite remarkable.

The final paragraph of Humphrey's letter was a tribute to Miss Crooke. 'I only hope', he wrote, 'that as (the men) go out with their new eyes you will have a real catch in your throat as you see the shuffle gone from their feet and their heads thrown back as they take a new outlook on life. No words of mine nor of theirs can thank you for your part in helping them to such new liberty as they may find.'

Miss Crooke's leading role in getting the experiment so successfully to this point was also recognised by Mrs Eustis, who told Eagar that Humphrey had nothing but praise and admiration for the work she had done, and 'as he is chary with either I feel that I should write you of it . . .'

The other three members of the 'nucleus', joined by Eagar, showed their appreciation of her achievement by presenting her, a few weeks later, with a pendant. Being a genuinely modest woman, it is not surprising that she did not keep the letter which accompanied the pendant among the many that were preserved. As time went on she became rather over-shadowed by others, although until she resigned in rather traumatic circumstances in 1940 she continued to play an important part in guide dog affairs. But, more than anyone else, she deserves the credit for getting the work started in Britain.

The balance sheet showed that the course had cost £145, which (as Mrs

Eustis had paid the trainer's salary) was accounted for by feeding, kennelling and equipment for the dogs, together with board and lodging for the trainer and the blind students. Among the papers left by Miss Crooke is a receipt made out to her for a silver cigarette case, which after 50 per cent discount and extra for engraving cost her £2.9s – a present for Debetaz, perhaps, as a mark of the gratitude and appreciation that she and the four blind men must have felt.

With the ending of the first class Debetaz leaves this chronicle. After a brief visit to Switzerland he sailed for America at the beginning of November, picking up Jock, one of the two dogs that were not used for the course, when the boat called at a British port on its way to New York. He resumed his work at The Seeing Eye and went on to become its vice-president in charge of training.

4

The Struggle to Survive

It had been agreed by the 'nucleus', on Mrs Eustis's insistence, that no further courses should be arranged until the first four guide dog owners had reported after six months' experience with their dogs. During this time, however, there were problems to be dealt with and other plans to be made.

One of the preoccupations was what they should call themselves and the dogs if the movement carried on. They clearly had doubts about the makeshift name under which they were now affiliated to the NIB (Committee of the Dogs as Guides for the Blind Training Scheme). Miss Crooke appeared to favour using the American title 'Seeing Eye' (at least as a corporate title) and despite a discouraging comment on this proposal at the end of October 1931 from Mrs Eustis she continued to put it forward in correspondence with Sington in the coming weeks. He thought 'blind-leading dogs' would be a better description of the guides, provided a hyphen was placed between the first two words to remove ambiguity. He wanted a short name, but not 'guide dogs' because that might suggest tracking, and was keen to have initials that could be used with a dog's name to indicate its status. PD (police dog) and TD (tracking dog) were used in Britain at that time and he suggested GFB or 'Guide for Blind'. This brief flurry of correspondence over a suitable name soon petered out, however, and a decision on the matter was put aside until it became necessary for them to make up their minds in July 1932.

Publicity was a headache, for a familiar reason: the press were getting the facts wrong and sometimes giving misleading accounts of the work. Particularly worrying was a report that the blind people had to spend three months at Wallasey learning how to use their dogs (the period was in fact three weeks). As Sington pointed out, the prospect of having to spend such a long time at the training centre would be enough to frighten off many potential applicants, to whom in any case the advantages of a guide dog were not yet proved.

The 'nucleus' were not too dismayed by the unreliability of press reports, however, and spread information about their activities wherever they could. Mrs Eustis did not attach much importance to publicity, taking the view that the money would come in without it and that once the dogs were in service they would carry their own publicity. Nevertheless, this was one subject on which the group did not follow Mrs Eustis's advice. They even gave demonstrations (at least, Mrs Bond did), something their mentor had discouraged.

'What does the average person know about a dog used by the blind for guiding?' asked Sington. 'Not one in a million know a thing and think of a beggar too probably. Demonstrations show it is something more than this I feel.'

The men had not long returned home with their new guides when the problems began. The only person with any experience of the work, Debetaz, had left for the United States and so early in November Miss Crooke wrote for advice to Jack Humphrey in Switzerland. He was being kept so busy by the Fortunate Fields kennels and L'Oeil qui Voit that he was at his desk by 3.30 in the morning and seldom stopped work until seven at night. Nevertheless, he offered some immediate 'first-aid' advice and passed Miss Crooke's letter on to Debetaz in America because he knew the dogs and the men and would be able to give more informed and detailed advice.

The six-page reply from America was, in fact, written by Willie Ebeling, who had joined The Seeing Eye to look after the training division, after discussing the problems with Debetaz. It makes interesting reading because it sets down some of the basic principles on which a successful partnership between a blind person and his guide dog depends. While great advances have been made over the years in dog supply, the training environment and some aspects of training itself, the guide dog owner's role still remains much as it was outlined by Ebeling.

The problems had arisen, he declared, because the dogs' masters had not adhered to the lessons they had been taught about the need to maintain accuracy in the details of the work until a 'complete working union' had been established. When the accuracy had become second nature, he continued, 'the work cannot help but be right and remain right'. He then proceeded to give a two and a half page analysis of the cause of Folly's nervousness, diagonal road crossing, distraction by other dogs and not stopping satisfactorily for traffic. The rest of the letter was devoted to Flash's inadequacy around obstacles and Lamb's difficulty in following Meta. Frankland seemed to be doing all right with Judy, although Ebeling was concerned that he was apparently just letting the dog take him without paying much attention to where he was. In the view of Debetaz it was a case of 'too much Secretary and not relying upon himself'.

The men were not correcting the dogs' faults as they arose, said Ebeling. Even more important, they were forgetting to praise the dogs when the work was done correctly. Folly's master, ap Rhys, was too hard with his guide, and was not following corrections with a reward or caress in a tone of voice that could be understood by the dog. 'Any caress which does not come from the bottom of the heart is almost as good as useless,' he told them. 'Get command into the voice and get joy into the voice to show the dog that the master is pleased with the obeyed command . . . the "attagirl" should be "sung" at the dog with the same joy as if the master were suddenly presented with a million pounds.' (The American 'attagirl' was not used as a term of praise for long in Britain but the corrective 'phui' that was introduced by Mrs Eustis's trainers continued until at least the late 1940s.)

Obedience exercises were very important, Ebeling insisted. During these exercises, the blind person was absolute master of his dog and if the dog accepted this many of the problems would be resolved.

Guide dog owners vary, of course, in their ability to be regarded as an 'absolute master' by their dogs, and people often assume that it is the dog that is master. There is the classic (even corny, perhaps) cartoon or joke about the guide dog owner who stops a sighted person to ask the way. The person then bends down and gives instructions to the dog. This may, of course, be just a comic view of the 'does he take sugar' attitude, but in fact many people do not realise that the dog's role is limited. It is trained to walk in a straight line and avoid obstacles; to stop at kerbs and places like doors and stairs; and to disregard a command to cross the road if its master has got it wrong and is about to get himself and the dog killed by an approaching vehicle. But that, with a few other subtleties which will emerge later, is all. It is the owner who is in charge and who decides when to cross the road by giving the command 'Forward'.

*   *   *

To many people in the 1930s, the idea of dogs leading blind people seemed incredible. News of the new development in mobility for the blind had spread to Ireland but, wrote Richard O'Farrell in Dublin to L'Oeil qui Voit, 'I cannot get either the blind or the sighted to take your movement seriously. They argue . . . that the whole idea is fantastic!' A later letter to Mrs Eustis, exploring the possibility that some of the doubters might visit her establishment in Switzerland, was signed, 'Your blind, dogless, but not despairing disciple'. Nearly half a century was to pass before a guide dog school was established in the Republic, although the British Association supplied them with dogs for some 25 years before they had their own facilities.

While the 'nucleus', principally Miss Crooke, was trying to keep the momentum of the new movement going and dealing, by remote control, with the aftercare problems of the first course, Eagar of the NIB was watching developments. He saw the potential value of guide dogs to blind people and was ready to help the pioneers get established, but he was also anxious to avoid conflict with existing services and appeals for the blind. He had kept Captain Hobbs of the Tail-Waggers informed about the progress of the first course and had been up to Wallasey to see the work for himself. During the latter part of 1931 and while plans were developing for a second course to be held at the end of 1932 he gave what advice and support he could and waited.

In the meantime, more problems were arising with the new guide dog owners. Towards the end of January Lamb wrote to Miss Crooke saying he would have to send Meta back because she was getting more nervous each time he took her out amongst a crowd. It was a condition that Ebeling and Debetaz had warned of when they wrote with advice a few weeks earlier. 'It is his not following the dog, his constant walking into the dog or bumping, and his being too far ahead of his dog's body which makes the animal nervous. With her teaching it is enough to drive her crazy and if this is not corrected immediately she will someday not go forward. She will plant herself and say: Try and make me do it, I value my own skin even if you do not value yours.'

Humphrey was philosophical about the matter, telling Miss Crooke that she would have to get used to the fact that a certain percentage of blind people found it difficult, if not impossible, to adjust themselves to the use of a dog. It's like a married couple, he suggested: sometimes they just cannot seem to get on together, but if you suggest they separate they decide to stay together. Ebeling offered further advice from America: try cutting the dog's speed down. A better understanding between dog and master was all that was needed. Sington seemed more concerned about formal qualifications for the dogs that would be recognised by the Kennel Club and dismissed Lamb's troubles impatiently: '(he) seems to be a complete mutt.'

Sington may not have been far wrong in that judgement because Lamb also failed to exercise much control over his dog at home. 'About the false teeth which Meta has eaten up,' wrote Humphrey. 'This is a new question . . . none of my trainers have false teeth.' Destructive behaviour in the house could be corrected as one would with any puppy or dog but, as he recognised, the problem with guide dogs (in those days) was that many of the young adult animals that they acquired for training had never been in a house.

Thomas ap Rhys was an outstanding competition walker and is seen here with Folly in 1939 training on Bangor pier. Six months after receiving his guide ap Rhys reported enthusiastically on her skill in avoiding obstacles and retrieving his hat when it blew off.

Caldwell's Flash had become jumpy when cars back-fired, a problem Ebeling attributed to its owner's reactions. All the dogs had been tested on loud noises and the reaction in the dog had arisen, he suggested, because Caldwell himself had probably jumped at the sound.

Despite the difficulties and anxieties, all four of the first class completed their six months' trial period and reported enthusiastically. 'Flash has revolutionised my working life,' wrote Allen Caldwell. 'Behold me now with a practically unlimited range, and able to proceed at a good, health-giving pace. Obstructions of any kind have no more terrors for me now, for Flash is so extremely sensible of my safety, consequent on her excellent training. Her piloting of me along a crowded pavement is so skilful, that it has to be seen to be believed.

'It is, however, in the crossing of a busy street that she is a triumph. No more unnecessary hanging about, for as soon as it is safe, off we go and often leave sighted people standing. Not only has my dog given me

Ap Rhys used guide dogs for 48 years and died in 1979 at the age of 82 while retraining with his sixth dog. With him in this picture, which was taken on the day of his death at the Bolton training centre, are John Bailey, who was then in charge of fund-raising for guide dogs in the north-east and was also retraining with a new dog, and Bob Steele, the centre's head instructor at the time.

glorious freedom and independence, never known since pre-war days, but delightful companionship, and an unfailing friend, from whom I always receive an exuberant welcome after even a very short separation.'

After praising Folly's skill in avoiding lamp posts and other obstacles, Thomas ap Rhys added: 'she takes me down the pier daily, conducting me to the proper turnstile and negotiating all the barriers and seats that are left about. Her training in picking up anything is proving a most useful accomplishment. This was brought home to me the other day when my hat blew off. There was no one else on the pier at the time but Folly found it and brought it back quite safely ... I notice that after a very few journeys, she learns to stop at a particular gate I want to turn into ...'

Ap Rhys concluded that 'the biggest advantage of a dog-guide to a blind man accustomed to walking about alone, is that all nerve strain is entirely eliminated.'

G.W. Lamb reported: 'Meta is going well at present, going a nice steady pace and taking me through the crowds beautifully ... I had rather an exciting experience the other night whilst out for a walk, the pavement was in course of repair, naturally I did not know this and when we got up to the barrier, Meta stopped and sat. People came rushing up to tell me the pavement was up; of course they were too late! ... I just gave her the order "left" and we went away merrily, the crowd saying what a good dog it was, and Meta seemed quite fussy too, hearing herself praised. She has indeed been a treasure ...'

Musgrave Frankland declared that 'a guide dog is almost equal in many ways to giving a blind man sight itself. I have walked with her for miles, scores of miles, down main roads with rapid motor traffic, up country roads with and without pavements, roads with awkward lamp posts, protruding trees, overhanging boughs, and I have never had the slightest mishap that could in the least reflect upon the guiding powers of Judith.' Unfortunately, Frankland's partnership with Judith was short-lived. Only a year after this glowing report was written the dog escaped from the garden while in season and was knocked down by a vehicle.

*   *   *

The four reports provided the impetus that was needed to establish the work on a permanent footing. Tentative plans for a second course were now moved on, financed partly by funds left over from the first course and partly by a contribution from the Tail-Waggers. 'Captain Hobbs ... is a stout fellow in every sense and I think will be most useful,' wrote Eagar to Miss Crooke. The NIB increased its commitment to the cause by nominating W.H. Tate, a member of its general purposes committee, to the guide dog committee, and from Switzerland Jack Humphrey promised a trainer who would come over early in July 1932. 'You will like him,' he wrote, 'a very quiet and conscientious boy, speaks very little if any English now (fact is he does not speak much in any language but gets along well with his blind) so you can practise your French.' The plan was to select eight dogs, of which six would qualify, and to have 'six good men ready and two held in readiness in case more than six dogs finish'.

Looking further ahead, Humphrey told Miss Crooke that when the work started in earnest two permanent employees would be needed: a trainer and a *paid* secretary and general manager. He urged her to consider taking the latter job herself: 'I know of no one who could fill the job better than yourself if you would accept it.' About two weeks later, in a 'private' postscript to an account of a meeting with Sington, Eagar noted: 'Captain Sington tells me that Miss Crooke is an artist by profession and finding times very hard. She might be persuaded to take a paid post with a salary perhaps of £100 per annum.'

The acquisition of a permanent trainer now became the subject of a great deal of debate and correspondence. In May Humphrey discussed a number of options. An English boy could be trained but that would take at least two years and many dropped out after three to six months when the novelty wore off. A Swiss boy was a possibility in a year to 18 months or, perhaps, someone from Potsdam. The committee were keen to have an Englishman and urged Humphrey to accept for training in Switzerland a 29-year-old ex-police dog trainer named Sly who had applied for the job. A great deal of time was spent exploring this possibility before he eventually withdrew his application. There the question of a permanent trainer rested for a while.

In the meantime, the committee met in London on 9 June 1932, after which Sington triumphantly announced to Humphrey 'that our scheme has definitely started ... and Captain Hobbs, secretary of the Tail-Waggers' Club, has taken us over as his official charity.'

The club that had given its support to the new movement was formed by Hobbs in 1928. It was the dogs, not their owners, who were the members and they were enrolled for life on payment of a subscription of 2/6d (12½p in today's money, although it was worth a lot more then). Members received a collar disc bearing their club number and the club's logo of crossed tails with the motto 'I help my pals'.

Hobbs's enormous energy and enthusiasm produced remarkable results. Largely through his efforts the club raised £20,000 in a year to build a veterinary clinic and hospital, the Beaumont, in Camden Town. Within two years of its creation the club had about 300,000 canine members, including several Royal dogs, who were given a separate series of numbers with the prefix R. The late Dukes of Windsor and Gloucester enrolled R.22, a great dane, in 1930 and Mick the Miller, the famous Greyhound Derby winner, became a Tail-Wagger in 1930. In addition to its fund-raising for charity the club also published a monthly magazine and sponsored worthy projects such as its Lost Dog Scheme.

After Hobbs's sudden death in December 1935 at the early age of 39, the club continued to support guide dogs, but the 1939-45 war led to a huge drop in the dog population, and consequently in club membership, as dog breeding was reduced and pet dogs were not replaced. Membership never again reached the pre-war level and the club was eventually closed, although its funds continue to be administered for charitable purposes by the Tail-Waggers' Club Trust.

*   *   *

Eagar was now growing concerned about the possibility of conflict with the NIB's National Unification Collecting Agreements and in July 1932 advised the committee that in order to give themselves greater freedom

Georges Gabriel, the instructor loaned by Mrs Eustis from L'Oeil qui Voit to run the second and third classes in Wallasey, training Tina in Liverpool in February 1933. He was described by Jack Humphrey as 'a very quiet and conscientious boy, speaks very little if any English now (fact is he does not speak much in any language) but gets along well with his blind.'

they should apply for their own registration as a charity. This they did, giving themselves the title Guide Dogs for the Blind in place of Dogs as Guides for the Blind which they had been using until then.

Humphrey arrived in England with a trainer, Georges Gabriel, on 11 July and after a meeting with Eagar and seeing some dogs in London, moved on to Wallasey via Birmingham, where there were more dogs to be seen. The training seems to have gone smoothly although the public were still liable to be a nuisance. One day Gabriel got into a heated argument with a man who was interfering with his work and dragged him over to the car Miss Crooke was driving for traffic training. Gabriel, of course, had very little English and so the man complained to Miss Crooke that the dog's collar – an ordinary check chain – was cruel, and that he was going to report the matter to the police. Thereupon, they bundled him into the car and drove off to the police station a couple of miles away where he was told not to be foolish. When he then complained that he had no money for his bus fare back home he got little sympathy from Miss Crooke and Gabriel, who drove off, leaving him to walk home.

The second class arrived to join their dogs on 15 October. Although it had been hoped to make up a group of six, the final number was only five

and one of these, the only woman, did not complete the course. Once again, three of the successful four were St Dunstaners: J.H. Burt from Southampton, whose dog Daphne worked with him until it was 12 years old; J. Worthington from Stockport whose Olga had nine puppies (all destroyed) during training and went on working (after 1934 with another owner) until she was about 13; and J.W. Birchall from Chadwell Heath in Essex who had a white bitch called Mona that died in 1937. The fourth man was Alfred Morgan, who worked for the Mersey Docks and Harbour Board as a clerk in the stores at the Coburg Dockyard. He did much in the coming years to publicise guide dogs and wrote a number of revealing and moving accounts of the impact they had had on his life. With his dog, Bella, he gave a demonstration to Members of Parliament in 1936, and travelled widely with her for another two years before finding her dead in her kennel one morning. She was only eight years old.

Alfred Morgan and Bella, who were on the second class to be held in Britain, in October 1932, giving a demonstration for MPs in Parliament Square in July 1936. Less than a year after training with Bella he wrote '. . . I have regained my freedom. The fact is I have another pair of eyes . . .'

The June 1933 issue of The "Tail-Wagger" Magazine reproduced extracts from a letter written by Morgan about his experiences with Bella in the short time he had then had her. The yard where he worked was in the south of Liverpool and he lived in the north, which meant travelling by tramcar. He was able to do most of the journey by himself but needed a guide to take him through the docks.

'I have to go over dock gates and bridges, and across great open spaces strewn with piles of cargo, motor lorries, railway trucks, cranes and engines of every description, and all the paraphernalia of dockland. No blind man on the face of this earth could negotiate it alone,' he wrote.

'Well, Bella and I manage it very nicely, thank you. We walk through the busiest part of the town – about two miles – to one of the big city railway termini, take a train – not always from the same platform – go through six suburban stations, and toddle off home, like Darby and Joan. In fact, that is exactly what some of our fellow passengers call us, in a friendly, amused kind of way.

'At first they were simply astounded, and did not believe that I was a blind man; in fact, some of them don't believe it even now. There are people who have seen me walking through the station for the last five months who get the shock of their lives when they accidentally find out.

'. . . I know, and appreciate, and at one time even envied, the way that some blind men can get about without a dog. There is just this difference. No blind man, no matter how clever he is, can cover the ground with the ease and speed that I can, with Bella's help. Now do you see what I mean by saying that I have regained my freedom? The fact is I have another pair of eyes . . .'

While Gabriel was completing the training of the dogs for the second class, the committee asked Mrs Eustis to let him stay on for a third class. She agreed and while in London at the end of September 1932 also went to the Ministry of Labour to get permission to send over a foreign trainer who would set up a training programme for British apprentices. Before she left she showed once again her appreciation of Miss Crooke's qualities: 'thanks *heaps* for being true to work with,' she wrote. 'Without you it would be Bedlam.'

The committee, which since July 1932 had included Mrs Schuster, were now becoming anxious about funds to finance future courses and put the work on a secure footing. At the beginning of October they wrote to the NIB asking for help, and as a consequence were invited to a meeting with Eagar and J.H. Batty, chairman of the Institute's finance committee. Eagar put his cards on the table: there had been great competition between collections for the blind, he explained, as a result of which the Institute, for some time past, had been unifying collections in different parts of England. Frankly, they did not want people who ordinarily subscribed to blind societies to be appealed to on behalf of guide dogs, and preferred that such organisations as the Tail-Waggers should be used to their fullest capacity.

The committee's immediate need was met by the NIB guaranteeing an overdraft of £100 should it be needed. The Tail-Waggers demonstrated their support by running an 'evening' at the Piccadilly Hotel which raised £160 for guide dogs, and followed this with another event at the Dorchester on 20 January. 'Scholarships' were given by Gordon Stewart, who bred great danes, and Mrs Hickman Morgan. The committee was strengthened by the addition of Lady Sackville and A.J.W. Kitchin, representing the NIB's finance committee, and an application was made to the BBC for a broadcast appeal.

St Dunstan's was still on the sidelines, although it demonstrated its interest in developments by sending Colonel Eric Ball to the committee's meeting with the NIB about finance. 'They are evidently beginning to wake up,' commented Miss Crooke. One reason for their interest, however, was that they were as concerned as the NIB to prevent a national appeal on behalf of guide dogs. They therefore resolved to work out with the Institute a policy that would recognise Guide Dogs for the Blind as 'a small experimental movement, subject to safeguards which would avoid the new charity making general appeals'. On 18 May 1933 the NIB's general purposes committee passed a resolution that led, shortly afterwards, to a joint memorandum with St Dunstan's which was sent to the Guide Dogs committee.

> The NIB and St Dunstan's cannot participate in or agree to the launching of a National Appeal addressed to the General Public. On the other hand, the NIB and St Dunstan's would favour appeals being made to dog lovers, papers, societies, and organisations generally concerned with dogs, and would do what is in their power to support the Guide Dogs Committee in making such appeals. They would, however, not favour attempts to reach dog lovers and dog organisations through the medium of the general national and provincial press, and of other such means as would conflict with the appeals made for the blind by the national and local societies for the blind.

To sugar the pill, the NIB offered clerical assistance should it be needed, but it was small compensation for a very restrictive proposal. So insecure did the members of the new movement feel, however, that they agreed to the memorandum without hesitation and immediately invited St Dunstan's to join the committee. Its nominee, Lieutenant-Colonel Charles Kerr, took his place for the first time in December 1933 and remained on the council (after 1942 as Lord Teviot) until 1962.

The committee was now growing fast. By the middle of 1933 there were 13 members, including one or two names that would figure prominently in the years to come: Roger Eckersley, who held an influential position in the BBC, Captain Hobbs of the Tail-Waggers and Ben Purse, a third representative of the NIB. They had all been elected for

Four early supporters of the guide dog movement in Wallasey in 1933. Miss Crooke, on the right, and, next to her, Lady Kitty Ritson, were members of the original 'nucleus' of four, which by the time this picture was taken had grown to a committee of 13. Lady Sackville, on the left, remained a member of the Association's general council until 1958 and Mrs Lucy (later Lady) Schuster was one of the main driving forces during the 1930s, becoming honorary organiser in 1936 and continuing to play a part in guide dog affairs until her death in 1950.

the practical help they could give and this soon yielded fruit. Eckersley persuaded Christopher Stone, a well-known broadcaster, to do a radio appeal on Sunday, 17 September 1933. It is not clear why such an appeal did not conflict with the agreement so recently made with the NIB and St Dunstan's, but there appear to have been no objections. The NIB's representatives were perhaps reassured by the decision to submit a copy of the text to the Institute for approval before the broadcast.

Ben Purse played his part by liaising with the Advisory Committee on the Welfare of the Blind and regional associations for the blind, and Lady

Sackville organised a fund-raising event at Knole House. Mrs Schuster had persuaded the Kennel Club to grant free registration for guide dogs, provided they were otherwise eligible.

The concern over money led the committee, at its meeting on 26 July 1933, to suggest that the NIB or St Dunstan's should be invited to take over the fund-raising responsibility. Kitchin, representing the NIB's finance committee, told them the invitation would almost certainly not be accepted and so they resolved to approach the Tail-Waggers' Club for the support needed to ensure the continuance of the work. It was a crucial decision, although it was to be another year before their approach was consummated by the formation of The Guide Dogs for the Blind Association, financially and administratively backed by the Tail-Waggers.

$$* \quad * \quad *$$

Gabriel's second course ended in April 1933, the students on this occasion being rather more comfortably accommodated in a house, loaned by a sympathetic Wallasey councillor, for which furniture had been borrowed or hired. The five men who had started on 25 March were described by Miss Crooke as 'not a very promising lot' and indeed one soon dropped out. Of the remaining four, three were again St Dunstaners: W. Johnston was a Boer War veteran living in Bradford; S.A. Worlidge had a poultry farm near Brigg in Lincolnshire; W.S. Castle's occupation is not recorded, but he lived in Birmingham. The one civilian was L.J. Owen, a Liverpool piano-tuner.

Unfortunately, Owen's dog, Dinah, soon began to show signs of aggression. Miss Crooke gave what advice she could and immediately wrote for further guidance to Gabriel, who had returned to Switzerland as soon as the class disbanded. Their efforts were unavailing, however, and despite a brief return to Wallasey for a 'refresher' the dog's behaviour continued to cause alarm. After attacking a boy in August she was withdrawn from work. Prospective buyers also found her aggressive and she was eventually put down. It was a sad fate, particularly as the dog had, in a few months, already made a profound impact on Owen's life – he was hardly recognisable, there was so much improvement, reported Miss Crooke.

Dinah had been donated by the committee's chairman, Captain Sington, and when Miss Crooke first reported her concern about the dog to the committee in May they questioned her handling of the case. The incident provoked her to try to do something about defining her role and how much the committee was entitled to dabble in the day-to-day running of the training activities. 'It must now be definitely understood that the trainer and I do our work and arrangements without interference from the committee in matters which they don't understand,' she wrote to Gabriel.

It was not the first time she had expressed her frustrations. In April, she had complained to Humphrey that at times she was supposed to know and see to everything, and at others to be a sort of typist. 'What am I supposed to be and do?' she asked. 'Can you tell me just what my job is, and what the committee should be and do?' Humphrey's response to these two letters was to advise Miss Crooke to lay down the terms under which she was prepared to continue and tell the committee to 'take it or leave it'. She should tell them that she had virtually given up her painting and other interests for the sake of guide dogs but would be very happy to return to them. He concluded by advising her to 'put a little rouge just in front and under your ears as that is the place a fellow first whitens up when he gets in a hot argument. And then pocket that little habit you have of not saying anything which is not nice and tell them what is what.' There is no evidence that she followed Humphrey's advice, but the impending alliance with the Tail-Waggers, added to her natural diffidence, may have led her to remain silent.

Also, Mrs Eustis had tactfully pointed out the distinct roles of committee and training department to Mrs Schuster and suggested to Miss Crooke that if she wanted to continue the work she should make herself more indispensable by spending some time in Switzerland acquiring a greater knowledge of the training. She accepted the invitation and spent several weeks at Vevey in July and August 1933.

Earlier in the year, while the third class was still in progress, the committee were pressing Mrs Eustis to let them know when they could have a 'head trainer' for two or three years or more. They were rewarded at the end of March with the news that their 'permanent instructor', Nikolai Liakhoff (k not pronounced), would be sent to them towards the end of September. His wife, said Mrs Eustis, 'was a brick, speaks very good English and could be used, I think, to do some work in the house.' The proposal was that he would stay until an English apprentice had been trained and would then be moved by Mrs Eustis elsewhere.

During a one-week visit to Vevey in August, Mrs Schuster met Liakhoff and was 'delighted with him'. Uncertainties over funds and complications over a long-term contract resulted in Liakhoff agreeing to come for one year initially, to keep the work going and give the committee time to make more permanent plans. Mrs Schuster then returned to England to help ensure funds to guarantee a year's work.

Liakhoff arrived in England in October 1933 with his wife Irena and young daughter Tatiana. After spending a few days at the Schusters' home they travelled to Wallasey where Liakhoff started work at a salary of £5 a week plus allowances.

5

Growing Pains

Nikolai Liakhoff was born in the Russian Black Sea port of Odessa on 17 April 1897 and followed his father, General Dmitri Liakhoff, into the army. He served in a Guards Cossack regiment, was awarded the Order of St George for bravery in the First World War and became an ADC to General Wrangel during the Civil War that followed. When the White Russian army was forced to evacuate the Crimea in November 1920, Liakhoff went to Constantinople (as Istanbul was then called) where he met Princess Irena Ourousoff, another refugee from the revolution. They married in 1925 and for the next few years led, like many others in their situation, a rather unsettled existence. For a while they lived in Paris, where Liakhoff worked as a taxicab driver, but in 1930 they moved to Switzerland, possibly because members of the Ourousoff family had settled there, possibly because of his health. He became a driving instructor for a time and joined L'Oeil qui Voit as an apprentice in the spring of 1932.

No sooner had Liakhoff started his new career than Mrs Eustis heard from Mrs Thomas Chadbourne, the American who had been underwriting all L'Oeil qui Voit's expenses, that due to the Great Depression that followed the Wall Street crash of 1929 she would have to cut her support by a half. Economies were immediately made, but they only postponed the inevitable and in 1934 Mrs Eustis closed down the school and kennels in Switzerland and moved permanently to the United States. She was probably anticipating the closure and thinking about the future of her staff in the early months of 1933 when Liakhoff was offered to the British committee as their permanent trainer. It was said in later years that she offered Liakhoff the choice of going to America or Britain, and that he chose the latter because it was a monarchy. The story may be apocryphal, but his daughter thought it could well be true. His choice may also have

Nikolai Liakhoff about six months after his arrival in Wallasey from L'Oeil qui Voit in October 1933. The original plan was that he would stay until an English apprentice had been trained and would then be moved by Mrs Eustis elsewhere, but in the event he stayed on to play a leading part in the development of guide dog work in Britain.

been influenced by the wish to remain near to his elderly father and only brother, who were both living in Europe.

When he arrived in England in October 1933 Liakhoff had had only some 18 months' experience of guide dog work. Nevertheless, he quickly won the committee's confidence and had a fourth class under way. Soon after it finished, in March 1934, Miss Crooke reported to Mrs Eustis that it had been a great success and that the four men and one woman had all liked Liakhoff very much. 'He is most awfully nice with them,' she wrote. 'I like his training with his dogs and with his blind people very much indeed . . . and he and Madame are both so nice.'

Sington confirmed the good impression: 'We are all delighted with Captain Liakhoff. He is the right man in the right place. He is an excellent trainer and is most sound in everything he does, and everybody likes him.'

There must have been some tricky, and often hilarious, moments during this and subsequent courses due to Liakhoff's lack of English. He used to say, in later years, that he knew only two words when he arrived: yes and no. One day, when he was out with a dog that had been treated with mercurochrome, he was stopped by two women who asked if it was blood. He smiled and said 'Yes'. 'Did you injure it?' he was asked. He smiled again: 'Yes', whereupon the indignant ladies lost no time in reporting him to the RSPCA. The story, which no doubt became embroidered with repeated telling (because he was a great raconteur), concluded with Liakhoff having to explain the incident to an inspector through an interpreter, presumably either his wife or Miss Crooke.

In the wake of previous courses problems had arisen with the dogs. The fourth course broke new ground in precipitating a domestic crisis. About three weeks after it finished one of the participants returned to Wallasey and asked Miss Crooke to take the dog back – 'or rather, he had been sent by his wife with a note asking me to do so,' wrote Miss Crooke. 'Trouble at home, he had become so independent and was able to go anywhere at any time that he liked, and did so, so she was jealous and threatened to leave him.'

As Miss Crooke commented, it was a great compliment to the dog and the work, confirmed by the fact that they had made the journey through Liverpool and across the Mersey on the ferry to the training centre on their own. She sent him home with a letter to his wife and followed it up by taking Liakhoff to visit them.

The man concerned must have been A. Gaffney, a St Dunstaner living in St Helens. Other members of the course lived too far away to have made the journey as described by Miss Crooke. The matter seems to have been resolved because the records show that he continued to use the dog until May 1936, when it was sold as a pet. 'Gaffney says he could not afford to keep and feed her,' Miss Crooke recorded. 'The dog had also shown signs of over-protection'.

'An unsatisfactory man,' she concluded.

It is instructive to follow the fortunes of the other dogs on this course, because it highlights some of the difficulties that bedevilled the early years. Flare, a black-and-tan bitch, went to H. Rotchell, who lived in Birmingham. In April, about six weeks after the class finished, the dog was back in kennels: 'Rotchell no good,' Miss Crooke noted cryptically in the record book. She was then given to J. Rawlinson on the next class in June that year and worked with him for less than two years before again being returned to kennels. This time the reason was thin skin on the pads of the dog's feet, which caused pain when she walked on grit or uneven surfaces. She was therefore sold as a pet for £3 and went to a home where she would mostly live on grassland.

Gwen was a grey bitch that was given to H. Ollington of Earlsfield in London. Just over a year later she, too, was back in kennels and was then given away as a pet. No reason was given, but Ollington does not appear to have had another dog.

The remaining two dogs seem to have fared slightly better. Kitty, a silver grey bitch, lasted a few months with the only woman on the class, Mrs E. Wells, and then went to J. Bailey of Birmingham on the next class, after which we lose track of her. Cora had the most settled, if not the longest, life with Peter Johnson, who kept her until she became ill and had to be put down in October 1939.

Stories such as these were commonplace in the days when the dogs were not specially bred and reared for guide dog work, when there were so few applicants from which to choose and there was so little opportunity to make good matches. Inevitably, there were other hazards as well. Edwina, from the third class, was returned only five months after qualifying, following a motor accident in which she and her owner, S.A. Worlidge, were involved. The dog ran off and for a week there was no trace of her. Then a boy reported seeing a dog wearing a harness wandering about the countryside many miles from Worlidge's home in Hatfield. During the next three days Worlidge and the boy walked about 60 miles calling the dog before at last the bedraggled and badly-shaken animal was found. The experience must have left it too nervous to be any further use as a guide dog because it was sold soon after as a pet.

Among the dogs from which Gabriel selected a handful for his second course at the end of 1932 was Lish, a dark sable bitch whose dam was Lona, the former German guide dog brought to England in 1928 by Lady Kitty Ritson and subsequently passed on to Mrs Bond. Lish had been sold for £5 to the training centre, but Gabriel found the dog, who was only 10 months old, too young and unsettled. Mrs Bond had therefore taken Lish back in February 1933 but wanted Liakhoff to take her for his first course starting in October that year. Liakhoff was not keen, but Mrs Bond nevertheless brought her and one other dog for testing, despite being told not to do so by Miss Crooke. When the three met in October on a Liverpool station, Liakhoff refused both dogs and Mrs Bond was so annoyed that she was extremely rude and unpleasant to Miss Crooke.

'After that', Miss Crooke noted, 'I would never have anything to do with her.' In fact, Mrs Bond had played little part in developments after the initial contacts with Mrs Eustis and the decision to start training near Miss Crooke's home in Wallasey rather than in Yorkshire where Mrs Bond had her kennels. She was, however, elected a vice-president in due course and when Miss Crooke was in difficulties with the executive committee in 1937 over her title and responsibilities, Mrs Bond supported her by threatening to resign. She had apparently put the incident on the Liverpool station behind her.

* * *

While Liakhoff was settling himself in at Wallasey, the Tail-Waggers' Club was considering the committee's invitation, issued in July 1933, to assume financial responsibility for the future of guide dog training in Britain. The approach to Captain Hobbs had been made by Mrs Schuster, and many years later Miss Lilian Shrimpton, who was then Hobbs's secretary, recalled how 'charmingly persuasive' she was. The club was still covering the immediate expenses but in June 1934 Hobbs responded to the committee's request with proposals for the formation of The Guide Dogs for the Blind Association with an executive committee that would comprise six members of the old committee and an equal number of representatives of the Tail-Waggers' Club. The Association would also have a general council of up to 25 members and an advisory committee drawn from representatives of blind associations and others willing to help. These proposals were accepted by the committee and the new Association was registered as a limited company at Somerset House on 30 August 1934. The first general meeting (special) and the first meetings of the general council and of the executive committee were held on 2 October at the offices of the NIB in Great Portland Street, where the old committee had met for some time.

As 'tail-wagger-in-chief' and secretary of the Tail-Waggers' Club, Hobbs clearly had a position of considerable power on the new executive committee, but he nevertheless declined the invitation to become chairman. He did, however, readily accept the post of treasurer. The man who was elected chairman was A. Croxton-Smith, who was chairman of the Tail-Waggers' Club. He was also a leading 'doggy' journalist, a breeder and judge of dogs and, from 1937 to 1948, chairman of the Kennel Club. Sington became vice-chairman and Miss Crooke acting secretary. She had been secretary to the old committee (for which she received an honorarium of £100 a year) and now agreed to continue in the post until more satisfactory long-term arrangements could be made. In due course the job was taken on by the Tail-Waggers' secretary, Miss Lilian Shrimpton, and all the appeals and committee work was done from the club's office. Miss Crooke then, in January 1936, accepted Liakhoff's invitation to become his assistant at a salary equal to the honorarium she had been receiving. It was an uneasy situation, however, and although her status was enhanced later in the year when she was given the title chief assistant and founder, conflicts over duties and responsibilities were not resolved until, at the beginning of 1937, she gave an undertaking to accept Liakhoff's instructions 'in all matters'.

At the first general meeting (special) on 2 October 1934 an impressive array of former patrons of the Guide Dogs committee became vice-patrons of the new Association. It was hoped to get a member of the Royal Family as patron but this was not achieved until 1938 when the Earl

In March 1934 the committee took on an apprentice, Bob Montgomery, seen here with Liakhoff during the short time that he stayed. The two men remained close friends, however, and some years later Montgomery reappeared on the scene as a member of the general council. When this picture was taken, and for several more years, the handles were fixed to the dogs' harnesses at shoulder level, the shafts passing through loops higher up. Some time around the end of the 1930s the fixing was moved to a position on the dog's back.

of Athlone accepted the position. Formerly Prince Alexander of Teck, he was Queen Mary's brother and in 1904 married Princess Alice, a grand-daughter of Queen Victoria. Among the distinguished vice-patrons were the Archbishop of Canterbury, a duke, three duchesses, a marchioness, three earls and two countesses, together with a dozen lesser lights. The position of president was left vacant until 1938, when it was filled by the Earl of Derby, but honour was done to those who had laboured to bring events thus far by electing as vice-presidents Alan Sington, Miss Crooke, Mrs Bond and Lady Kitty Ritson. A number of benefactors, including Mrs Harold Baring, Miss M.J. Chadwick, C.B. Cochran, Mrs Hickman Morgan and Mrs Schuster, were elected life members.

All this wooing of titled patronage was, of course, largely to add distinction to the letter-heading and to give the obscure and untried Association respectability and status. The vice-patrons were not really expected to do anything and very few did. There were, however, many titled people who supported guide dogs very actively over the years.

The union with Tail-Waggers was the highlight of 1934, but it was by no means the only notable event of the year. In March, in a fit of over-enthusiasm, the committee took on an apprentice, Bob Montgomery, despite Liakhoff's lack of experience and advice from Switzerland that he should be allowed some time to get settled. Perhaps because the committee had acted too hastily he did not stay long with Liakhoff in Wallasey, but the two men remained close friends and some years later Montgomery reappeared on the scene as a member of the general council.

The first publicity film was made in 1934, although Sington had some anxieties about whether it would infringe the agreement with the NIB and St Dunstan's, which he described as 'really an iniquitous one'. This is the first record of the vexation and resentment that was felt by guide dog supporters at having to restrain their fund-raising activities.

By 1934 the early difficulty in getting sufficient applicants for guide dogs was over. Whether it was due to the grapevine within the blind community or the efforts of the NIB, there were 'heaps of blind people wanting dogs,' according to Miss Crooke, 'far more than we can supply'; and more applications were coming from young, civilian blind people. The advantage of this large pool of applicants was that Liakhoff was now able to select for training only those people most likely to persevere in the face of the inevitable difficulties they would encounter and most capable of handling dogs that were often far less suitable for the work than they are today.

Articles in the NIB's annual report and its journal *The New Beacon* must have played a part in encouraging applicants. 'A blind man and his dog' was once a synonym for dependence, the Institute's 1932–33 annual report declared, but 'a blind man and his guide dog' had now become a synonym for independence. *The New Beacon* tackled the old prejudices head-on. The image of the blind beggar and his dog was a relic of the past, it claimed, but a blind man would always need a guide to some extent in a busy world with increasing traffic dangers. Even the most independent blind man needed a guide to cross busy roads and his independence would be that much greater with a trained dog than if he had to wait for the attention of a passing stranger.

'Apart from its value to the busy independent blind man, the guide dog is an enormous asset to the nervous blind man – the blind man who does not often venture out alone in the streets, because of the strain on his nerves, because of his sensitiveness in asking strangers to lend their aid,'

Liakhoff in the summer of 1935 wearing blacked-out goggles while testing Kitty with an obstacle blocking the pavement.

the article continued. It urged that 'the blind should not hesitate to acquire a trained guide-dog if they love the companionship of dogs, and can care for and accommodate them,' and it concluded by giving Miss Crooke's address in Wallasey.

A pamphlet produced at about this time for home teachers, visitors and prospective applicants pointed out the financial advantage of having a guide dog. 'The average wage for a human guide is from 10s to 15s per week for a day of eight to ten hours, plus meals and fares. A guide dog costs about 5s a week to maintain and its hours are its master's.'

Unfortunately, the upsurge in interest that was created by the publicity was not matched by an increase in the output of guide dogs. Supply did not come anywhere near meeting the demand for decades. Whereas Germany was very quickly turning out hundreds of trained dogs every year, in Britain progress was painfully slow. By the outbreak of the war in 1939 there were no more than 76 working guide dogs in the country and during that year only 28 blind people passed through the training centre to get dogs.

In Britain, of course, the work was not State backed, as it was in Germany. The Association was run by a group of charitably-minded people in their spare time and they were slow to exploit the enormous fund-raising potential of their cause. Inevitably, therefore, they edged forward cautiously, lacking both the financial and the managerial resources that would have ensured a faster rate of growth. Progress might have been faster if the 1939–45 war had not diverted people's energies and thrown everything into confusion, but for many years after the war there was still a very long waiting list.

*   *   *

By the end of his first year in Britain Liakhoff, with Miss Crooke's help, had trained 19 pairs of dogs and blind people. But in order to find those 19 suitable dogs 80 had been taken in at Wallasey for testing.

A note written by Miss Crooke late in 1934 or January 1935 gives a vivid picture of the dog supply situation. 'We finish a blind class and immediately the new dogs must arrive. It is necessary to arrange for at least three times the number of dogs to be seen than we actually need. There is a difficulty in getting a large number of young bitches between the ages of 14 months and two years, to arrive on one or two certain days.' If people were asked to hold a bitch which was then rejected, they would ask for the cost of board while it had been kept.

Dogs were never taken straight into kennels: there was not enough room and the health risk was too great. They would first be seen by Liakhoff, who would decide whether to take them in for the full approval time.

'I have two men who meet and look after the dogs arriving,' Miss Crooke recorded. 'This is also necessary as some dogs arrive at midnight, early morning, or two or three at different stations at the same time.

'One of the chief difficulties is the people. They think that we want a dog, so, this week, next week, or next month will do to send it.' Furthermore, even those people who bred, showed and trained dogs for obedience work did not understand that for guide dog work characteristics and sensitivities of which they had never needed to think had to be taken into consideration. They had their own firm ideas on temperament and suitability for training and thought that if they judged a dog was suitable there was no need for it to come on approval.

On the other hand 'dogs which we have been told are untrainable have sometimes turned out exceptionally well, often this is a case of the dogs being more intelligent than the person.'

She noted that suitable dogs had an elusive combination of qualities which could be found in good specimens, cast-offs from good kennels, pets and dogs bred by very poor people. She and Liakhoff were very interested in the possibility of certain characteristics running in families but this was difficult to follow up because they seldom got closely related specimens and rarely any useful knowledge about the parents.

Looking speculatively, but prophetically, into the future, Miss Crooke concluded that 'it is unlikely that this will come to a definite enough thing to go by, unless the time ever arrives when it is possible to arrange and control the breeding of our own dogs.'

The note, which finished with the information that since his arrival at the beginning of November 1933 the head trainer had seen 103 dogs, of which 38 had been bought, must have been thought by Liakhoff to have implied a criticism of his record and so he sent Hobbs his own report on the work. It may not be reading too much into these two communications to see in them the seeds of the insecurity and distrust which was a feature of the row that blew up in 1940 and led Miss Crooke to resign. Her early enthusiasm for Liakhoff was perhaps beginning to cool when her only reference to the head trainer in a letter to Mrs Eustis in May 1935 was 'the Liakhoffs seem all right.'

Hobbs, as tail-wagger-in-chief, was the Association's main prop as well as its treasurer. He therefore kept a close eye on the expenses. After getting in a group of dogs at the end of 1934, Miss Crooke prepared for him a list of all the ones that had been seen, with their sources and the costs associated with them. Dealers, kennels and individuals who had replied to advertisements were all listed, together with comments where appropriate: 'we have already had four good dogs from this man, bred by him, he also tried to get dogs for us'; 'I have met her at shows and she has already sold us a dog. She also lets me know if she comes across any'; 'Had to part with his dog, someone at an alsatian training class told him to come to me.'

The report finishes with a summary of the work and costs: correspondence about 36 dogs, saw 20, bought 7; purchase price £21.7s.6d, advertisement 7s.6d, cost of meeting, boarding, returning and refunding carriage where necessary £9.8s.10d; total £31.6s.4d, or an average of £4.9s.7d per dog bought.

Miss Crooke also prepared for Hobbs and the executive committee a list of the amounts paid by the blind people for their dogs. After the first course it had been decided to ask recipients of guide dogs to pay what they could reasonably afford for them, not so much to help cover the costs but so that the people would feel that they had made a contribution and were not entirely dependent on charity. By the end of 1934 all except one had paid something. Of the 29 who did subscribe, one had paid 16 guineas, one £15 and three £10, with 12 between £1 and £5 and 12 under £1.

The work was now well established, but progress was being hindered by the lack of a decent, permanent training establishment. Dogs were still being kept in the makeshift kennels at the Cardigan Road garage; the empty house was still being taken for a month at a time for each class, with the hired or borrowed furniture being moved in and out on each occasion.

Then early in 1935 the Wallasey Corporation came to the rescue by lending the Association 'The Cliff', a large old house built on a red outcrop of rock called Red Noses which, like the Cardigan Road quarters, was in the northern suburb of New Brighton. Later in the year they made a more permanent arrangement by renting the house and grounds for a nominal sum and at the beginning of 1936 the dogs were moved in. A secure and integrated training centre was at last a reality. The Liakhoff family, now increased by the birth of a second daughter in 1935, continued living for a while in the rented house that had been acquired for them in Ellesmere Grove, but in due course they moved in to part of the building.

The training facilities were much improved in 1935 when the Wallasey Corporation first loaned and then leased to the Association for a nominal sum a large old house in the northern suburb of New Brighton. A member of the first class to be held at The Cliff was A. Pink, seen here leaving the training centre with Judy. The ground sloped away on the other side of the house towards the beach and on that side it was a two-storey building.

Another member of the first class held at The Cliff in March 1935 was Miss W.D. Archer. Liakhoff watches as she negotiates a pavement obstacle with Yvonne.

The move to The Cliff enabled Miss Crooke to have an office in which to do the administrative work not being done at the Tail-Waggers office in London, and she therefore moved all her papers and records from her father's house in Warren Drive. Her father, who was a respected local GP, was also helping the work by lending his spare car for traffic training and other purposes, an arrangement which continued until the Association was able to buy a second-hand car of its own for £10 at the end of 1936.

The main beneficiaries of the new quarters were, however, the dogs and the blind people. The Cliff had a large garden which at that time, before the promenade was built, ran straight down to the beach, and in it the dogs soon had more spacious kennels and runs. There were also separate facilities for dogs on trial and sick animals in the stables. For the blind students there was more comfortable accommodation and better food. Miss Phyllis Robinson went there, as a very shy young woman of 23, for her first guide dog in the summer of 1937 and clearly remembers her first meal of fresh salmon, which she didn't like. The permanent centre made a more flexible training programme possible and so there was not the same regular pattern of classes as there used to be: only one other student was in training when she arrived, J.K.W. McLay from Glasgow.

The staff comprised Liakhoff; an apprentice, Bernard 'Bunny' Holmes, who had been taken on in 1936; Miss Crooke; Charlotte Windsor, the cook-housekeeper; and Primley the gardener, whose name Liakhoff always got wrong. 'We used to train three times a day', Miss Robinson recalled, 'and every time we met Mr Primley Captain Liakhoff used to say "Good morning Mr Plimley", whether it was morning, afternoon or evening.'

One of the first two guide dog owners in Scotland was A. Gilzean, who was a member of the first class to train at The Cliff in Wallasey in March 1935. He was still using Lady in Edinburgh in November 1943 when the Association's journal Forward *reported on eight guide dog owners then working in Scotland. By that time, however, Miss M.T. Melling, who had preceded Gilzean at Wallasey by three months, was no longer a guide dog owner.*

By then, Liakhoff's English had improved considerably, although he still had a strong accent. In time the accent became less pronounced, although he would always turn it on for comic effect or when it suited him. In fact, he quickly gained a very good command of the language, but he could never understand the Liverpool accent. 'Neither could I,' said Miss Robinson. Charlotte Windsor spoke broad Liverpudlian, McLay broad Scots and Liakhoff fractured English. 'It was terrible,' she recalled. 'Only Miss Crooke spoke good English – beautiful English.' Mrs Liakhoff had learnt English as a girl and spoke the language well, but she was in Switzerland with the children at the time of Miss Robinson's stay in Wallasey in 1937.

Miss Crooke used to muck in, as they all did, and help with everything. There was no artificial obstacle course in the grounds at that time so one of the training staff always had to go ahead with the wooden frame or the bicycle that was used as a pavement obstacle, moving it when the student had passed and then rushing ahead to the next spot where it was to be placed. Two training staff therefore had to be on hand: one to deal with the obstacles, the other to watch over the student.

'It was usually Bunny Holmes that put the obstacles up,' Miss Robinson recalled. 'Miss Crooke would follow.' She also used to drive the car for traffic training and taught Miss Robinson how to groom and feed her dog.

Learning to use a guide dog is not an easy experience for a blind person. Euphoria at the prospect of greater mobility and getting acquainted with the new dog is soon offset by the stress of mastering new techniques and discovering how difficult it is to handle the dog effectively, particularly with the dog's previous (expert) handler hovering not far away. To the mental and emotional stress that this induces is added, for many first-timers, the physical exhaustion of all the walking after leading a relatively inactive life. The improvement in health that results from taking more exercise is, of course, one of the many benefits of owning a guide dog, but in the early days it can be a very tiring experience.

'You nearly always have a second week "drop",' said Miss Robinson, but Liakhoff would always get them through it with great understanding and kindness. 'He was very good with us. He had men that were fed up, women in tears, but he would take them away and have a little talk and all would be well. His patience was unbelievable.'

The dog Miss Robinson acquired in Wallasey in 1937 was Flash, a silver-grey alsatian of unknown pedigree that had been bought for £3.10s from Jack's Pet Stores in Blackpool. Unfortunately it developed skin trouble, became lethargic and had to be changed for another guide in 1939. Judy, the replacement, did not last long either although it was an excellent guide dog. It became over-protective and had to be withdrawn, after which it found its true vocation in Scotland as a guard dog.

Miss Robinson went on to own other dogs and in 1987, 50 years after getting Flash, she was leading an active life with her 10th dog, Corrie, in Leamington. At the time of writing Corrie and Miss Robinson are still going strong.

*   *   *

The acquisition of The Cliff as a permanent training centre may, at the time, have seemed like a turning point in the Association's fortunes. But the remaining years of the 1930s were still beset with problems, among them: dog supply; getting the right kind of applicants; NIB doubts about the value of guide dogs and the administration of the Association, as well as discussion of a takeover; and continuing unrest over Miss Crooke's position and her relationship with Liakhoff.

Several of these concerns surfaced together in July 1937 in a letter from Lady Schuster, as she was now, her husband having inherited a baronetcy in 1936, to Ben Purse, head of the NIB's services to the blind department and a member of the Association's executive committee. She had heard that he and Sington had been discussing the possibility of a takeover by the NIB and reminded him that a similar proposal had been turned down four years previously. She continued: 'I still feel with you that that would be far the most desirable thing that could happen.' Tenure of The Cliff was uncertain, they needed more and better dogs and were getting a long waiting list of candidates. The solution, she believed, was 'to get someone to make a bit for us, and to build up a sum which will bring us in an assured income and then go to the NIB again and see if they will take us over.'

Purse's interest in the idea was due not to his enthusiasm for guide dogs – indeed, he had considerable reservations about them – but to his concern over an increasing number of appeals being made by charities for the blind. 'These innumerable appeals are becoming a source of trouble and weakness to all the agencies undertaking blind welfare work,' he commented to Lady Schuster.

She was keen to appoint an appeals secretary to help raise the sum she believed necessary in order to attract the NIB, and proposed Lieutenant-Colonel Percy Battye for the job. Purse would have none of it: tell the NIB of your difficulties, he proposed, and ask them to include guide dogs as one of the objects for which their general appeals were launched.

'That means that you should be able to get sufficient money to finance your undertaking and free you of the liability of supervising and controlling appeals secretaries with all their weird and wonderful ways,' he maintained. When she repeated her conviction that substantial capital was needed to avoid another refusal he responded that he thought the NIB would judge the issue on its merits and that if they took over the appeals work it would be because they believed in the work, not because there was a substantial bank balance.

Purse made no secret of his personal view of guide dogs. 'I am not convinced myself of the real utility of the service in blind welfare work,' he wrote. 'I know it can only have a very limited application . . .'

Lady Schuster retaliated by acknowledging that it was not an economical service and was, of necessity, a limited one. 'But in trying to help must one always put money first and must one always think of the majority? . . . I feel that these dogs have brought some happiness, comfort and independence into the lives of some people which they otherwise might not have had. But you and your colleagues know so much more, and if you all decide that what we do is not worthwhile I shall very sadly have to bow to your decision.'

Purse protested that she had exaggerated his reservations, but in defending himself gave a revealing insight into his own attitude to mobility. 'For people who lose their sight in middle or late life, guide dogs are certainly of enormous help, but for younger people – whose education is such as to enable them to utilise and develop the faculties they possess – I am convinced that it is a mistake to induce them to rely upon external agents for the help which can be secured from the development of their own faculties.'

After these exchanges, discussion of an NIB takeover seems to have died down – but not for long. Lady Schuster got her way over the appointment of Battye as appeals organiser and in April 1939 he lunched with Eagar, the NIB's secretary general. They were obviously exploring the merger question, because Eagar replied to Battye's thank-you letter with ' . . . I would like to fit the Guide Dogs into the general scheme of blind welfare. Whether that is possible or not, you can count on my goodwill, good wishes and admiration of the vigorous way in which you have tackled the Guide Dog problem. I do not think we can force the pace and we cannot go forward with any plan until we can see just how it will work. In the meantime let us keep on friendly terms and consult each other . . .'

When Battye rejoined the army the following summer, following the outbreak of war, he wrote briefly to Eagar ' . . . I am sorry that our scheme did not materialise of the NIB taking over the Guide Dogs.' The NIB apparently came to regret it as well. When the two organisations were at loggerheads in 1949 over the fund-raising agreement the view was expressed that they should have taken over guide dogs years earlier when they had the opportunity.

Purse continued to have anxieties about the Association's fund-raising efforts, and he also had a poor opinion of its financial control and committee organisation. He had expressed these concerns in an internal NIB memo to his secretary general in July 1937, and they surfaced again in a note that he was asked to prepare when an appeal for funds was made by the Association to the Gardener's Trust for the Blind in 1939.

'Neither the officials nor members of the committee know sufficient about blind welfare work to enable them to function to the best advantage,' he wrote. There was a tendency for them to think that every blind person should use a guide dog, which was 'a palpable absurdity'.

'I should have thought that for all practical purposes the money at the disposal of the committee is sufficient to meet their needs,' he continued. (Income for the previous financial year was £4,076, sufficient to give them an excess over expenditure of £482, bringing their reserves of cash on deposit to £5,065.) As to the way the training programme was run, it was 'economically unjustifiable to keep a large house open, with all its attendant expenses, for one or two candidates only.'

Purse may well have been justified in his criticism: the Association was not well managed. Liakhoff was an effective head trainer, but had little skill or experience as an administrator. Office services were provided by the Tail-Waggers' Club, but they suffered if there was a pressure of club work. Members of the executive committee had other interests, were scattered and met only once a month. No matter how able they might have been individually, they were no substitute for an efficient full-time management team.

*   *   *

With the death of Captain Hobbs in December 1935 the executive committee lost its treasurer as well as one of its most active members. He was succeeded by Mr (later Sir) Victor Schuster, a member of Rothschild's bank who was persuaded by his energetic wife to take the post. When Croxton-Smith resigned at the end of 1937 he rather unwillingly became chairman and in 1939, after the office of treasurer had been left vacant for two years, Lady Freda Valentine stepped into his shoes. She had been brought onto the committee in 1937 by Lady Schuster, who had tried to rope her in earlier in the 1930s. But Lady Freda, who had married in 1931, said she could not commit herself until she had finished having children and could devote herself properly to the work. She remained treasurer for nearly 39 years and became a legendary figure: slightly eccentric, rather awesome, always liable to ask penetrating and awkward questions and unwavering in her concern for the welfare of the Association and everyone associated with it. When she was reminded once of her reputation for keeping a tight hold of the purse strings she retorted, 'Well look where it's brought you!' She was justifiably proud of the part she played in putting the Association on its feet and of the CBE she was awarded in 1979 in recognition of her work.

Lady Schuster was the real driving force in the 1930s, she maintained. 'She was very good-looking, with enormous energy and charm. She had

Lady Schuster with Lord Teviot, who as Lieutenant-Colonel C.I. Kerr joined the Guide Dogs committee as the representative of St Dunstan's in 1933. He remained a member of the general council (after 1942 as Lord Teviot) until 1962. This picture was taken some time during the 1940s.

great charisma – everyone melted before her. She made things go and persuaded people not to resign in a passion.' She was also very protective of her husband. 'Everything had to go right with Sir Victor – he hadn't to be annoyed.'

The Schusters both had musical interests and she was a fine violinist. They were also prominent in the dog world and owned the Nunneshall kennel of alsatians and wire-haired dachshunds. Of Lady Schuster it was said, on her death in 1950, 'she was the kindest woman . . . and never refused to help anyone.'

In 1936 Lady Schuster was given the title of honorary organiser. In that capacity, and as the most active member of the executive committee, she went with Liakhoff to visit the Potsdam guide dog school in June 1937. The purpose of the visit appears to have been the pursuit of ideas for solving the dog supply problem and to compare training methods. What they saw was interesting, but it did not solve the problems.

'They can obtain as many dogs as they like', they reported to the executive committee, 'and the percentage of unsuitable dogs is 30 per cent, while here in England the supply of dogs is very limited and of that supply 75 per cent, or even more, are absolutely unsuitable.'

The German method of training was based on correcting the dogs severely which gave good, quick results in some parts of the work, but was quite unnecessary in others. 'A very sharply spiked collar, leather with nails inside about an inch long, is used during all the training, so that a very small jerk on the leash, which may be unnoticed by the public, is very effective for the dog.'

In Germany, the blind people used sticks to feel the kerbs and to give commands, which made the work easier and required less precision from the dog. The report concluded that 'the sharp collar, used without exception there, may only be used in rare cases here', and that the use of a stick by blind people was undesirable because they often needed the right hand free to carry things.

Liakhoff followed the report on the Potsdam school with a review of the dog supply problem in Britain, which was preventing an increase in output. There had been months when none of the dogs which had come on trial could be accepted. 'I'm sure there must be plenty of good dogs in England,' he said, but the training centre only got those people wanted to get rid of.

Among the ideas he offered for improving the position was one for which he gave the credit to Lady Schuster: the establishment of a special society or club for improving the temperament of the breed, with prizes for temperament offered at shows. Nothing came of the proposal, however, and it was another quarter of a century before the Association started to develop a breeding programme of its own on any substantial scale.

Liakhoff also talked about rearing puppies – another early appreciation of one route to greater success. A very basic programme was, in fact, already operating. Offers of puppies were received and there were people willing to rear them, but the success rate was low because the Association did not have the resources to see all the puppies and check the conditions in which they would be reared. Nevertheless, in 1938 the programme was being developed with some enthusiasm and the annual report for that year noted that 130 puppies were being walked. The momentum was not maintained, however, and puppy-walking was little more than an inter-

W. McGarry left Wallasey with Skippy in January 1939 and the pair continued working together until 1950 or '51. The PDSA apparently recognised the dog's achievements with the award of a medal.

mittent activity of limited value until it was taken up by Callum McLean, an enterprising member of the general council, in the 1950s and placed firmly on the path that has made it such an important programme today.

In an unsuccessful attempt to improve the supply of dogs a letter was written at the end of 1936 to alsatian clubs and canine societies. Further promptings during 1937 still failed to get results and so in November Lady Schuster suggested that dog dealers should be invited to see the work at Wallasey and offered a bonus of £1 for every dog they supplied that successfully completed its training. A visit was eventually arranged on 19 March 1939, when 67 representatives of alsatian and canine associations in the north, the Midlands and Scotland turned up and resolved to help as well as to visit any puppies being 'walked' in their area. Lady Schuster arranged a meeting for a similar group of people in London. Whether these efforts would have produced results we will never know because the war soon prevented any good intentions being realised.

In fact, the threat of war had already led to a reduction in the supply of dogs. In the crisis atmosphere that followed the annexation of Austria

The crisis atmosphere that followed the annexation of Austria and the invasion of Czechoslovak Sudetenland by Germany in 1938 caused an abrupt decline in pedigree dog breeding and so with fewer alsatians on offer the Association turned its attention to other breeds. Border collies then dominated the scene for some years but other breeds, such as the keeshond Aga seen here in 1938 with Miss Luff, also helped to fill the gap.

and invasion of Czechoslovak Sudetenland by Germany in 1938 pedigree dog breeding declined and so, with fewer alsatians on offer, the Association turned its attention to border collies, which, as a working breed, were still available. A variety of breeds had been tried, including labradors, golden retrievers, flat-coated and curly-coated retrievers, keeshonds, dalmatians, collies, airedales and any number of crosses and mongrels.

Only the border collies were judged to have the qualities needed. It may seem surprising that the labrador, which was to dominate the guide dog population in later years, found no favour but it must be remembered that in the 1930s they would mostly have been bred as show or gun dogs and that the specimens sent to Wallasey may not have been very good ones anyway.

Liakhoff did not consider the change from alsatians to border collies a disadvantage. On the contrary, he believed that the temperament of male collies would enable them to be used as well as bitches; and the cost of feeding a smaller dog was less. 'The fact can be stated,' he claimed confidently, 'that the main handicap to the work, the supply of dogs, though not yet ideal, is greatly improved and gives the hope of an even greater improvement in the future.'

Despite the threat of war hanging over the country, the chairman's report at the annual general meeting in 1939 also struck a remarkably confident tone. 'I think it is clear from the events and activities of the past year ... that the Association has made great progress towards the attainment of a position where the school may confidently be expected to carry on its work without interruption either by financial difficulties or lack of dogs.'

It was, perhaps, a rather complacent statement in the circumstances. Not only did it ignore the strong possibility of war and the disruption that would cause, but it indicated no determination to tackle the growing waiting list of applicants by more vigorous fund-raising and an increase in training resources. There was, all the same, some cause for satisfaction. A successful radio appeal by the comedian Leslie Henson in 1936 had raised over £3,500; the Tail-Waggers appeal had added another £2,100; two paid appeals organisers were beginning to generate a useful return; and fund-raising branches, including one in Scotland, were starting up. The financial situation was reasonably satisfactory for the limited needs and ambitions of the moment. The work was also becoming better known; it had featured in a television broadcast in 1937 and a second, much better film had been made in which Vivien Leigh had appeared.

Within a few months of the chairman's optimistic review of the prospects, war broke out. The Cliff was immediately taken over by the 267th Battery, Royal Artillery, an anti-aircraft unit, and the Association found itself once again having to do the best it could with makeshift training facilities.

6

The Dogs of War

With a savage war about to erupt in Europe, a minor conflict was brewing in Wallasey. The trouble began in the spring of 1938 with the return of Mrs Liakhoff and her two daughters from a stay in Switzerland. Mrs Liakhoff had a fiery temper and an extremely jealous nature, which were quickly directed at Miss Crooke and her work. Although she had no recognised position and was receiving no salary, she insisted on dabbling in Miss Crooke's administrative and training activities, frequently quarrelling or creating scenes. After one incident Miss Crooke asked Liakhoff why he had to bring his family into the work, to which he replied that unfortunately he could not help it.

'They were continually having the most awful rows between themselves', Miss Crooke recorded, 'before the blind people or anyone. She had to have her own way always.'

The trouble got worse as time went on. 'Captain Liakhoff has had to take one thing after another from me and give it to her until only the work with the dogs and the blind people was left,' she told Sington. Mrs Liakhoff had taken to opening all the mail and on one occasion opened a letter addressed to Miss Crooke and threw it on the fire in a fit of temper. The charred remains were kept by Miss Crooke as evidence of the intolerable situation that had developed.

Matters came to a head in May 1940. The switch to border collies had resulted in a plentiful supply of dogs and so Miss Crooke was able to advance from giving general help with training to having dogs of her own to train. Between September 1939 and May 1940 she turned out six dogs. It was while she was out training a dog one evening in late May that another scene occurred which brought Miss Crooke to the brink of despair. Liakhoff was helping her by putting out the obstacles and Mrs Liakhoff started complaining loudly that they were upsetting the work she was doing with a dog. She then turned and shouted for some time at Miss Crooke.

When Liakhoff and Miss Crooke returned to The Cliff (where the dogs were still kept) the abuse started again. 'She was shouting at him and as I went towards the dog room she shouted that I was in love with him and other such things,' Miss Crooke reported to Lady Schuster. 'There were soldiers standing about at the door of the house. She was in an uncontrollable fury.'

It was not the first time Mrs Liakhoff had interfered with the training. The previous November she had got in the way, shouted at Liakhoff and ended by 'throwing the obstacle off the car in the middle of Victoria Road.' Obviously in great distress, Miss Crooke concluded her letter to Lady Schuster: 'You have no idea what things are like, sometimes I just don't know what to do . . . Capt Liakhoff is quite a different man to what he used to be. Will you help me please?'

A day or two later further trouble erupted over Liakhoff's insistence that even letters addressed to Miss Crooke personally should be delivered to the flat where he now lived. It was the final straw, and on 28 May she resigned. She retained her position as a vice-president and a member of the general council but she seldom, if ever, attended meetings and never again played an active part in the Association's affairs.

It was a sad fate for the person who was recognised as 'the founder' of the Association. Although she always gave credit for the part played by Liakhoff, she dominated the early years and deserved better from him and the executive committee. Some years later Liakhoff acknowledged that he had treated her badly when he wrote: 'I do not deny that you have grounds to hold something against me personally.'

If the committee ever considered intervening in support of Miss Crooke they probably dismissed the idea fairly quickly because, of course, they were completely dependent on Liakhoff. Holmes had completed his apprenticeship and become a qualified trainer in 1939, but Liakhoff was the only one with any real experience. The thought of losing him would no doubt have sent shivers down their corporate spine.

Although the foregoing account of events leading to the crisis of May 1940 depends largely on documents written by Miss Crooke herself, there can be little doubt that she gave a fairly accurate picture of the circumstances. Mrs Liakhoff was, as many people have testified, a jealous, quick-tempered and difficult woman who often made life disagreeable for her husband and others. But there was another side to her character as well. Nora Robinson (later Kirienko), who was first a kennel maid and then a trainer in the early 1940s, remembers her as 'very warm-hearted, very up and down, but a lovely person.' Many others found her likeable, although, as one of them put it, 'she was trouble'.

In 1974 The Seeing Eye in America honoured Miss Muriel Crooke by giving her the Buddy Award, named after their first guide dog, 'in recognition of her foresight, integrity and unflagging effort' in establishing The Guide Dogs for the Blind Association in Britain. The award is here being presented to her by the Earl of Lanesborough, who was then the Association's president.

Miss Crooke's distress at having to give up the work with which she had identified herself so closely, and which had come to occupy her life so fully and enjoyably, was fortunately soon replaced by the satisfaction she was getting from an interesting war job in a censorship office. After the war she resumed her interest in dogs and in addition to breeding, training and showing her own dogs, was a judge at championship shows, including Crufts in 1968. Despite her early promise as an artist in the 1920s, when she studied in Paris for 18 months and exhibited at the Royal Academy and elsewhere, she never resumed painting seriously.

In 1959 she moved to Gloucestershire, living first at Kemerton, near Tewkesbury, and then Charlton, near Evesham. She kept in touch with guide dog affairs and was occasionally seen at events, but she was so retiring that she would seldom even allow her photograph to be taken. She died on 6 December 1975 at the age of 74.

*   *   *

By the end of May 1940, when Miss Crooke resigned, negotiations were under way to buy one of two properties in Leamington Spa as a training centre. At Wallasey, the only parts of The Cliff left to the Association were the kennels and one little stone outhouse. The Liakhoffs had moved to a flat, Holmes and the blind students were lodged in nearby boarding houses. A few months earlier Nora Robinson, who lived in Wallasey, had joined Liakhoff as a kennel maid and she remembers that in the evenings they would sometimes sit in the primitive quarters to which they had been banished at The Cliff and Liakhoff would talk about Russia and cook a meal on a primus stove. 'He was a very good cook. He didn't cook for the multitude, because he didn't have the time. He could turn his hand to anything.' When the bombing started they would give bromide to the more nervous dogs and sometimes stay with them all night.

In July, negotiations over one of the Leamington properties, Edmondscote Manor, were concluded and the house, together with some 13 acres of ground and various outhouses, was acquired by the Association for £4,000. The training staff had to wait some months before taking possession of their new home, but by 1 November dogs, kennels, fencing, furniture and records had been moved.

Alfred Morgan thought it was 'a swell place'. He described it to Miss Crooke shortly after visiting the Manor in July 1941.

'The house is old, but in very good condition. It is, roughly, I should say, about the same size as "The Cliff". There is a large entrance hall with a corridor running to right and left the length of the house. The pupils have what used to be the drawing room, which is a fine large room looking out on to the gardens at the back of the house. The room next to it is used as "the office", and the other rooms on the ground floor are used by the Liakhoffs in various ways. That is to say, they *will* be used by them when times are normal, but at present they have no indoor staff except a daily woman, and, to make the work easier, the Liakhoffs have all their meals with the pupils.

'There are 3 bedrooms for pupils, 2 containing 3 beds each, and 1 with 2 beds, and with plenty of room, so that they would really be capable of extension if needed. There is also a "guest" room in this part of the house. I am not exactly sure what this means, but it probably means "ex-pupil" guests. There is also a bathroom to this part. Anyhow, the place is quite capable of dealing with at least a dozen pupils at a time, with a little readjustment. The other half of the house is taken up by the Liakhoffs.

'There is a fine large courtyard with stabling for 9 horses, including loose-boxes, and 3 coach-houses, which, of course, are now garages, with electric light. There is also a harness room and one or two other places which are used as "dog rooms" by Miss Robinson. There is also another fine large yard, with accommodation for several cows and other domestic animals. All this is very handy indeed, and is capable of great development. There is hot and cold water everywhere, and steam radiators in the pupils' bedrooms. Oh, and before I forget, let me explain that over the garages is what is called "the flat". Miss Robinson lives here with her mother, who has been bombed out of her home in Wallasey, and they appear to be very happy there. Miss Robinson was delighted to hear about you and has probably written by now.

'So much for the house; and now for the grounds. These are in as good condition as the house, and are really quite extensive – 13 acres, I believe. The front of the house is fairly close to the main road, but a sort of flattened "S" drive, well "wooded", makes it quite secluded. There is also a side drive to the stables. Everything else, of course, is at the back and sides of the house. The kitchen gardens (there are two) cover 4 acres, and contain everything needed (and more) to feed all the pupils they will be able to deal with. There is every kind of vegetable, apples, pears, currants, every sort of berry, tomatoes, peaches, and a vine, and that rarest of all delicacies, the onion. The gardens are a riot of roses and lavender, and there are several large lawns and a nice large summer-house (very useful, for sitting out with the dogs), a tennis-court (no use to us), a huge rock garden, and crowds of huge, ancient trees. There is a large meadow on the bank of the Avon, which goes past the foot of the grounds. Then, of course, there are the runs for the dogs. These are not yet fully developed, for Captain Liakhoff cannot get enough wood and wire, but they are capable of huge expansion.'

Although Liakhoff and the committee could be well satisfied with their acquisition of a permanent home, they were less pleased with the staff situation and financial circumstances. Holmes, the newly-qualified trainer, had been called up and was serving in the navy, which left only the Liakhoff family and one kennel maid, Nora Robinson, at the school. In Miss Crooke's opinion Holmes was no loss to the Association: 'never worthy of his certificate'. But the committee had other views.

'We are in despair over our apprentice,' wrote Lady Schuster, who seems to have forgotten that Holmes was now a qualified trainer. 'All our efforts to get him released have so far been unavailing', she continued in a letter to the NIB's secretary general, Eagar, on 17 December, 'but I have just been informed that there might be a slight ray of hope if you and Sir Ian Fraser put in a word.'

Bernard 'Bunny' Holmes was taken on as an apprentice in 1936 and became a qualified trainer in 1939. Lady Schuster was 'in despair', however, when he was called up for service in the navy, leaving only the Liakhoff family and one kennel maid to run the new training centre in Leamington. She secured his release in January 1941 but he was dismissed by Liakhoff at the end of 1942. (Fox Photos)

The committee's efforts to get Holmes released were fuelled by their anxiety over the health of their only source of expertise. 'Captain Liakhoff is far from strong,' Lady Schuster told Eagar. 'He has had TB and is always liable to get pneumonia and also suffers from a duodenal ulcer'. Eagar promptly wrote to the Admiralty, who agreed to Holmes's release a few weeks later.

With one anxiety removed, the committee now turned their attention to the financial situation. At the end of September 1940, when the Association's financial year closed, the balance sheet showed cash reserves of £4,288. This was soon virtually wiped out by the purchase of Edmondscote Manor, and although its loss made little difference to the Association's income – bank or building society deposits had contributed only £64 in interest to the year's running expenses of £3,818 – income from other sources had fallen drastically in 1940 and the committee used the acquisition as a peg on which to hang a special appeal for funds in 1941. The Gardener's Trust for the Blind were approached again, on this occasion giving £300, despite another unenthusiastic comment from Ben Purse of the NIB, who was 'compelled to say that my attitude towards the Association is as stated two years ago.' Another £300 was given by the NIB and some time later, in August 1942, St Dunstan's gave 100 guineas.

In its anxiety over funds, the Association turned to America for help. Prompted by Lady Sackville, a member of the executive committee who was herself American, the chairman, Sir Victor Schuster, wrote what he called an SOS to Mrs Eustis. He did not ask for support from The Seeing Eye's own funds, but hoped they might appeal on behalf of British guide dogs throughout the United States. There is no record of any response to this request.

The BBC were also approached for another broadcast appeal, which led them to consult the NIB about the merits of the application. 'The real question,' Eagar replied at the beginning of September 1941, 'is not whether the Society is worth supporting but whether its case is stronger than that of other agencies for the blind which might broadcast their needs to the public. It certainly has been hard hit.'

A month later Eagar followed this rather non-committal response with the suggestion that any wireless appeal should 'definitely be of a doggie character addressed to dog lovers.' The NIB had 'very carefully steered them', he said, 'to the position that they will appeal, so far as possible, to the dog-loving rather than the interested-in-the-blind public.'

Despite the NIB's rather lukewarm comments, but no doubt encouraged by Roger Eckersley, a member of the general council who worked for the BBC, the Association was offered a 'Good Cause' broadcast, and the appeal was made by Leslie Henson, who had made the previous broadcast appeal in September 1936. Although the £2,375 yielded by the second appeal was disappointing by comparison with the £3,500 of the earlier broadcast, it nevertheless made the balance sheet look a good deal healthier.

Eagar's comments to the BBC on the proposed guide dog appeal provide an interesting insight into the NIB's reasons for keeping the Association at arm's length. 'We affiliated them, but would not accept responsibility for their operations, chiefly because we did not wish to involve ourselves in any guarantee that a blind man led by a dog is safe in traffic.' This is a somewhat surprising attitude because there appears to have been no suggestion from any quarter that a guarantee of this sort was considered necessary by the pioneers in the guide dog field. Indeed, no such guarantee is given today and it is well recognised by the users of guide dogs, as well as their trainers, that accidents may happen in some traffic conditions and that it is therefore best to seek sighted help in crossing a particularly difficult road. It is up to the guide dog owner to judge when that help is needed and sometimes he will get it wrong, but traffic accidents involving guide dogs are rare.

If traffic safety was a factor in determining the NIB's attitude towards guide dogs, it was probably only one of several considerations. They held back, one feels, largely because there was insufficient conviction among NIB staff and committee members of the value of guide dogs. They were not, however, prepared to see the movement fade away and when the Association was in difficulties in 1939 over its school at Wallasey and Lady Schuster wrote to the NIB and St Dunstan's for their opinion on continuing with guide dog training, they both replied praising the usefulness of the work.

*   *   *

Although the Association's income fell sharply at the beginning of the war, the setback was brief. In 1938 and again in 1939 over £3,500 had been raised through subscriptions, donations, branch activities and scholarships. In 1940 this plunged to £2,161 but thereafter, despite losing Lieutenant-Colonel Battye to the Royal Fusiliers in August 1940, income started to rise again: £2,554 in 1941, £3,141 in 1942 and continuing upwards until, in the final year of the war, 1945, over £13,000 was raised.

During these years, although more staff had been engaged and some money had been spent on Edmondscote Manor and its kennels, expenditure had risen a good deal less than income. As a result, in September 1945 the Association had investments of £20,000 and bank deposits of £5,700.

How does one account for the Association's astonishingly successful war record? In the year following the outbreak of war, five of the eight branches closed down and income from this source was only £172 in 1945. £10,000 of the £13,200 raised in 1945 is described in the annual report for the year as 'general donations', and although the chairman declines to specify the largest donors, 'as there may be a widow's mite which merits our greater gratitude', he does single out Mrs Kingdon Ward, a member of the general council and of the executive committee, as the most successful of the voluntary collectors. She could not have been the only member of the general council who was using her influence and energies in the interests of guide dogs.

The truth is probably that the biggest factor was the emotional appeal of guide dogs which the NIB had predicted and feared: the level of donations was, as the chairman put it, a gratifying and encouraging mark of public approval. There were still only 97 working dogs at the end of 1942, but they were often featured in the press and had quickly acquired a large body of admirers. Furthermore, The "Tail-Wagger" Magazine, with its huge circulation, carried monthly articles about guide dogs, publicising fund-raising activities and, at times, an 'SOS for funds', as well as tugging at the heartstrings with appealing stories about the dogs and their owners.

The situation might have been very different, too, if the Tail-Waggers' Club had not continued its administrative support. Miss Lilian Shrimpton, who was secretary of both Tail-Waggers and the Association, never

Siesta time for a brood bitch and her litter at the breeding centre. Eighty per cent of dogs from the breeding and puppy-walking programmes now complete their training successfully, compared with only 20 per cent that became guide dogs when the training centres had to rely on dogs from other sources.

Puppies are reared in the homes of puppy-walkers until they are about a year old and mature enough to start their training. During this important first year pups become completely socialised. They are also introduced to the noise and bustle of town life so that they become thoroughly conditioned to the environment in which they will eventually be working.

The first hesitant steps on public transport.

Opposite: Guide dog training is no longer a tough 12-week crash course. The dogs now acquire their skills over 10 months or more in a programme that places the emphasis on encouragement rather than the excessive use of correction. During the early weeks the dog is gradually taught basic tasks such as walking in a straight line and stopping at kerbs. The harness is not introduced until later.

Above: Fifty of the Association's dogs (plus two babes in arms) gathered on the lawn of Tollgate House, the breeding centre, in September 1987 for this special retirement picture in honour of Derek Freeman, who started and built up the breeding programme. Four training centres sent 10 dogs each and Tollgate supplied 10 breeding stock, seen sitting at the back of the picture.

Towards the end of a dog's training its instructor wears a blindfold in order to put the months of learning to the test with a handler who cannot see. Another instructor watches over the pair in case help is needed.

Shirley Rosario and Nell learning to work together on the obstacle course at a training centre.

When confronted with an obstacle that blocks the pavement as completely as this a guide dog will take its owner to the kerb so that they can continue along the road – a manoeuvre that obviously has to be mastered thoroughly if it is to be performed safely.

An instructor keeps a watchful eye on John Dove and Ishka as they gain experience in dealing with traffic. The dog has brought them to the kerb and it is now up to the handler to judge when it is safe to cross and give the command 'Forward'. The dog will then proceed unless it sees danger of which its owner is not aware, in which case it will sit tight. This is the most difficult area of the work and on very busy crossings guide dog owners are advised to seek sighted help.

At the end of every class the students and their guides pose for a 'graduation' photograph. When they return to their homes they are rather like drivers who have just passed their test – reasonably competent and safe, but needing some months of experience before they are able to get the best out of their mobility aids.

Immediately after qualifying, new guide dog owners are visited at home by an instructor in order to go over regular routes together and discuss potentially difficult spots. Here, in 1986, Mrs Janette Stainton returns home to the Isle of Lewis at the end of her training with Syd Duncan, an instructor from the Forfar training centre. The immediate aftercare visit is followed by others at regular intervals or in response to a request for help.

The 100 or so dogs in training at each centre are now provided with accommodation that makes the old wooden kennels of the Wallasey and early Leamington days look like a shantytown. The modern facilities include a hospital block such as this one at Forfar where a patient is wearing a hood to prevent it getting at a surgical wound or dressing.

Over 600 guide dogs and their owners were among the congregation of 2,000 that gathered in Westminster Abbey on 18 July 1981 for a thanksgiving service to celebrate the Association's golden jubilee.

The only sounds to come from the dogs were one or two half-hearted barks, a few yawns and the tinkling of chain leads when they moved.

Countless young people have been introduced to guide dogs for the first time by BBC Television's Blue Peter *programme. Goldie, the programme's dog during much of the 1980s, had two litters, both sired by studs from the Association's breeding centre. Six of the second litter, seen here in 1986, became guide dogs, one became a stud dog and the eighth, Bonnie, took over from her mother as the programme's resident dog.*

The Association's training services and appeals activities are run mainly from the seven regional centres, seen here in the order in which they were opened: Leamington, Exeter, Bolton, Forfar, Wokingham, Middlesbrough and Redbridge. The last picture shows the kennels and the H-block design that is now a standard pattern at all centres.

missed a day at the office in Gray's Inn Road during the war, working long hours to keep the two organisations on their feet during the worst of the bombing and other disruptions.

Although the Association prospered financially as the war went on, its training record was less successful. In 1938, the last year before the upheavals of the war, 27 blind people received guide dogs. In 1939, when the training staff were evicted from The Cliff, 21 guide dog owners were trained. A low point was reached in 1940 with only 17, after which there were three years when the output stayed at 22. It rose by one in 1944, but collapsed dramatically to nine in 1945 due, apparently, to a decision to concentrate on training apprentices who would help to expand output in the future.

It is hardly surprising that output fell to 17 in 1940. In his report for the year Liakhoff paints a sombre picture of the difficulties. To begin with he was mainly concerned about the time wasted because he could not find a boarding house for the students that would allow their dogs to stay as well. Later, when air raids started, the Anderson shelter at the boarding house would get so crowded that students were often unable to sit down, with the result that they were frequently tired and unwilling to do much training. The bombing also affected the nerves of some students, which further interfered with training. Before long Liakhoff decided to stop calling blind students for training and to concentrate during the second half of 1940 on looking after the dogs and preparing for the move to Leamington.

With Holmes in the navy, Liakhoff was left with the task of putting up the kennels and constructing fences out of the old wood brought from Wallasey. Each piece of wood had to be sawn to size and although there was a gardener at the Manor he was still employed by the previous owner and could not be used by Liakhoff until 18 November. Even then, there was so much work to be done that Liakhoff was not able to start training again until January 1941, the month in which Holmes was released from his brief service as a naval coder.

One difficulty the war brought was in feeding the dogs. For the first year at Leamington, Liakhoff was able to get some meat from a local horseflesh dealer, but the supply was erratic and the meat was often bad. This poor and irregular feeding was, in Liakhoff's view, the reason for an unusually large number of cases of hysteria and epileptic fits during 1941. The meat supply improved the following year when he was able to deal direct with a slaughterer, but in 1941 the situation would have been desperate had the Ministry of Food not been persuaded to grant a special permit for the supply of cereal foods for guide dogs.

Liakhoff's other preoccupation in 1941 was the supply of suitable dogs for training. It was not a new anxiety, of course, and it was to continue for years after the war. But once he had dealt with the immediate tasks demanded by the move to Edmondscote, Liakhoff decided to tackle his recurring supply problem by taking in more puppies than adult dogs. Puppy-walking had been tried and abandoned before, but on this occasion young puppies were taken in to the training centre where they were reared under the supervision of the staff. After Alfred Morgan visited Edmondscote in July 1941 he told Miss Crooke that there were 50 puppies ranging from four to ten months of age at the centre. They were being fed, he reported, on 'minced horseflesh boiled in with bran and oat mash, with variants of brown bread and hound meal and so on.'

In some respects this approach was no improvement. Many of the puppies that arrived at the centre were poor creatures bearing little resemblance to the description given in the appeals that were made, and some brought disease with them. 'As a result', Liakhoff reported, 'the percentage of suitable dogs from these puppies was not actually any larger than the percentage obtained from the grown-up dogs taken on approval under the previous schemes.' There were significant advantages, however: suitable puppies had greater potential as guide dogs because of their supervised rearing; and they were able to start some form of elementary training sooner.

Liakhoff also took the obvious step to deal with the weakness of the puppy programme: he started to breed his own. By the end of 1941 he was able to assess the results of two litters. From the first litter of only three, two were successful. Of the second litter of six, one died, one was under-sized and unsuitable in temperament, and four were successful.

The experiment was, as Liakhoff recognised, far too small to provide definite proof of its value. Nevertheless, he was justified in claiming that it gave hope of transforming the supply position to one in which only 25 or 30 per cent of dogs were unsuccessful.

He foresaw that the Association would eventually have to supply all its own dogs, 'and the sooner the better', but also recognised that there were formidable practical obstacles to achieving this on the scale required. The main difficulty, he believed, was that a breeding programme would require blind people to be separated from their guide dogs for about three months, which few of them would welcome. He saw, rightly, the necessity to breed from animals whose temperament and physical qualities had been proved, but at the end of 1941 he apparently did not envisage building up a separate breeding stock. He did make this suggestion a few months later and was authorised to purchase brood bitches from time to time 'as opportunity presented itself', but little seems to have come of the idea.

Dog supply therefore continued to be a problem. At the end of 1942 Liakhoff reported that 'after each appeal for dogs the kennels were overflowing with them.' A large number were no good and were difficult to dispose of. All the small puppies that were received had to be kept until they were at least eight months old before their temperament could be assessed, and then many proved unsuitable.

'I did not refuse to take puppies', he comments, 'as I was afraid of being without dogs. I am trying this year (1943) to avoid having small puppies, but I am not sure that this will not affect the supply.'

*   *   *

In 1942 St Dunstan's started to take a greater interest in guide dogs. Early in March the director of their home in Shropshire visited Edmondscote Manor and commented that until he had seen the work he had not realised just how much independence a guide dog brought to its owner. A contribution of 100 guineas followed a few months later and was continued every year until 1949 when it was raised to 500 guineas, the level at which it remained for the next 20 years. In 1970 the donation was doubled and has continued at £1,000 a year since then.

St Dunstan's commitment to guide dogs was further assured in January 1946 by the election to the Association's executive committee of their secretary, W.G. Askew, an astute man who was to be an influential figure in guide dog affairs for some years.

A surprising development in March 1942 was that two more apprentices were taken on. Despite the limited finances and bleak outlook Diana Crofton and Hilda Riley, youngsters of 18 and 17 respectively, joined Nora Robinson, who had by then graduated from kennel maid to apprentice. Not that this addition to the staff made much impact on the centre's costs. For the first three months they were boarded and lodged at Edmondscote but apparently received no pay. After this probationary period they received £1 a week for six months, with increases of 10 shillings (50p) every six months until they reached £2.10s a week and were fully qualified.

Another addition to the staff was guide dog owner Phyllis Robinson, who was taken on in December 1941 as shorthand typist and continued working for Liakhoff until 1958. Mrs Liakhoff's position at this time was still not properly established. In May 1940, the month that Miss Crooke resigned, she was appointed apprentice/secretary for a trial period of three months at a salary of 30 shillings a week. Phyllis Robinson recalls that when she started working at Edmondscote Mrs Liakhoff was occupied mainly in the office, but also tested approval dogs and did the ordering. In fact, it was not until November 1942 that the executive committee confirmed Mrs Liakhoff as secretary to the manager, compensating her for the delay with a gift of £30.

By 1942, when this picture was taken, Nora Robinson (centre) had moved up from kennel maid to apprentice and during that year two more apprentices were appointed, Hilda Riley (left) and Diana Crofton. The kennels behind them were brought from Wallasey in 1940. (Popperfoto)

All three apprentices were keen students and good workers, Liakhoff reported at the end of 1942: 'punctual in starting work and very willing to do any extra work such as meeting or despatching dogs in the evenings or at weekends, attending to sick dogs through the day and night if necessary.'

He did not mention domestic duties. 'We all had to have a week on house duty,' Nora Robinson recalled, 'which meant we trained our dogs as well as cooking the meals for the staff and students.' A combination of the apprentices' cooking skills and food rationing kept the menus simple. 'Macaroni was about all you could get – and Spam. I still can't look at Spam.'

House duty naturally included clearing the table and washing up. It also ran to putting the children to bed. Liakhoff and his wife liked to go down to the pub in the evening for a couple of hours and so it was left to the duty apprentice or Phyllis Robinson to look after the children. They would come back about 10.30, and on a summer evening it was not at all unusual for him to take a student out for some late obstacle training. On more than one occasion Nora Robinson was summoned from her bed to put out the obstacles and found herself cycling around town in her night clothes. On other evenings, after returning from the pub, he would talk to the students about how they were getting on.

'He was delightful – charm a bird off a tree,' said Nora Robinson remembering the warm, happy atmosphere that used to prevail. 'Wonderful with the dogs and a very, very good trainer of us and the students. He told us that we could criticise the students as much as we liked, but that we should always finish with praise. Even if they'd done nothing well and had a miserable walk we had to find something to praise. He was a good psychologist.'

There was also plenty of social life in the evenings. 'When Captain Liakhoff came back from the local, he'd teach us Russian folk songs. Sometimes we learnt the words, although we didn't know what they meant. Sometimes we just sang the tunes – all in parts. We'd sit around until 12 or 1 in the morning – the students loved it.'

*   *   *

The war was a testing time for guide dogs and their owners. A familiar route could become a waste land overnight and there are some striking testimonies to the remarkable way in which these hazards were overcome. Alfred Morgan, the guide dog owner who worked in the Liverpool docks, described how his border collie Fly guided him safely through nine months of regular blitzes, getting him to and from work. 'without the loss of a single hour'. Morgan called her his 'war dog' because he brought her home on 2 September 1939, the day before war was declared, and because it was the war that brought out her best qualities.

On one occasion, when all the possible ways ahead were blocked, Fly 'turned on her tail and walked back a few vehicles to where there was a small space, and so gained the pavement. The way was still blocked in front of us, so she hesitated a second, and then deliberately went down a small side street and then along another at right angles, and rejoined our usual route about 200 yards further down.'

The dog's actions had been witnessed by a number of people. 'She made a . . . of a sight better job of it than most of *us* would have done,' commented one observer.

'Do you realise,' Morgan wrote to Miss Crooke in December 1941, 'of all the blind people in Liverpool, only FOUR are going about, and have been going about, in their normal way.' They were all guide dog owners. 'Those who are not evacuated', he continued, 'are now handicapped worse than ever by the loss of many of their "landmarks" by the raids . . . *Our* problem isn't landmarks, but obstacles. And *they* are not really *difficulties*, they are merely disconcerting when one comes on them suddenly. The dog does the rest.'

Alfred Morgan walking through the Liverpool docks, where he worked, with Dawn, the guide dog he acquired after Bella's sudden death in 1938. The partnership was brief, however, and Dawn was replaced by a border collie, Fly, in September 1939. Morgan called her his 'war dog' because he brought her home the day before war broke out and she showed such outstanding qualities during the air raids, getting him to and from work 'without the loss of a single hour'.

Morgan's account of the plight that many blind people found them-selves in is also a resounding tribute to the superiority of a guide dog over other mobility aids (except possibly a sighted guide) when faced with unfamiliar or unexpected conditions.

John Bailey, a guide dog owner who is now the Association's senior appeals manager, tells a similar story which illustrates that landmarks can also disappear in peacetime with disastrous consequences. Not long after losing his sight in a car accident in 1956, and before getting a guide dog, he was going home one night after his usual weekly visit to his parents. He got off the bus for the last stage of the journey, a half-hour walk that he knew like the back of his hand. He crossed the road, mounted the pavement on the other side and turned left to follow a wall. Tapping his way along with his cane he came to some railings that turned to the right. On this occasion, however, a gate had been left open and he turned in thinking he was at the corner. He was now lost, but kept going until he tripped over. In fact, he was in the parish churchyard and had fallen over a grave.

'If you cry for help from a churchyard at that time of night, no-one is going to help you,' he said, recalling the incident. Fortunately, some youngsters passing by did respond to his cries and he eventually got home considerably later than he had planned to a very worried wife.

'It was that incident that finally decided me to apply for a guide dog,' he declared, 'that and people treating me like an old man when I was still in my twenties.'

*   *   *

Alfred Morgan's travels through Liverpool and further afield were tragically interrupted in September 1942 when he was knocked down and seriously injured by a lorry when crossing the road with Fly. The tragedy did not shake Morgan's faith in guide dogs or his adventurous spirit, however, and he recovered to carry on undaunted with another guide dog for several more years.

The accident occurred one morning on the way to work. A noisy horse wagon was drowning other traffic sounds and he was about half way across a road with Fly when the wagon stopped. He described what happened next in a letter to Miss Crooke from hospital four months later. 'In the comparative silence I heard a motor coming down the hill at a good pace . . . I sensed that something was going to happen and stood firm for a second. Fly struggled to get me along, but I stood firm. When I did move it was too late. A sighted person would have jumped for it, but a blind person always stops. We do not know which way to jump, so stop to allow the driver of the vehicle to clear us if possible.' On this occasion, however, 'the back of the lorry skidded and the back wheel got me.'

Morgan woke up about ten minutes after the accident in a casualty station to find himself being attended to by a doctor and a nurse, and Fly 'dashing about the waiting room and taking running jumps at the door to the room in which I was, trying to burst it open.' He told them to bring her in to him and she quietened down when he put his hand on her head. A short time later one of his friends arrived and Fly consented to leave with him.

The wheel had gone over both Morgan's legs above the knee. At first he was not expected to live but he was fit and strong and was soon out of danger. Six days after the accident, however, his right leg was amputated.

The left leg had sustained a clean break, and after 16 weeks in a splint he gradually got the full use of it again.

Shortly before writing to Miss Crooke in the middle of January 1943, he had been measured for an artificial leg. 'What will be the end of all this fuss and bother?' he enquired rhetorically. 'My own idea is very definite indeed . . . to go back to the Yard, and to have a dog again . . . I *must* have a dog; if I can't the whole arrangement will collapse as far as I am concerned.'

Morgan wanted his 'war dog' back again, but Liakhoff dismissed that proposal because Fly was too fast for someone with an artificial leg. By the end of August, however, Liakhoff had devised a solution.

'I have prepared a dog (a small crossbred alsatian bitch) very gentle and not pulling hard. In the meantime Forbes's dog died . . . His way of walking is somehow awkward, as he has something wrong with his legs and this has increased since he had his first dog. In order to give Morgan's dog a real experience I thought I would give her to Forbes temporarily and see how he gets on. A month or two before Morgan comes I will take the dog back, will try it and adjust anything that is necessary . . . The old man was very nice about it and said that he would do anything he could and would give the dog back with the greatest of pleasure knowing that he was helping someone else.'

The technique used by Liakhoff to 'adjust anything that is necessary' included strapping up his own right leg to simulate the way Morgan would walk.

Although Morgan was disappointed not to get Fly back he found her a happy home with the mother of the nurse who had looked after the bitch in the casualty station immediately after the accident. Nurse Greene turned up on Morgan's ward at the hospital some time later and had so taken to the dog that she offered a home for it believing that he would never use a dog again.

'They are all very happy and comfortable together', said Morgan, 'and the nurse, when she goes home for her weekly day off, is very envious and wishes she could have Fly at the hospital with her.'

At the end of the year Morgan went to Leamington to collect his new dog, Betty. But no sooner had he returned to Liverpool with his new guide than more trouble struck: someone left open the door of the house in which Morgan lodged and Betty slipped out. All that day he and his landlady, Mrs Hartley, searched the neighbourhood, but the dog had vanished. The next day the headmaster of the local school allowed him to enlist the help of the two top classes and 60 or 70 boys joined the hunt.

'The boys were far more useful than the police,' Morgan reported. 'They told me all about her movements and tried to get her, but unfortunately they thought of it as a "round-up" and when they got her cornered, made a grab at her, and off she went.'

It was six days before a policeman called Morgan and Mrs Hartley to a field in which he had spotted Betty. They walked up and down calling her name and the dog soon emerged from some bushes.

'She stood and looked at us for a moment, and then ran towards us. But there was a great 6ft barrier of barbed wire between us, and she couldn't get through. Then she ran along the wire towards the gate. It is quite a large field, quite a quarter of a mile in length. The policeman saw her coming and made to keep her in the field, but she got scared and leapt over a high wall into the road. Mrs H left me standing in the field and gave chase. People and children kept her on the track and at last, after chasing up several streets, she found her crouching down in a corner. She called her quietly and Betty ran up to her. Mrs H was so excited that she couldn't put on the harness or the leash, which she had, but picked her up and carried her back to the taxi, and when Betty saw me she simply flew at me, shrieking with joy. The rest was easy.'

Six days on the loose had apparently done the bitch no harm. But she had escaped just as she was coming into season and returned pregnant. Liakhoff's advice was to have the pups put down at birth but Morgan was all for keeping two or three of them, for Betty's sake, even if it meant losing her as a guide for some weeks. It appears that he did send Betty somewhere to have her pups, but there is no record of what happened afterwards. In any event, she cannot have lasted long as a guide dog because Nora Robinson, who in 1944 married a Russian serving with Czech forces in Britain, remembers training a dog for Morgan in 1945, when she resumed work after having a baby. 'She was a wonderful bitch. When they got to the pavement he would put his head right down to the dog's ear and say "Forward"; and they would shoot across the road. He wasn't a very tall man, so he didn't have far to stoop. We couldn't get him to stand up and say "Forward".'

Morgan's adventures are recounted at some length, not because he was unique, although he was certainly a remarkable man, but because he demonstrated in striking fashion the determination possessed by so many blind people, a quality without which they can never realise the full potential of a guide dog. His story is an eloquent reminder not only of the joy that guide dogs have brought to so many lives, but also of the courage and perseverance that are needed to enjoy the fruits of this remarkable partnership between man and dog.

*   *   *

The security that the committee had acquired for the training programme by arranging for Holmes's release from the navy in January 1941 was shattered at the end of 1942 when Liakhoff asked for permission to dismiss his only qualified trainer. He complained of rudeness, insubordination and refusal to comply with orders, leaving the committee with little alternative but to write to the Ministry of Labour informing them that Holmes was no longer essential to their work.

'I have always thought you were mistaken in keeping him and giving him his trainer's certificate,' said Miss Crooke when she heard the news; 'he is just no good as a trainer and unsuitable for training or handling blind people.'

Liakhoff put a brave face on things and claimed he was better off without him. Despite the loss of about 30 dogs due to an epidemic of distemper and trouble with his knees he maintained that he would produce more dogs than he would have done with Holmes's help.

It is not clear how his knee trouble arose. A story has been handed down that they were damaged when his horse fell on him during his days as a Cossack. What we do know for certain is that he was in hospital for nearly three weeks in the summer of 1942 when it was hoped that an operation might be possible. It was not, and so he had to endure the conflicting advice of different specialists. One recommended putting him in plaster for three to six months; another said that remedy would finish his knees for good and recommended horse riding. Not surprisingly, Liakhoff decided to follow the latter's advice, bought himself a polo pony called Brenda for £10 and was given a grant of £25 a year by the committee to help with its upkeep. They seemed to think he could use the pony instead of his bicycle in the training work. In practice, he only used Brenda occasionally and Nora Robinson often exercised her around the paddock.

Mrs Kirienko (as Nora Robinson became in 1944) does not remember Liakhoff's knees giving him any trouble, but he maintained that specialists had predicted that he would be crippled completely in a few years. As a result, he prepared a scheme 'in which semi-trainers (I have three girls now) will be able to carry on the training up to a certain point and the last stage of it will be done by blind trainers.'

'I am making experiments with this with Miss P. Robinson', he told Miss Crooke in January 1943, 'and have every hope that this scheme will not only keep the quality of the guide dogs on the same level, but may even raise it.' It was a somewhat optimistic outlook for a scheme based on such uncertain foundations, and like some of Liakhoff's other ideas it never got very far.

Not long after telling Miss Crooke of his new scheme Liakhoff lost one of his three girls, Diana Crofton, apparently because her parents were dissatisfied with the pay. Coming on top of Holmes's recall to the navy, this drastically depleted his training resources, and at a meeting in July 1943 of the house sub-committee, which had been formed at the end of 1941 to deal with training centre affairs, concern was expressed that the output of dogs was not increasing. They were also worried once again by what would happen if they were to lose Liakhoff for any reason.

'I gather that one or two people, including the chairman, talk of resigning,' Captain Sington informed Miss Crooke soon after the July meeting, 'and Lady Schuster said her husband spoke of closing the school – or rather suggesting it but there are people who will have something to say to the contrary should he make such a proposal.' Sington thought the difficulty could be overcome; 'the disgruntled people are those who take little interest, or know little about the work, or have never in two instances, I believe, even visited the school (including the chairman)!'

Liakhoff had told the sub-committee of his plan for breeding his own dogs and using blind trainers, and Sington seems to have been reassured to some extent by these proposed solutions. The subject was to be pursued further, however, and Sington commented acidly that the next executive committee meeting ought to be held in Leamington 'so people can look into things on the spot, seeing so many have never been to the school.'

At the executive committee's next meeting (in November at the NIB's offices in London) no anxiety about the situation seems to have been expressed. The minutes record simply that the house sub-committee presented a report dealing with the activities at its meetings in May, July and October, and that it was unanimously adopted.

The executive committee did, however, touch on another subject which had been worrying Liakhoff. An important source of funds that had been used by Mrs Eustis and adopted in Britain from the very beginning was the 'scholarship' scheme, whereby a certain sum of money was collected or donated to sponsor the provision of a dog for a blind person. The sum was originally fixed at £50 but by 1943 costs had increased and so it was raised to £100.

Liakhoff was aware of the great financial benefit of scholarships, but it was very uncomfortable, he declared, when the collectors of scholarships insisted on having the blind recipient in their own town.

'When the blind man leaves the school with his dog he is far from perfect,' he wrote, 'far away from being an example of how the man and dog should work together. He has too many faults which affect the dog's work. During this time he must be left alone to carry on persevering and if, at this time, he is followed by people, the dog's work is inspected and criticised and this criticism passed on to him which makes him feel uncomfortable, impatient and even sometimes shakes his confidence in the dog, it is not only very difficult to get a good result from the work, but there is also the risk of much bad propaganda.

'Moreover, the people who collect scholarships sometimes select the candidate to receive it and their selection is not always correct. The refusal of such a candidate, however, often offends them. I do not think it is advisable at present, in view of the fact of our poverty, to put any restrictions on the scholarship system, but I mention this point as one of our difficulties.'

It was not long, however, before the difficulty was tackled. At the AGM in March 1945 the chairman asked the donors of future scholarships to allow their funds to be used 'to the best advantage of the blind, without restricting us and chaining us down to the narrow stipulations which are sometimes specified, as we often find this a great embarrassment . . .'

This request eventually became enshrined in the anonymity rule that applies today. The scholarship scheme now takes the form of fund-raising targets, but it is no longer possible to sponsor a dog for a particular individual. The blind person's right to freedom from the attentions of sponsors (who are no doubt well-meaning but unaware of the difficulty, embarrassment or worry they can cause a guide dog owner) is regarded as just as important as his freedom of mobility.

*   *   *

With the end of the war in sight and a steadily-improving bank balance, the Association began to take seriously the task of expansion. In October 1944 Sir Victor Schuster resigned from the chairmanship that he had held since 1937 and was succeeded by Captain V.M. Deane, who had been the NIB's representative on the Association's general council and executive committee for some years. Deane, who was blind, took over the chair better informed than some others on the committee, having spent two weeks at Edmondscote Manor a few months previously. He immediately announced that it was his ambition to double the output of guide dogs and to improve the accommodation at the centre. Unfortunately, ill-health forced him to resign in January 1948, when Sir Victor Schuster took over again, but in his short reign a good deal was achieved.

By the time the war in Europe ended, in May 1945, three new apprentices, two men and one woman, had been taken on. Nora Kirienko had returned after having a baby and was within a few months of completing her apprenticeship and becoming a fully-qualified trainer. The kennels had been rebuilt and work was about to start on a reconstruction of the house and stables to provide more rooms and greater comfort. It was the beginning of a long post-war development that is still continuing.

7

Domestic Dramas and the Coming of Age

'On Christmas Eve 1949 the position appeared almost hopeless,' Liakhoff recorded in July or August of 1950, 'and it seemed that the Association's constructive work of 17 years was to be destroyed.'

'On that day', he continued, 'all the training staff left, after having given one week's notice, taking with them the only experienced kennel maid (the fiancée of one of them). The real reason for this action is still unknown to me, though they stated in the press that it was due to their dissatisfaction with the administration here and the Association's policy in general.'

Liakhoff was being disingenuous in claiming that he did not know why the training staff had walked out on him, as will become clear later. But how did he land himself and the Association in this pickle? When the war ended, the prospects looked bright. Indeed, until the crisis suddenly blew up, the late 1940s appeared to be a time when the Association was coming of age and setting out on a long period of steady, untroubled growth. The financial position was improving, more staff were being taken on and Edmondscote Manor and the kennels were being given a face-lift.

Conditions were still far from ideal, of course. John Weeks, who was taken on as an apprentice early in 1946 and survived the turmoils of the next decade or so to become regional controller for the south-west, remembers that his first impressions of the Manor were of, 'a pretty decrepit-looking hovel'. The furniture 'wasn't second, it was more like nineteenth-hand', and according to Liakhoff's younger daughter, Abou*, it was mostly bought by her mother at auction. On one occasion, apparently, Mrs Liakhoff bid for the wrong lot and sometime later a vanload of deer's heads arrived at the Manor.

The feeding of the dogs was a pretty basic business. Raw meat was

*The name she acquired as a baby because it was the first intelligible sound she made. She was christened Catherine, with Mrs Schuster, as she was then, standing as godmother.

bought from a family at Kineton who were farmers and butchers. 'We used to go out there in the evenings to collect the flesh,' Weeks recalled. 'It would be anything in the fields that was on the point of death that they would bump off and drag in. Sometimes we would drive across the field in the van and one of them would sit on the wing with a 12-bore, and if he saw a rabbit he would bang off at it. Then when we arrived at the shed where the meat was stored the headlights would shine in (there was no electricity) and we would collect our supplies.

'As a sideline he had a vast chest in which he cultivated maggots for sale to fishermen and if you lifted the lid off this it was like hearing the tide coming in. There was a heaving mass of great fat maggots.'

Back at Edmondscote Manor the meat would be tipped into a large boiler and cooked for hours, 'until it looked like a great chunk of brown coal'. It was then minced, mixed with terrier or hound meal and given to the dogs without any fuss about adjusting the quantity for each dog.

'But the dogs prospered, they didn't look bad at all,' Weeks remembers. 'The real problem in those days was that there was no vaccine that gave protection against distemper and there were some horrendous outbreaks, really heartbreaking, especially if you had a string of dogs nearing the end of their training.

'You would take them out one day and they would not be quite as sharp or enthusiastic. The following day they would be lying down and there would be mucus running from their eyes and noses; and probably by the end of the week you would be taking them down to the destructor. It was highly infectious, and by the time you had spotted it in one it would already have spread to half a dozen or more. We would have perhaps three outbreaks a year.'

Weeks's grim recollections are substantiated by figures that Liakhoff submitted regularly to the committee. In the 12 months prior to October 1947, 55 dogs died or had to be destroyed – nearly twice as many as were trained as guide dogs. Over 100 were disposed of in other ways; usually returned to their owners as unsuitable, or sold.

When Weeks joined the Association there were three other apprentices: Betty Bridge, Charlie Green and George Sheppard. John Appleton was also taken on with Weeks, and a few months later Paul Holden arrived. However, in October 1946 Charlie Green was sacked after a row with Liakhoff and shortly afterwards John Appleton left before completing a year at Leamington. The training staff, which briefly boasted six apprentices was, therefore, by the beginning of 1947, only four strong. One of them, Betty Bridge, had just qualified as an instructor, and lost no time in expressing to the executive committee her dissatisfaction at the pay for women, £3 a week plus board and lodging, which compared poorly with the rate for men of £5 per week. She was therefore given £4 a

week, which is perhaps as good as might have been expected in those days. In fact, however, the following year, after further representations from Miss Bridge, her salary was raised to the same level as the men's. It was a minor triumph that the committee could well afford to concede, but it is interesting to reflect that it must have placed the Association among the few employers in the country who at that time paid women fairly for the work they were doing.

Unfortunately, the management's apparently enlightened attitude to women was shown to be nothing more than expediency when, in October 1949, the finance and general purposes committee endorsed a recommendation of Liakhoff's that no more female apprentices should be engaged. He presumably gave reasons, but they are not recorded, and after the early 1950s it was over 20 years before women were again offered the chance to become qualified instructors.

With the training staff comprising Liakhoff, one qualified instructor and three bright young apprentices the training centre's output rose. In 1946 it increased to 21 (although the target had been 30) and then to 30, 42 and 57 in the next three years.

One event of interest in 1947 was a month-long visit made by Liakhoff to guide dog schools in Germany, Holland and Belgium. He returned

Two of the post-war intake of apprentices, George Sheppard, on the left, and Paul Holden, in one of the runs at Leamington, probably in 1948. Disease was a big problem among the dogs, and the wastage rate from this and other causes was 70 or 80 per cent. In 1947, 55 dogs died or had to be destroyed – nearly twice as many as completed their training. (Keystone Press Agency)

'satisfied that in practically every way our standard of training is higher', and with an idea which led the executive committee to call for plans to use the grounds of Edmondscote Manor 'as they are abroad, for the working of obstacles . . .' Before long, artificial obstacles were being used inside the grounds as well as on pavements outside the centre.

With output on the move more kennel accommodation was needed. One reconstruction had been completed in 1946 and had resulted in 'rows of fine new kennels, brick-built and concrete-surfaced, with movable wooden floors raised off the ground with heating pipes below.' Runs had been wired in and asphalted, with separating fences to allow the staff access to one part of the kennels without having to go through other parts. Prior to this, the outer fence dividing the Edmondscote grounds from the adjoining property consisted of old army beds standing on end and wired together, and much of the other fencing was made of the old pieces of wood brought from Wallasey.

But the 1946 improvements were already inadequate and in 1948 further extensions were built and officially opened by Anthony Eden, the local MP, in June 1949. So pleased was he with progress that the chairman, Sir Victor Schuster, was moved to call 1948 'a year of fulfilment'. In his annual report for 1948 he boasted of 'a comfortable house for the students and staff: the most perfect kennels for the dogs: and four enthusiastic young trainers working under the supervision of the Director.' By the standards of the time the kennels no doubt rated three stars or more. In retrospect, one can see that they were far from perfect and compared poorly with the accommodation provided today.

When Derek Freeman arrived at Edmondscote in 1959 he found 'little, dark kennels that were like condemned cells. They were cosy, clean and warm to a certain extent, with straw. They looked nice, but the dogs saw nothing – it was terrible.' It is only in the last 30 years that people have come fully to understand the importance of kennel environment, along with breeding, puppy-walking and a less intensive training programme, in reducing wastage and producing better-adjusted dogs.

*   *   *

Despite the healthy appearance given by the post-war intake of apprentices and the rising output, there was clearly a deep-seated feeling of insecurity among the members of the council about the Association's administration. Documents circulated among the council members show that in 1947 a suggestion was being considered that St Dunstan's should be asked to take over the Association. When that charity's representative on the council, W.G. Askew, was consulted on the matter, however, he firmly rejected the idea as undesirable. He also dismissed another proposal that he should become chairman of the Association on the grounds that, in his view, it was wrong in principle for the paid official of one organisation for the blind to become the chairman of the governing body of another organisation for the blind.

The administration at this time was still in the hands of the Tail-Waggers' Club, but the war had taken its toll on their membership and in 1948 they decided that they could no longer continue their sponsorship or to provide administrative services (for a small fee) from their offices in Gray's Inn Road. The years of support had been crucial to the survival of guide dog work, but the split now led the Association to set up its own London office at 81 Piccadilly. It also gave them the full-time services of Miss Shrimpton, who had previously been serving both organisations as secretary.

The growing output and size of the training staff, together with the extra cost of new kennels and a London office of its own, led the committee to appoint Roger Eckersley as part-time appeals organiser to bring in more funds. He had recently retired from a senior job in the BBC and had also been a useful member of the general council since the 1930s, in particular helping to arrange the radio appeals that brought in very substantial donations. On taking up his new job in April 1948 he resigned from the council.

The only other paid appeals worker at this time was Miss Gertrude Lawis, who had been raising funds in Sussex since before the war, principally through the Everyman's Dog Show, which she organised annually. Branch activity had revived, however, and a new breed of 'voluntary organisers' was emerging who were paid an honorarium of £25 a year.

Eckersley's appointment soon paid dividends. The BBC was persuaded to allow another 'Good Cause' broadcast in July 1949, which brought in over £3,500, and a charity matinee performance of *Oranges and Lemons* at the Globe Theatre in London, attended by Princess Elizabeth (now the Queen), raised over £2,000.

The broadcast was notable because it was given by a guide dog owner, Miss Nina Barrett, and because it was aimed particularly at raising money for a second training centre. 'Although in recent years we have considerably increased our output, applicants still have to wait from three to four years before their turn for training comes,' reported *Forward*, the Association's magazine, in the autumn of 1949. Despite the public's generous response to the broadcast, more money was needed before a second centre could be launched, and readers were urged to help.

All these efforts enabled the committee to balance its books satisfactorily. Nearly £10,000 was raised other than through the BBC appeal and the Globe Theatre matinee, the NIB contributed its annual £500 and St Dunstan's the slightly larger and certainly more elegant figure of 500 guineas. The total enabled the Association to meet its expenses with £728 to spare.

Legacies of £2,400 were also received but the practice had already started of treating these as capital, rather than income. They were therefore credited to the balance sheet, which, by the end of September 1949 showed a total value of nearly £40,000, of which about £26,000 was cash or investments. It may not have been the strongest position from which to plan for another training centre, but nevertheless the committee did so. In May 1949 two members of the finance and general purposes committee, J.E. Walker and W.G. Askew, were appointed as a sub-committee to deal with the setting up of a second centre as a matter of urgency. However, when they presented a report to the general council in July showing that capital of £30,000 and additional annual income of about £6,000 would be needed, caution prevailed and it was decided not to acquire premises 'until we see our way clear to the acquisition of the requisite capital sum.'

*   *   *

Whatever tensions may have been building up between Liakhoff and the training staff in the late 1940s, life at Edmondscote Manor was obviously very pleasant for the students during their stay of about three weeks. Many blind people who had spent a good part of their lives in institutions and expected to find a similar atmosphere at Leamington were delighted to find how relaxed and informal the place was: 'the home atmosphere was more stressed,' wrote one student. In the evening they were asked if anyone wanted to visit the local pub and later, over a cup of tea, Liakhoff talked to them informally about dogs, their training and being a guide dog owner. 'It was packed with good sense and understanding.'

They were always 'asked' to do something, never ordered. The training staff were not over-protective, the emphasis being on rehabilitation in its widest sense, psychologically as well as getting about physically. A blind person going to Edmondscote Manor would find, 'a "home", where the guests are made to feel welcome from the moment they come to when they leave with their new friend.'

Another correspondent in 1948 spoke for many when she wrote of the happy time she was given at Leamington. 'If the Edmondscote atmosphere could be spread around a bit, the world would be vastly happier,' she maintained. 'The training was hard, and the beginning of training at home was hard, but it is worth it over and over again.'

But beneath this tranquil surface the conditions were gradually being created for the crisis of Christmas 1949. Early symptoms of the trouble could be seen in the circumstances of Charlie Green's dismissal in 1946. Executive committee minutes for October 1946 merely record that

Captain Sington had been to Edmondscote at Liakhoff's request and concluded, after a lengthy interview with Green, that there was no alternative but to dismiss him. John Weeks's recollection of events reveal something of the underlying problem. Liakhoff wanted Green to make some changes in the training of a dog that he (Green) had been working with for some weeks. Green demurred, pointing out to Liakhoff that he usually insisted on consistency in handling dogs. Liakhoff exploded, demanded that it should be done as he ordered and was told by Green that he would only do so if he thought it was right.

Some hours later Liakhoff called a meeting of all the training staff (except Sheppard, who was ill) in order to reassert his authority. 'But Captain . . .' said Green at one point. 'You will call me Sir,' Liakhoff demanded. 'I will not,' Green replied, 'I don't have enough respect for you.'

Green then left and Liakhoff told Betty Bridge that she must call him Sir. 'Yes, Captain,' she replied cheekily. To John Weeks he said, 'You can call me what you like. You can call me Nicky if you like. I do not mind what you call me, but I will have respect.' But, of course, as Weeks later commented, his behaviour did not earn him respect, at least not among his training staff. He had quite a different relationship with the blind students, who posed no threat and did not challenge him.

'Almost every day, it is his habit to drink a whisky or two in the morning, then to drink beer from 12 till 2pm – eat a large lunch in about 10 minutes, sleep till 4.30pm or 5pm, do a little work, then spend all the evening in the pub. Mrs Liakhoff drinks even more than he does, but is less affected by it.'

George Sheppard gave this account in March 1950 in the course of telling Miss Crooke about the events of the previous Christmas. He continued: 'It was terribly galling here to have these habits referred to by the local people. A voluntary collector here told me long ago that he was frequently refused subscriptions by people who said, "I'm not giving a penny for those Liakhoffs to spend on drink".'

Liakhoff's well-known drinking habits might not in themselves have eroded the respect of his staff. But his drinking, which contributed to his deteriorating health, increasingly affected his work. There were other factors as well. 'He could be very irritating at times,' John Weeks recalls. 'He would follow in a car while you were working with a dog, then drive past and wait 100 yards up the road, smoking and reading a newspaper, or pruning his eyebrows. He had incredibly bushy eyebrows and he'd be setting them. He was quite vain about his appearance.'

Liakhoff would play off one member of the staff against another, exploiting the rivalries that inevitably existed within the group. He managed to create an uneasy, insecure atmosphere among them. In return, they could be provocative. By 1949, they all had several years' experience behind them and began to ask more searching questions about the work.

> 'We all asked them,' John Weeks recalled, 'but we asked them of one another. Paul Holden was the one who would suddenly say in the car returning from town, "Tell me, Captain, why is such and such?" Nick would fumble. I don't think there was actually any muted laughter but there was certainly an atmosphere of cynicism in the car which must have indicated to Nick that his stock was sinking lower. He would persist in the most silly concepts and maintain that there were good scientific reasons for these without telling you what they were.
> At this point his English would become fractured. Paul was a very knowledgeable, clear-thinking individual; an obvious candidate for promotion. I think Nick realised he would be a bit of a thorn in his side. He felt he could manage George Sheppard, and he could certainly manage me.'

The incident that caused this simmering pot to boil over was, in itself, a minor one. Holden made a remark about the Liakhoffs keeping some food for themselves (it must be remembered that rationing still persisted) and the remark was quickly reported. Later, Liakhoff was overheard asking the chairman, on the telephone, if he could come to see him the following day because he thought it was necessary to dismiss a member of his staff.

That night the staff put their heads together and when George Sheppard was asked by Liakhoff the next morning to drive him to the station Sheppard said that if he was going to London to secure Holden's dismissal all the staff would resign when he came back. Liakhoff continued his journey and on his return was handed the resignations.

George Sheppard's explanation for their action was that they had no confidence in the Liakhoffs. 'We knew that our work was not the deciding factor in our employment,' he told Miss Crooke. 'That we were liable to be dismissed at the personal whim of either Capt. Liakhoff or Mrs Liakhoff, no matter what specious argument was put to the Committee against us and about our work.'

They also believed the committee would always accept Liakhoff's very plausible account of events rather than theirs and that their only course, if they were not to drift on and find themselves individually being compelled to leave at one time or another and find different work, was to make a clean break and continue together.

Trying to explain Liakhoff's behaviour and personality, Sheppard continued:

> 'I really should not be surprised if by this time he has completely and honestly forgotten that anything *was* done before he came. In the years I have known him he has never mentioned it, though he has frequently

spoken of the struggle of the early days – always a struggle between the public on the one side, and himself alone against them on the other. Mrs Liakhoff seems even more jealous of his reputation in this respect than he does.

'Captain Liakhoff is something of an enigma. He does, I think, live in a dream and see circumstances as he wants to see them, not as they are. He exaggerates enormously even though he should realise that the person to whom he speaks is aware of the true state of affairs. He does not consider that possibility, however, as I am sure that he does, temporarily, honestly believe his own version. There's probably some simple psychological explanation for this, but perhaps it all boils down to vanity. I got to know him pretty well, but I cannot say that I dislike him. I know that his code of honesty and fairness is a most unusual one, and that he is willing to devise facts if convenient ones do not exist to support his temporary points of view, but he has a peculiar charm that prompts one not to classify him as a downright liar so much as a sort of reincarnation of Munchhausen.* Mrs Liakhoff falls into quite a different category in our estimation, the least said of which the better. Without her I think he could have been a much "bigger" man.'

*Baron Munchhausen was the subject of a series of fantastic adventure stories written in English by R.E. Raspe during the 18th century.

When John Weeks read that analysis of Liakhoff in 1988 he commented that it was, 'as good a description as you could expect to get of his personality'. Nora Kirienko, who had been with Liakhoff in Wallasey and left Leamington long before the trouble erupted, was a detached but saddened observer of these events. 'They really *were* different in the early days – kinder altogether, and I suppose I still see them that way,' she wrote to Sheppard early in March 1950. 'But don't think I am blinded to seeing how things stand now.'

*   *   *

And so it came about that on Christmas Eve 1949 Liakhoff found himself on his own with 80 dogs in kennels and only four inexperienced kennel girls. He was booked to go into hospital on 15 January for three months, probably for treatment for his duodenal ulcer, and a class of four blind people was due to arrive on the 16th.

To his great credit, he did not panic. He cancelled his hospital appointment, rejected three of the dogs scheduled for the class and brought forward three more that were trained intensively to get them ready, recalled a guide dog owner who needed some additional traffic training and worked, by his own account, not less than 12 hours a day, seven days a week. It was a punishing programme for a man in poor health.

He then proceeded to rebuild his staff. In January he promoted three of the kennel girls to apprentice trainers and took on one man. In February he engaged Arthur Phillipson, who was later to become the Association's director of training, and in March his wife's nephew, Michael Bibikoff.

Meanwhile, members of the finance and general purposes committee were salvaging what they could from the wreckage. Some members of the committee, in particular Askew and Walker, acknowledged that the staff had cause for resigning. They were reluctant to lose the services of four experienced trainers, who in any case had announced their intention to set up a rival organisation to train guide dogs, but recognised that they could not and would not work with Liakhoff. They therefore brought forward the plan that had been put on ice a few months earlier and suggested to the breakaway group that they should establish a second centre under George Sheppard which would be completely independent of Liakhoff. Their first proposal was that, 'in view of all the circumstances and Captain Liakhoff's state of health,' Sheppard and his team should operate at Edmondscote and Liakhoff should be given three months' sick leave during which time the other centre could be obtained.

In the event, presumably because of the way Liakhoff had taken matters in hand at Leamington, things worked out differently. The four trainers agreed to stay on but it was they who set up the second centre. George Sheppard and John Weeks made an intensive tour of numerous properties all over the south and west of England and by the spring of 1950 they were turning Cleve House in Exeter into a training school.

The events of Christmas 1949 brought into prominence a member of the finance and general purposes committee, W.G. Askew, who had been elected to the general council as a representative of St Dunstan's in 1946. 'I had enormous respect for him', George Sheppard said, and it was no doubt the esteem in which he was held that enabled him to bring about a reconciliation. Had he not done so there might well have been two organisations in Britain providing guide dogs, because Sheppard claims that he had good connections and the promise of financial support. However, he does not regret the outcome. Although it can be argued that an element of rivalry between two separate organisations might have had some benefits, he shares the view of many others that there is enough fragmentation in the field of blind welfare without having two charities providing guide dogs.

Askew's skill and hard work in negotiating the settlement earned him the unusual tribute of a 'very hearty vote of thanks' from the other members of the finance and general purposes committee and from the general council. His services were never called on again in quite such desperate circumstances, but in the remaining 17 years that he was a member of the general council he was clearly a very influential figure.

'Askew was the really important one,' recalled Callum McLean, who joined the general council in 1954. 'He was so capable. He really knew how to run a committee. I didn't always agree with him, but if I disagreed I found he always won. I learned a lot from him.'

As long as Askew was on the general council and the finance and general purposes committee, of which he was chairman from 1958 to 1962, the Association had a source of shrewd, practical advice that was of incalculable value, and when he left in 1967, the year before his death, his loss was deeply felt. Like John Walker, who was another forceful and valuable member of the council in the 1940s and '50s, Askew's background and life were very different from that of some other council members. Walker had a science degree and worked for the National Farmers Union in East Anglia. Askew joined St Dunstan's in 1919 as pensions officer and progressed to become its secretary and a key figure in the organisation. He was appointed CBE in 1951 and Lord Fraser, the head of St Dunstan's for many years, once wrote of him that 'there is no single individual member of the staff to whom St Dunstan's owes more . . .' John Colligan, a former director general of the RNIB, as it became in 1953 after the grant of a Royal Charter, called him 'the wisest man I ever met'.

Despite the Association's apparently critical condition when the new decade dawned, the 1950s turned out to be a period of considerable achievement. It began with a swift resolution of the resignation crisis and was followed immediately by the appointment, in April 1950, of Roger Eckersley as the Association's first general manager. He was already 62 at the time of his appointment and a more ambitious council might perhaps have chosen a younger man, but it was a safe choice, and a step in the right direction – the first tentative move towards the development of a professional management.

It took a long time, however, before a clear distinction was drawn between the roles of the general council and of the management. It would be tedious to trace the evolution of this relationship in detail, but it was not until the chairmanship was taken in 1964 by Sir Joseph Napier, a man who had considerable business experience, that the principle of a division between policy-making and 'trusteeship' on the one hand, and executive responsibility on the other was clearly laid down. Even then, despite further progress made by Napier's successor, Ken Butler, and his director general (as the general manager had by then become), Tony Clark, the principle was not fully implemented until the arrival on the scene in 1983 of a director general, Major-General John Groom, who was a good deal more aggressive than his predecessors. It seems strange now to see in the records that in November 1955, for example, the management sub-committee of the general council were considering such details as the purchase of a toaster for Exeter and potato peelers for both centres.

A member of the sub-committee was, of course, the legendary Lady Freda Valentine, who was honorary treasurer from 1938 to 1977. She was

Lady Freda Valentine in December 1956. She was a member of the general council between 1937 and 1982, for nearly 39 of those years as honorary treasurer, and acquired a formidable reputation for her energy and penetrating attention to detail. She was awarded a CBE in 1979 for her outstanding contribution to blind welfare and continued to take an interest in guide dog affairs until her death in 1989 at the age of 93. (Anthony Buckley)

renowned for scrutinising training centres' bills and querying the smallest items of expenditure. She once demanded to know why Leamington had found it necessary to buy six-penny-worth of parsley when she knew there was some in the garden. When she was told that the garden was covered in two feet of snow and they couldn't find the parsley, she briskly informed them that they should follow her example and put canes in the ground to mark the spot.

She was scrupulously fair, however, and could be generous if the circumstances demanded it. Arthur Phillipson remembers how hard up he was as a young trainer at Leamington in the early 1950s. While out training a dog, he used to stop and look longingly in the window of a 'gents outfitters' at a pair of corduroy trousers to replace the threadbare pair he was wearing. One day the shopkeeper came out and asked him if he wanted them. 'I can't afford them,' Phillipson replied. The shopkeeper was obviously touched by Phillipson's plight because he fitted him out with the trousers, shortened the legs and asked for a shilling a week until the debt was paid off. In fact, Phillipson continued paying him a shilling a week until the man retired – his only credit customer.

About this time Phillipson married and found it almost impossible to live on the pay he was getting. He wrote to the general manager explaining his predicament and was summoned to a committee meeting where Lady Freda and others enquired minutely into his circumstances. 'How on earth do you manage?' they enquired.

'Well, that's really why I've come,' he replied. Lady Freda then asked how much he wanted. He was drawing roughly £5 a week and, reluctant to push his luck too far, asked for £7.10s. Lady Freda's reaction, he recalled, was to thump the table and cry, 'Nonsense, you can't live on that.'

'I think they put it up to £12.10s,' he said. 'I couldn't believe it. I could actually buy a pair of shoes.'

*   *   *

In Exeter, Sheppard and his team were not having an easy time, but they did have the advantage of enthusiasm and a determination to succeed that was rooted in the certain knowledge that there were a number of people who would be very happy to see them fail. In the aftermath of the resignations and reconciliation, sides had inevitably been taken and Sheppard was not always sure of the support he was getting. He not only distrusted Eckersley, who was 'very much a friend of the Schusters' and pro-Liakhoff, but was frustrated by the general manager's inefficiency.

'Half the time I don't know whether to blame these failures on the part of Eckersley to his age, a natural stupidity or a wilful desire to make things difficult,' he wrote to Miss Crooke in July 1950. 'I write to him on quite important matters and never get a reply, or only an evasive answer, and the matters which should be discussed by the sub-committee he very often sits on and does nothing about.

'I suppose things will come right in the end. What I should like to see would be a few more Askews and Walkers on the committee. Some new blood might do good.'

Sheppard and his colleagues had taken over Cleve House in March. The building was a fine 16th century manor in about 14 acres of grounds, in good condition but in need of decoration. To keep costs down Sheppard and the other two men concentrated on building temporary kennels, while Betty Bridge got on with training dogs for the first class. By July they were living at the centre, 'more or less under camping conditions', and the first class of students was scheduled for September. Dog supply was proving to be a problem because they had been told they must not tread on Leamington's toes in finding suppliers. Some of the teething troubles the new centre was to experience could be put down to difficulty in getting suitable dogs: a big enough problem normally, but made even worse by the restriction that was placed on them.

Meanwhile, Liakhoff, in his struggle to recover from the disaster of the previous Christmas, was issuing optimistic reports about new ideas with which he was experimenting. They were received with some scepticism, however. John Walker's view was that although it was good to know that Liakhoff was looking for new methods to keep up the output, one had to be careful that his theories were not being developed to fit the circumstances, rather than the facts.

'It would be a little strange', he remarked in a letter to Sir Victor Schuster in July, 'if after 17 years or more of development of one method of training, a better method should be evolved in the course of a few months. At any rate it would be strange if the finding of that method should coincide so precisely with the change of circumstances.'

Walker's influence on the course of events at this time is nowhere better demonstrated than in this letter to Sir Victor. After expressing his view of the training experiment he continued: 'On the main point of your letter, I must make my own view clear. If, in the future, we should attempt to force upon the trainers at Exeter, "supervision through the Director of Training", that, to my mind, would not be compatible with the undertaking we gave to Mr Sheppard and the other trainers. To that extent, so far as I am concerned, it would not be honourable, and I could not be a part of it.'

His good sense is shown in the conclusion to his letter. 'If we can leave time to look after these things, I believe it will do so ... they (the two training centres) will, ultimately, come together, and much of the present bitterness between the personnel will be forgotten.'

Liakhoff was clearly doing what he could to discredit Sheppard and his colleagues, as two surviving letters from him to Miss Crooke and Lady Freda Valentine demonstrate. John Walker was aware of it when, in September, he told Miss Crooke that 'Liakhoff is using all the methods – which you know perhaps as well as any of us – that he can use to discredit the boys, but those methods are beginning to cut a little less ice. Askew is a good man on the committee, and between us I believe we are beginning to get things straightened up.'

Liakhoff was also ruffling a few feathers by proposing to give his nephew, Michael Bibikoff, the salary of a fully-qualified instructor only six months after his arrival at Leamington, his argument being that Bibikoff had already done 12 months' work with him in the Wallasey days.

John Walker was not convinced, however, and asked Miss Crooke how much work Bibikoff had done at Wallasey. Not much, she replied. 'He was a nice lad, but showed no special interest in the work. He was always willing to do odd jobs. I used to give him 2s.6d to do the kennels for me on Sunday mornings when it was my weekend . . . Michael also fetched dogs from the station for us occasionally, but he did not work as a trainer . . . one of his chief occupations was playing table tennis with some other boys, on most afternoons, at some club . . .'

She added that Mary Knowles, who 'used to help us a lot with odd jobs, traffic work and all sorts of things, and was constantly at "The Cliff" . . . remembers Michael Bibikoff very well and says that to the best of her knowledge he never did any work or took any particular interest in the work . . . She says that she never saw him do anything with either dogs or blind people.'

The enquiries seem to have prevented the immediate attempt to provide 'jobs for the boys', as Walker referred to it, but Liakhoff was not thwarted for long and Bibikoff became a qualified instructor on 30 May 1951, little more than a year after arriving at Edmondscote. Two months later Arthur Phillipson, who had been taken on shortly before Bibikoff, in February 1950, also qualified.

Nepotism soon raised its head again. In July 1953 the general council decided that Liakhoff, who was both director of training and controller of the Leamington centre, should move from Edmondscote Manor to concentrate on the first role and that someone else should be appointed to the controller's post. A year earlier, Liakhoff had managed to persuade Sir Victor Schuster, who was then in the final months of his chairmanship, and others that a number of Exeter's aftercare cases had been mishandled and that he should therefore be allowed to take responsibility once again for all 'technical' work.

The effect of this decision was to give Liakhoff responsibility for the work of two centres, instead of one, and the council declared that one purpose in separating the roles of director of training and controller of Edmondscote was to allow Liakhoff the time to supervise two centres. It would also allow him to compile a training manual and to direct a small breeding experiment that had recently been started in Runcorn. Behind this decision probably lay the wish to relieve Liakhoff of the pressure of day-to-day activities in running a training centre. In January 1951 he had had one serious operation, for a duodenal ulcer, and he was in hospital again for an operation in the middle of 1952. (During one of his stays in hospital, it was said, he got fed up with the diet to which he was restricted and persuaded his wife and Miss Shrimpton to smuggle in some pork pies.)

Liakhoff had, not surprisingly, recommended that Bibikoff should succeed him as controller at Leamington, despite the claims of two much more experienced trainers at Exeter: Paul Holden and John Weeks. (Betty Bridge had emigrated to New Zealand at the end of 1950, and subsequently moved to Australia to start guide dog training in that country.) Anticipating trouble, the new chairman, Lady Freda Valentine's half-brother, the Earl of Lanesborough, had gone to Exeter and told Holden and Weeks that it was no good them applying for the job because they wouldn't get it: if it didn't go to Bibikoff, Liakhoff might leave and the council were not prepared to contemplate that outcome. However, Holden was not inclined to let the job go unchallenged and submitted a formal application.

It was no good, of course. Bibikoff got the job, which he took over at the beginning of January 1954, and in March Holden and Weeks resigned. The appointment was a mistake, but it typified the combination of expediency and muddle that hampered the Association's growth and caused it to lose many valuable and experienced training staff over the years. Bibikoff held the controller's post for only 18 months and then went to South Africa to start a guide dog school.

Bibikoff's departure, and Liakhoff's failing health, prompted Lord Lanesborough to ask Weeks at the end of 1955 if he would like to return – but not to the vacant post of controller at Leamington. At Liakhoff's insistence, the less experienced Arthur Phillipson became head trainer and subsequently controller at Leamington, while Weeks had to be content with the job of deputy controller at Exeter. He did not have to wait long, however, before another upheaval led to an improvement in his position.

The trouble started with a refusal to recognise that Weeks was entitled to hold a new, higher training qualification that was being introduced – an ironic situation because he had played the major part in working out the new idea. In January 1957, exasperated by the decision, Weeks offered his resignation and was strongly supported by George Sheppard, the controller at Exeter, who also resigned, adding that he was dissatisfied with what he considered unjustified interference by the chairman in training matters. When Sheppard declined an invitation to reconsider his position John Walker immediately resigned from the council, presumably in protest at the way the affair had been handled.

Liakhoff and the council had by then conveniently discovered that there had been a misunderstanding over Weeks's qualifications. They offered to rectify the position immediately and asked him to withdraw his resignation, which, after some hesitation, he agreed to do. He then became controller of the Exeter centre and remained at Cleve House until he retired in 1988 as regional controller for the south west. He had the opportunity to become director of training in 1975 but did not care for the financial terms of the offer.

It would be wrong to attach too much importance to these futile clashes and differences. They were certainly wasteful of talent and experience and distressing to some of those involved. Greater stability and better administration might well have solved recurring problems, such as dog supply, more quickly and led to faster growth. This, in turn, would have reduced the long period (several years at this time) blind people had to wait for a guide dog, a highly desirable outcome, of course.

But growth was surprisingly rapid during the 1950s, despite the problems. Between 1950 and 1957 the annual output of trained dogs rose from 38 to 89. The fund-raising effort was thriving and savings were building up again after being drained almost entirely by the £25,000 needed to purchase, renovate and equip Cleve House. By the end of 1953 there were already about 100 branches or voluntary organisers and new ones were being formed at the rate of 40 or 50 a year. The Scottish branch, formed in 1950, was alone bringing in £1,000 a month in 1957.

The result was that in the 1956/7 financial year income exceeded expenditure by £8,500 *after* transferring £30,000 into a fund for new training centres. Another £16,000 worth of legacies was tucked away on deposit or in investments, and savings altogether amounted to about £140,000. When the decade ended Askew, as chairman of the finance and general purposes committee, was able to boast of a 'flourishing' financial position and Schuster, who was still a member of the general council, of the 'radical change' and growth that had occurred.

*   *   *

Among the landmarks of the fifties was the consent of Princess Alexandra to become president (later patron) of the Association. She became president in September 1954 and in the following May and June visited the Leamington and Exeter centres respectively. On these occasions, as on the many other visits that she has made to the Association's growing number of locations over the next 35 years, she won everyone's affection for her warmth and sincerity.

It was in the fifties that the white harness was introduced. Up to 1952 the leather harness had been brown, but following the first fatal accident to a guide dog owner, Miss Agnes Wilson, in November 1951, Liakhoff explored ways of increasing their visibility at night. The National Federation of the Blind had suggested white harnesses, but initially it was decided to paint them with a luminous paint. This was unsatisfactory and in 1953 white-painted harnesses were adopted.

The fatal accident occurred on a rainy night just as Miss Wilson finished crossing a road. At that time the dog was taught to stop at 'up' kerbs (from the road to the pavement) as well as 'down' kerbs (before crossing the road). This procedure had the advantage of giving the blind person a very

The Association's first Royal patron was the Earl of Athlone, who accepted the position in 1938. Formerly Prince Alexander of Teck, he was Queen Mary's brother and in 1904 married Princess Alice, a grand-daughter of Queen Victoria. Princess Alexandra became president in 1954 and patron in 1957 after the death of the Earl of Athlone. She is seen here arriving for her first visit to the Leamington centre in May 1955 with the Association's chairman, the Earl of Lanesborough; and later that day walking blindfold with a guide dog under the watchful eye of Arthur Phillipson, who was then controller of the centre.

clear indication that he had reached the kerb, instead of relying on his ability to feel the dog stepping up ahead of him. However, its disadvantage was that it prolonged the exposure of dog and owner to traffic danger. It is difficult to pinpoint exactly when this practice was changed, but some time after the accident the 'up' kerb stop was abandoned, except in rare circumstances.

Towards the end of the fifties a long-running dispute with the RNIB

over fund-raising finally came to a head. Guide dog supporters had increasingly been appealing outside the 'doggy' circles to which they were supposed to restrict themselves by the agreement made in 1932. Despite protests by the RNIB, who were anxious about the inroads being made on their sources of funds, and meetings between the two sides which led to limited concessions on certain activities, the guide dog tide could not be stemmed. When Captain Deane, who represented the RNIB on the

The Duchess of Kent deputising for her daughter, Princess Alexandra, at the annual general meeting on 26 March 1958. She presented awards for service to the Association to Sir Victor Schuster, seen here receiving his guide dog 'replica', and others. On the right are the Earl of Lanesborough and Charles Maton, the general manager. (Central Press Photos)

council, reported that he had been asked unofficially whether the Association would agree to being taken over by the Institute, the matter was accorded only the briefest reference in the minutes. As John Colligan, secretary general of the RNIB, admitted in 1952 to one of his committee chairmen, the Institute was in a weak position and little could be done about it. 'To some extent', he recognised, 'it is an act of grace on the part of the Guide Dogs Association to discuss the avoidance of overlapping in money raising at all.'

Further irritation was caused by the use on the Association's notepaper and fund-raising literature of the phrase 'affiliated to the Royal National Institute for the Blind'. The Association was perfectly entitled to the use, the affiliation being part of the early arrangement between the two organisations, but by 1958 the RNIB felt that it was time to disaffiliate. In agreeing to the proposal, the chairman, Lord Lanesborough, hoped that even though 'this last material tie' had been severed and the Association was free to go its own way, friendly co-operation would continue.

'I think you have over-simplified the understanding to which we came,' replied Godfrey Robinson, the RNIB's chairman, who maintained that the disaffiliation did not nullify the fund-raising agreement. The correspondence continued for some weeks, with Lord Lanesborough claiming that it was unreasonable to be tied by an arrangement which restricted only the Association's activities and that he was not convinced that 'it is in our interests, to put it bluntly, to be bound by a one-sided agreement'. He did assure them, however, that the intention to enter into cut-throat competition with the RNIB was 'the one thing furthest from our thoughts'. The RNIB had little option but to accept the situation and hope that they would do less harm by leaving things as they were than by fighting on.

A natural consequence of the disaffiliation was that the Association decided it would be inappropriate to continue having RNIB representatives on its general council. The existing representatives would, if they wished to continue, have to be elected and serve as individuals and not as nominees of the RNIB. In fact, only one of the two, Captain Cochrane-Barnett, was re-elected.

While the RNIB drama was being played out thoughts were turning towards the need for more training facilities. In 1956 the Mayor of Blackburn apparently offered £150,000 to the Association over a period of four or five years if a new training centre was established, presumably in his area, but nothing came of this other than focussing attention on the north-west, and when, in January 1958, the planning sub-committee recommended that a new training centre should be opened 'as soon as convenient' in order to deal with the growing demand, no reference was made to Blackburn. In the event, it was the Nuffield Foundation that provided financial support for a centre in Lancashire and at the end of 1958 a suitable site was found in Bolton. Nuffield House, the Association's first purpose-built training centre, was opened by Princess Alexandra in 1961.

Perhaps the dominant event of 1958 in human terms, at least, was Liakhoff's retirement as director of training to become a consultant. His health had been deteriorating steadily and although he was very reluctant to give up the post, the general council decided that it was the only sensible course.

He had undergone an operation for a duodenal ulcer in January 1951, after which he was off work for several months. He was taken into hospital for another 'emergency' operation on 12 June 1952, although it was, in fact, not performed until the 23rd of the month. He became ill again during April 1954, as a result of which the surgeon who had operated on him in 1952 said his condition would not improve unless he altered his way of life, including taking more regular meals. An appointment was arranged with Sir Horace Evans, who reported that there was some possibility of chronic pancreatitis but found difficulty in suggesting treatment. He thought there was no reason why Liakhoff should not resume work when he felt able.

A year later Liakhoff was in hospital again, for yet another operation, but he was fit enough to attend a meeting at the end of November 1955 and to re-start aftercare visits the following February. However, he continued to smoke and drink heavily and needed from time to time 'to take medicine which has a sedative effect', as his doctor described it in a letter to Lord Lanesborough on 26 April 1956. Other evidence suggests that he may have been injecting pethidine, a narcotic pain-killing drug that is less potent than morphine but has similar effects. The extent to which Liakhoff used the drug, and for how long, is unknown. In October 1957 he was prompted to refute criticism from staff that drugs were affecting his judgment by telling the general manager that his prescription had run out 18 months ago. On that reckoning he had been taking nothing since April 1956, the month in which his doctor had informed Lord Lanesborough that Liakhoff was in need of sedative medicine from time to time. The explanation for this apparent conflict is possibly that Liakhoff's memory was at fault and that it was not until later in 1956 that he ceased taking the drug. He was off sick again for several weeks towards the end of 1956 and it is clear that his health was now seriously affecting his work.

After handing over control of the Leamington centre to Bibikoff at the beginning of 1954 Liakhoff had moved into a house bought for him by the Association in Reading, which had good rail links with both Leamington and Exeter. From this base he was supposed to concentrate on monitoring the training work and undertaking aftercare visits, which at that time were still infrequent. In theory, at least, an 'immediate' aftercare visit was supposed to be paid by training staff within three months of the blind person returning home with his dog, and Liakhoff would deal with any subsequent visits that were needed. He had rashly promised to visit all guide dog owners, of which there were then about 400, within 12 months but was being rebuked by the chairman in January 1955 for the small number of visits carried out, for not going to the training centres enough and for training two blind people himself at Reading when he should have been concentrating on his other responsibilities.

For some time Liakhoff relied on Abou, his younger daughter, to drive him on aftercare visits, but when she married Bibikoff in 1955 he was forced to employ apprentices or trainers as chauffeurs. Their experiences provide further evidence of the sad decline in Liakhoff's powers. Journeys would be delayed, interrupted by stops for a drink or the need for Liakhoff to rest, and sometimes abandoned with little, if any, work done.

His impending retirement to become a consultant was announced at the annual general meeting in March 1958, and it became effective on 16 July. On the same day Bob Montgomery, his old friend and apprentice for a short time in 1934, resigned from the general council, of which he had been a member for several years. Arthur Phillipson, who had succeeded Bibikoff as controller at Leamington, was made 'chief control- ler' (he had to wait until 1965 to be given the title of director of training), a situation with which he must have been well pleased considering that he had started as an apprentice only eight years earlier. John Weeks, who had been controller at Exeter since the departure of Sheppard early in 1957, was the only other possible candidate for the post and, indeed, had longer experience than Phillipson. But having joined the revolt in 1949, resigned in 1954 and gone off for 18 months, then resigned again (but withdrawn) in 1957, he would not have been Liakhoff's choice and the council probably thought Phillipson was safer.

Liakhoff's remaining years were not happy ones. His whole life since coming to England had been bound up with guide dogs and he had had little time, or perhaps inclination, to acquire other interests. His enormous contribution to the development of the work was acknowledged by the award of an MBE in the New Year Honours List of 1953 and by the tributes that were paid to him at various times, particularly by guide dog owners and those who had been associated with him in the 1930s and during the war when the Association was young and struggling. After 1958, as a consultant, he was no longer involved with the day-to-day work and felt rejected and without purpose. His physical condition deteriorated further and he was in hospital again at the beginning of 1960. At one time he weighed barely six stone which, even for someone of his short stature, gave him a startlingly frail and cadaverous appearance.

Liakhoff continued to be employed by the Association as a consultant until 16 April 1962, the day before his 65th birthday according to the Gregorian calendar in general use today. He died two weeks later on 30 April, his 65th birthday on the Julian calendar that was used in Russia at the time of his birth there in 1897.

It is sad that Liakhoff's pioneering achievements could not have been followed by happier circumstances in his later years. But nothing can detract from the acclaim that is due to him for helping to lay the foundations of the work, or from the esteem in which he was held by the many blind people he trained. If relationships with his colleagues were not always so harmonious, it was because he felt they were a threat to him. His nomadic life in Europe between the collapse of the White Russian army in 1920 and coming to England in 1933, taken with his position as a foreigner (although naturalised) in this country must have left a legacy of insecurity which explains, at least in part, some of the later problems. Arthur Phillipson recalls that he would say they must not train too many blind people because there would not be any left who wanted guide dogs and then he would be out of a job. Others have seen how he felt challenged or threatened by staff who were acquiring knowledge and experience which previously only he had held. His tragedy was that the talents and qualities that served him and the Association so well as a pioneer were not so well suited to the more complex circumstances of a growing organisation.

It is easy to make too much of the dark side of things. Liakhoff may have had his faults, but so did others who have not had to stand in the glare of the spotlight, and he has to be admired for his extraordinary ability to face disasters and survive. Even in the worst moments, he improvised and the work continued. His ingenuity always found a solution and his tenacity kept him going.

He deserves to be remembered for all his great qualities and achievements, for his skill as a trainer and for the affection he inspired in nearly everyone who knew him. He was worshipped by many guide dog owners, and even those colleagues who became impatient of some of his ways found him a genial and likeable companion.

At the time of Liakhoff's death the third training centre, Nuffield House in Bolton, had been operating for nearly a year. In Scotland the citizens of Forfar had given the land for a fourth centre and construction of the main building and kennels was under way. A planned, well-organised puppy-walking scheme was at last taking shape, inspired and led by Callum McLean, who had joined the general council in 1954 and was now devoting a good deal of time and energy to a programme that he was convinced would have a profound effect on dog supply. He was right – and it is to the way in which this persistent problem was solved that we will now turn our attention.

8

From Street Dogs
to Puppy-Walking

For 30 years or more the training centres obtained their dogs from farms, dog dealers, breeding establishments of varying quality, and a host of other uncertain sources. It was like trying to build a racing car out of bits of scrap metal. The dogs were neither bred nor reared for their highly-specialised and demanding work and it is remarkable that they succeeded as well as they did.

Those selected for training were a very small proportion of the total number taken in for assessment. Some would be rejected almost immediately. There are heart-rending accounts of training staff going down to the railway station to collect dogs that were in a dreadful state: mangy, half-starved or dying from distemper. Others would die later during one of the periodic outbreaks of disease in the kennels. As time went on the isolation of new intakes of dogs and the use of vaccines became more common, but as long as large numbers of 'approval' stock were arriving from uncontrolled sources there was always a health risk.

Collecting the dogs when they arrived at the local station also presented another risk – to the training staff. The dogs would be chained inside the guard's van and many of them, particularly those inclined to be nervous or apprehensive, would be extremely aggressive by the time they arrived. They were supposed to be wearing muzzles, but sometimes they managed to get them off. Arthur Phillipson remembers one dog that ate its muzzle; all that was left was the end of the strap.

Many of Leamington's dogs arrived on a train that was scheduled to stop at nearby Milverton station for one minute, and on many occasions a long delay was only avoided by unhooking the guard's van and leaving it in a siding while an unfortunate trainer patiently calmed the dog so that he could release it without losing his hand. One technique was for the trainer to lie on his stomach, which the dog would recognise as a submissive posture, and gradually creep forward, talking all the time.

'You had to watch its reactions,' Arthur Phillipson recalled. 'Sometimes it would take an hour or more. On a winter's night, after a hard day, we used to curse the telephone when it rang just after 11 o'clock and a voice said, "Milverton station here. We've got a dog for you."

'When we got the dog off, we had to take it down to the kennels, prepare bedding, feed and water it, give it some exercise – by then it was well after midnight. Of course, coming in like that set all the other dogs off and the barking would disturb the neighbours.'

Many of Bolton's dogs arrived on trains that were going through to Manchester and Steve Lambert, who joined the centre as an apprentice in 1964 and is now regional controller for the north west, also has vivid memories of dealing with half-crazed animals in guards' vans that had to be left in a siding. Bolton staff would often use a dog-catcher – a loop on the end of a long pole – and on one occasion were even driven to throwing the dog a piece of meat doped with a tranquilliser in order to calm it down.

The assessment period for these 'approval' dogs lasted up to three weeks, by which time 70 or 80 per cent would have been rejected, largely for reasons of temperament, such as nervousness, aggression or sound-shyness. Disposing of the large number of rejects took up a good deal of valuable time. Some would be returned to the senders, but often this was not possible, and the reason for rejecting the dog could make finding a home for it difficult. The Association's reputation suffered, too, because people would take a reject thinking the dog would be all right in their loving home, and then blame the training centre when the dog was still being anti-social some months later. They usually failed to recognise that the dog's behaviour was a product of its earlier background.

The dogs that emerged successfully from the selection process were still a pretty mixed bunch: generally tough and streetwise, often of uncertain age and nearly always badly behaved in one way or another. It was quite common for them to be cat-chasers. Derek Carver, a former director of training who became an apprentice in 1954, remembers seeing a working guide dog take off after a cat that it had spotted, dragging its bewildered owner over a low wall and halfway through a hedge before it gave up the chase.

'That sort of thing was quite common,' he observed. 'But the owners were expected to deal with it and they regarded it as a bit of a laugh. It was assumed that dogs would chase cats.'

Nevertheless, there were some remarkable individuals among them. John Weeks trained a German shepherd that was much quicker at learning than most:

'I remember going out with her and coming across a branch that was perhaps 14 feet long. The dog went over to it and looked up at me and I said, "All right, go on then". The branch was quite thick at one end, tapering off at the other. She didn't try to drag it away. She picked it up and, half releasing it from her mouth, worked her way along until she found the point of perfect balance. Then she walked off with maybe four feet sticking out of one side of her mouth and ten feet out of the other.

'I used to play a game with her where I threw a ball into a bucket of water and she would pick it out. On one occasion I threw a ball that sank to the bottom. This puzzled her for a bit, but when she spotted it she put her paw in the bucket and found she could move the ball. The next bit sounds incredible, but I swear it happened. She stirred the water with her front leg until the ball came to the surface and she was able to snatch it out with her mouth.'

The dog went to May Walker, a teacher and the sister of John Walker, but in the classroom she was not able to exercise enough control over it and what started as a little 'muttering' developed into aggressive behaviour and the dog had to be withdrawn.

Some of the dogs are remembered for being 'characters' as much as for any outstanding abilities. Arthur Phillipson trained a beautiful rough collie called Baron which went to a Mr Jones. While Jones and Baron were out training one day in Leamington, under Phillipson's eye, they stopped at a kerb beside a shop in which there was a Yorkshire terrier.

'He was a nasty little devil,' Phillipson recalls. 'On this occasion he flew out of the doorway and growled at Baron, who was sitting quietly at the kerb. Baron just picked him up by the scruff of the neck, Jones gave the command "Forward" and they set off across the road with the terrier getting a good shaking as they went!'

After Baron released his persecutor the little dog ran off squealing with his tail between his legs. 'Serves him right,' said his owner, the shop-keeper, when Phillipson hurried across. 'He's always doing that.' Jones, meanwhile, carried on quite unaware of the adventure in which his guide had been involved.

On another occasion Phillipson was out supervising three students who were working their dogs around the town. One of them, a young woman, had a golden retriever who was tempted by a pheasant that was lying on the open slab in front of a fishmonger and game dealer's shop. As the dog walked past, and without pausing, it took the pheasant in its mouth and carried on, tail wagging and pleased as Punch with itself. Again, the dog's owner was not aware of what had happened until Phillipson spotted them and intervened in order to return the pheasant.

One of his more unusual trainees was an 'approval' dog called Patch that was probably a cross between a greyhound and a whippet. It was given to the Reverend Glyn Thomas, who was very strict chapel and a teetotaller. The dog's previous owner obviously wasn't, however, because one morning Thomas and his guide disappeared while out on a training walk and were eventually found sitting at a table in a pub. It was a summer's day, the bar had just been cleaned and the doors left open, so the dog decided to take its owner in. Realising he was lost, but not where he was, the minister sat down, waiting to be rescued. He was horrified when he discovered how his guide had led him astray.

Despite this inauspicious start, Thomas and Patch settled down well together. The story has a sad ending, however, because Patch was killed one Christmas in a quiet little Welsh village where Thomas had gone to stay with a friend. He'd let his dog out for a run, after being assured that it was quite safe because there was never any traffic. Unfortunately, on that occasion there was just one motorcyclist who came racing down the lane and hit Patch.

One truly remarkable dog was Sweep, a large collie, possibly crossed with a German shepherd, that had been neglected on a farm before being acquired by the Leamington centre. Derek Freeman, who was then the centre's reception kennel manager, recalls that he wasn't a bit protective and was more like a puppy-walked dog.

'He'd never been off a farm, never been into town, never had any experience or education apart from farmyard language he'd picked up himself. I remember taking him up to the top of the Parade in Leamington. There are wide pavements so I gave him plenty of room. There were cars coming past and periodically he would stop and look at them. He didn't panic. If you could have ever said a dog had a human expression that scruffy dog did.

'As we went on I was talking to him and I remember a woman coming out of the butcher's shop at the end of the Parade with a pushchair. As he rounded the half-blind, it flapped. Then this jet-propelled pushchair came straight at him, enough to make a number of experienced dogs run. He just stood back from it. As the pushchair went past he smelt the scruffy kid in it and his tail was going like mad. I thought, Funny! it must smell familiar (like a farmyard, I suppose). I showed him red buses on top of the Parade and he didn't panic at all as I stepped on and off the platform.

'His expression at the things he was seeing was absolutely amazing. I took him in shops and as soon as he felt the slippery floor he hesitated, but with a bit of encouragement he got going. At first, it was as if he was walking on hot cinders, not spread-eagled like a lot of dogs would at that experience. He was walking just as if the floor was hot, picking his feet up like a horse trotting.

'Then he could hear people talking over the counter and he looked up, fascinated by it all. I wish we could have got it on camera. Then he was confronted by a big flight of steps. Well, I gather he'd never seen steps before because there was no way he knew how to tackle them. That was the first time I'd seen a bit of apprehension in him. He wanted to rush them but, after several attempts up and down, he got the measure of them.

'He didn't know about travel because he hadn't done any. So we took him with us when we went out purchasing pups. He was a good traveller. He was good with cats. We also checked him on food. We took food from him and gave it back to him. In the end he looked upon this as a game.'

Sweep went to Mike Tetley, who lost his sight fighting the Mau Mau in Kenya, but refused to allow blindness to spoil his enjoyment of life. A great climber and walker, he decided to put Sweep to the test with a 33-mile walk from Luton, where he lived, to London. They did the journey in 12 hours, with an overnight halt, made only one mistake which Tetley was able to correct himself and asked for help on only one occasion, to cross the busy A41 where it met the A5.

'I had walked in shorts', Tetley recorded, 'and thereafter, every time I put on shorts Sweep thought he was in for a long walk.

'When I first got Sweep home he was an escape artist. Our garden had a fence six feet high. He jumped this. I put it up to seven and a half feet. He jumped this. Only when it was eight and a half feet and inclined inwards did we stop him. But not for long. Sweep found a packing case in the garden measuring about four feet in every direction. This he pushed with his nose until it was about five feet from the fence. Then he ran back, turned, ran forward, jumped on the case and then over the fence. Just to make sure that this was not coincidence I moved the case. He then replaced it and repeated his performance. I therefore had to remove the packing case.'

Sweep retained his herding instinct and if the Tetley children brought any of their friends into the garden the dog would look upon them as a flock of sheep, keeping them together either by nibbling their fingers or using his body.

Tetley described how Sweep used his body to clear a way for him through a crowd.

'On some occasions, when I was in a hurry to catch a train, if the way was blocked by a number of women talking and dawdling he would come up behind them, stick his nose between their legs, lift their skirts and blow. If this did not work he would put his shoulder against their knees and push them out of the way, making sure that my right shoulder never touched anybody.'

*   *   *

The list of breeds tried and used in varying numbers at times in the past makes surprising reading today, accustomed as we are to seeing very little but labradors and golden retrievers, or their crosses. From 1931 to 1938 the only variation from alsatian bitches were four alsatian males, two golden retriever bitches and three crosses. After 1938 border collies arrived in increasing numbers and soon dominated the scene, males being used as much, if not more, than bitches. Alsatians reappeared after the war in greater numbers but in the search for animals of the right temperament and in sufficient quantity two dozen or more recognised breeds were tried, not counting the crosses or mongrels. Many of them never made the grade as guide dogs, but among those that did were boxers, poodles, dalmatians, a bull mastiff, samoyeds, pyreneans, an old

Before the breeding and puppy-walking schemes developed sufficiently to cure the chronic dog supply problem that arose as output increased after the war, the training centres used dogs of any breed that was of a suitable size and temperament. Boxers, such as John Podmore's Honey, were often used, but Trevor Clarke's bearded collie Shandy and Albert Veitch's old English sheepdog Melody were more unusual.

English sheepdog, an airedale and an afghan. The failures included pointers, setters, dobermanns, ridgebacks and elk hounds.

This picture of an almost frantic search for dogs is drawn from the detailed dog record books kept at Exeter between 1950 and 1957. Other breeds were tried at Leamington, notably keeshonds and Alaskan mala-mutes, and even when the breeding and puppy-walking programmes had made giant strides in meeting the need for dogs, the occasional unusual breed would pop up.

By the mid-1950s, however, the dog supply system (if it could be called that) was clearly being strained to breaking point. One obvious way of improving the position was to reduce the huge wastage of dogs, and it was recognised as far back as the 1930s that puppies reared in the right

This mixed bunch of breeds, crosses and mongrels was photographed at Leamington in the early or mid-1960s. (Daily Telegraph)

conditions were more likely to succeed as guide dogs than animals that had grown up without any special conditioning. 'Notes on the Rearing of Puppies' that have survived from the Wallasey days (pre-1940) show that the principles were well understood, but attempts made by Liakhoff and others to develop puppy-walking programmes failed because of lack of resources, supervision and resolve.

Proposals for breeding schemes had also arisen over the years, partly to improve temperament, partly to deal with the irregular supply problem. Again, they had amounted to little more than wishful thinking or small-scale experiments.

In late 1952 Liakhoff put up a proposal to run a breeding experiment in Runcorn in kennels that had been erected by a Mr Owen. Four or five bitches were to be kept and the puppies reared there until they were a year old. The elementary training that the puppies would receive as they grew up would, he anticipated, reduce the time needed for their training at a centre, thus off-setting some of the cost.

The paper in which Liakhoff put up his proposal in September 1952 is interesting because it shows that although he recognised the benefit of rearing puppies in a home environment, he was more preoccupied at the time with how to provide a 'home life' in a big breeding establishment than with the development of a network of puppy-walkers. However, in January 1953 he did recommend the introduction of a scheme that had been proposed by Harry Rule, a member of the general council and chairman of the finance committee, to take puppies offered to the Association and place them in private homes to be walked.

The Runcorn experiment went ahead but lasted little more than a year and although there were continuing anxieties over dog supply, Rule's puppy-walking scheme lay dormant. In the early part of 1955 another breeding and rearing proposal, this time from a Colonel Briggs in Bournemouth, was explored and rejected, but in October it was decided to put an advertisement in *The Times*, for people willing to rear a puppy. They were to be paid a maximum of 10 shillings a week towards the cost. Only three replies were received to the advertisement, whereupon R.W. Pilkington argued that the scheme would be a costly failure and that the Association would get plenty of suitable dogs if it was prepared to pay £50 to £75 each for them (£20 was the maximum at that time). He wanted to ask members of the Alsatian League and Club to rear puppies, but it was pointed out that unless one had assurances on the way they would be raised the scheme might not provide animals that had been reared in a home environment.

The Pilkington idea got no further, but Callum McLean, who had joined the general council in October 1954, now drew the attention of his colleagues to a puppy-walking scheme run in America. He already knew something about guide dogs and puppy-walking, having visited Wallasey with his wife while home from the east before the war. After the war he got in touch with Liakhoff again and, in fact, reared two or three puppies for him. It was while he was in Java on business that he read about a programme run by The Seeing Eye in America which he thought might help to solve the dog supply problem in Britain.

Seeing Eye pups were being raised between the ages of 10 weeks and 14 months in the homes of members of the 4-H Club, which was sponsored by the Department of Agriculture in each state. The purpose of the club, according to Debetaz, who responded to a request for details, was to educate young people in the best farming methods and make them better United States' citizens.

'The raising of Seeing Eye pups is one of the important 4-H projects here in New Jersey,' he wrote. 'The youngsters are doing an excellent job for us. We have about 125 pups with 4-H boys and girls all the time. We have one young man, who is more or less liaison for this 4-H work, checking on the temperament and health of each pup during its stay with the family.' Debetaz also reported that the rest of their dogs came from individual families. They seldom accepted kennel-raised dogs.

Liakhoff agreed with everything in the Debetaz letter except the age at which training should start. 'Mr Debetaz thinks this should be 14 months; but I am convinced by experience that with gentle handling, training can commence sooner, so that, at 14 months, or just after, the dog is really trained and is ready to begin work with the blind person.'

With the 12-week training schedule in practice at the time some British guide dogs did in fact start their working lives at 14 or 15 months of age, but the unpredictable sources of supply meant that many were a good deal older than that. Modern practice is to start the training of labradors, golden retrievers and their crosses at about the age of 11 or 12 months, and German shepherds, which take longer to mature, at about 14 months.

Having created interest in The Seeing Eye's scheme, McLean was asked, at the end of May 1956, if he would help to develop a similar puppy-walking scheme in the Woking, Guildford and Reading areas, where he, Montgomery and Liakhoff respectively could supervise the work. It was planned to place the puppies at four months old, at which age Liakhoff felt it was possible to assess whether they were likely to become guide dogs.

In the surge of activity on rearing, the importance of getting the right type of material to start with was not overlooked. The Seeing Eye's breeding programme, which had been running since the beginning of the war, was by January 1956 providing one-third of the 180 guide dogs being produced annually by their training school. Although they were breeding German shepherds, Debetaz, in referring to the large number of other breeds they had used as well, reported that he had found 'that a mongrel gives much better results in training, not only from actual work, but as far as health is concerned and length of service to a blind person'. By 'mongrel' he meant a 'pure mongrel' or what is called in Britain a cross-bred. This was also favoured by Liakhoff, his preference at that time being for a labrador/alsatian cross, and he was therefore instructed to experiment with one litter of this cross at each centre. A year later, however, he was having to apologise for failing to carry out the instruction.

In the meantime, McLean was making headway on puppy-walking. Despite a disappointing response to his initial appeal for puppy-walkers he soon had three pups with walkers in the Woking area. By March 1957 these pups were in training at Leamington and he had five more homes waiting – if only he could get the puppies. He wanted to expand the scheme by taking up an offer from The Alsatian League of Great Britain to appeal to its members to give the Association one puppy from each litter bred. The general council, however, cautious as always, and reluctant to spend money, decided against expansion and The Alsatian League were politely thanked for their offer.

McLean's patience was sorely tried by this hesitant approach to the dog supply problem. What was the policy, he asked the finance and general purposes committee in June 1957? Were they going on with the scheme or not? After a good deal more talk Liakhoff was instructed once again to get on with breeding the crosses and McLean was assured that the policy was to carry on the scheme.

Some urgency was injected into the programme, however, when in September the chairman, Lord Lanesborough, announced that the training centres were having to restrict their intake of blind people because of the shortage of dogs. It was immediately resolved to extend the puppy-walking scheme through the two centres and by increasing the number of walkers supervised by McLean. The total of puppies walked up to then was only 27. Eighteen months later, in March 1959, 349 had been

It was not until the late 1950s that puppy-walking was anything more than an intermittent activity in Britain. Credit for launching the programme that exists today, and providing the drive that saw it through its early years, belongs to Callum McLean, who joined the general council in October 1954 and began puppy-walking in Surrey in 1956. He is seen here (left) with Ted Harte (centre), who joined McLean in supervising the work in 1958 and later became a member of the general council, and the chief controller, Arthur Phillipson.

walked, 45 per cent had succeeded as guide dogs and one-third of the centres' output was puppy-walked dogs. It was a remarkably swift and effective advance, for which most of the credit must be given to Callum McLean. He succeeded where others had failed in the past, partly because the dog supply problem gave a greater incentive, but mostly because of the drive and supervision that he provided. Although he was fully occupied in his family business he found time to visit puppy-walkers, check on the progress of their charges and give what advice he could. In this he had the help, from the early part of 1958, of Lieutenant-Colonel Ted Harte, who later became a member of the general council.

When Derek Freeman came on the scene as reception kennel manager at Leamington in January 1959, his job was mainly to select adult approval dogs. He quickly got drawn into providing expert advice to McLean's and Harte's puppy-walkers – a task that until then had fallen to Phillipson, the chief controller – and in March 1960 he was made responsible for running the scheme as well as supplying dogs to the two existing centres and the new one under construction at Bolton. McLean maintains modestly that he and Harte were very naive and that it wasn't until Freeman came along that expert advice became available to puppy-walkers. Nevertheless, they established the foundation on which Freeman was able to build and also taught him skills which he had not acquired as a breeder and trainer of dogs.

'They taught me an awful lot about relationships with people that I knew nothing about.' Freeman recalls that Harte used to keep details of the puppy-walkers that he visited in a diary so that he would not forget what they were doing and could talk to them about their lives, not just about the dogs.

McLean and Harte also played a crucial role in supporting the scheme in committee or council whenever it came under attack. For a long time there were reservations about its cost, and other challenges would sometimes arise, perhaps from a more modest scheme promoted by a training centre. Their commitment, not just to puppy-walking, earned them a high regard among staff, who appreciated the way they never failed to enquire about the work, the conditions or morale and showed a real concern for what was going on. There were, of course, many other council members who gave themselves with equal dedication to the guide dog cause.

Callum McLean continued to supervise puppy-walking in the Surrey area until 1964, when he moved to Scotland. His work was then carried on principally by Ted Harte and Marjorie Woolmer, who also became a member of the general council in due course.

Although the programme has developed enormously in the last 30 years, the basic principles are the same today as they were in 1960 or in the 1930s when puppy-walking was only an unfulfilled dream. This is not the place for a detailed account of the day-to-day routines of puppy-walking, but the essence of it can be given in one word: conditioning. A puppy that is carefully introduced to the roar of traffic, the press of crowded pavements, swing doors, lifts, busy shops and countless other features of the modern world is very unlikely to become nervous, sound-shy or aggressive, as so many adult approval dogs used to be. Without the conditioning that puppy-walking provides, it is doubtful whether guide dog work would be possible today. Freeman, and others, all agree that many of the dogs they were able to acquire in the 1950s and earlier, tough though they were physically, lacked the conditioning that would have enabled them to stand up to the hectic environment of the modern world. They would have become nervous wrecks in no time.

Being brought up in a loving home, often with children, now ensures that guide dogs are adjusted to family and social life in a way that dogs raised in kennels or on a farm would never be – and it must not be forgotten that guide dogs spend far more of their time off-duty as pets

Guide dogs never – well, hardly ever – chase cats, as Elgar demonstrated during National Pet Week in April 1989. Their tolerance is the result of growing up with cats, just part of the conditioning process that helps to make them good guide dogs. (Northcliffe Newspapers Group)

The Association's brood bitches, of which there are about 200, usually have their litters in the homes where they have been adopted as family pets. Some, however, are taken for the birth of their pups to the breeding centre near Warwick, where this picture was taken in 1989. (Birmingham Post & Mail)

than they do guiding their owners. In the past many guide dogs that were effective workers were not always very easy to live with.

The dogs also learn to live in peace with cats from an early age. The breeding centre keeps two or three that can often be found curled up with a litter, and many of the brood bitch holders and puppy-walkers own cats. Part of the puppy-walkers' job is to discourage any bad habits, so that by the time the dogs are about a year old and ready to start their training they should have learnt to overcome any chasing tendencies. Their immunity undergoes a severe test at the training centres, however, where resident cats seem to enjoy trying to provoke the young trainees.

During the early years of the puppy scheme, walkers would be given a pup when it was 12 to 16 weeks of age or more. Today they go at six or seven weeks because it is now recognised that at this age they enter a highly-formative period of their lives which lasts about two months.

About 80 per cent of the litters are born in the homes of the families with whom the brood bitches live as pets, and even in the nest the pups begin to become accustomed to the human voice and presence. By the time they are six or seven weeks old the pups are already confident with people and can leave their dams without trauma. Litters are first taken to Tollgate House, the breeding centre at Bishops Tachbrook, near Warwick, where they stay for two or three days while they are checked and assessed. Anyone with reservations about taking the pups away from their dams so young has only to see them playing together and eating heartily within hours of their arrival to be reassured.

During their stay at Tollgate, the pups also receive their first immunisation against distemper, hepatitis, leptospirosis and parvo-virus. This is much earlier than most pets would be inoculated, but it allows the process of conditioning to start as soon as the pups are given to the puppy-walkers. It is a gradual process, of course, and it is not recommended that in the early weeks they are taken into parks or other places where dogs are found. But they can be walked in clean, suburban areas and taken about to start adjusting to the world. The early inoculation is followed by full immunisation after 12 weeks.

Because of the importance of regularly exposing the puppies to a busy town environment, homes in the country are seldom suitable for puppy-walking. There is also a preference for homes in which there are not too many other dogs, so that the puppy only has to find its place within the human pack.

Puppy-walkers are visited at least once a month by experienced supervisors who give advice about feeding, house-training and behaviour generally, checking also on the pup's progress. As soon as it starts walking on a lead, the pup is encouraged to stay ahead of and to the left of the handler, not to heel. As time goes on its horizons widen with visits to railway and bus stations, restaurants and shops – even the butcher's where self-control is put to a severe test. It learns to tackle stairs of various kinds and floor surfaces that range from deep pile carpet to slippery marble.

Puppy-walkers are often asked how they can bear to part with an animal that they have reared in their homes for about a year and to which they have inevitably become very attached. The usual answer is that it is very hard. One woman who walked 35 puppies said that she always dreaded the day they left. On the other hand, the walkers recognise when they take on the job that they are only 'foster-parents' and have the reward of knowing the value of their work. Some puppy-walkers also take comfort in the knowledge that they will not have the distress of watching a much-loved pet grow old, decline in health and possibly have to be put down by the vet. 'My memories are all of puppies going out through the gate happy and healthy,' said one.

With around 700 puppies being reared in homes throughout the country, the Association now has a small army of puppy-walkers: dedicated supporters who are proud of their key role in producing good

Phil Drabble talking with puppy-walker Mrs Ann Kay during the filming by a BBC television crew of a programme about guide dogs in 1979 for a series entitled It's a dog's life. *Between them is producer Peter Crawford and, on the left, puppy-walking supervisor Miss Fiona MacDonald.*

guide dogs. They are organised in groups around each centre and once a year there is a 'puppy day', which is one way that the centre shows its gratitude. Another recognition of their contribution is the award of a bronze, silver or gold trophy for 50, 100, and 200 months respectively of puppy-walking.

The puppy-walkers are now almost 'a movement within a movement'. Some of them have established local clubs or publish their own newsletter, often containing hilarious or moving accounts of the antics or troubles of their charges. One could fill a book with stories of wrecked gardens, ruined furniture and homes destroyed not once, but several times by successive juvenile delinquents. But we must leave these for another occasion and stay, for the moment, with other, less sensational matters.

*   *   *

The 1960s were the years in which the dog supply problem was, if not resolved, at least dragged out of the muddle that it had been in. The decade opened with the puppy-walking scheme in its infancy, but a lusty child nonetheless. It closed with a separate, specialised centre for breeding and puppy-walking about to open. The programme did not grow all that fast after the initial surge. Between 1963 and 1970 the annual output of puppy-walked dogs rose from 105 to 144, while the total production of guide dogs went up from 172 to 300. A few came from separate rearing schemes at Exeter and, later, Bolton and Scotland, but there was still a heavy reliance on adult 'approval' dogs to make up the balance. The problems and wastage associated with this source of supply did not improve, and it is surprising to find that in January 1965 not all controllers, apparently, accepted the superiority of puppy-walked dogs. They were, of course, relatively expensive: £100 up to the end of the walking period, which led some people to argue that it was only justified if a high proportion became guide dogs. In fact, only a half made the grade, some being withdrawn during walking, others being rejected during testing or training. Even so, it was a far better record than that of adult dogs acquired from outside sources, of which less than 20 per cent tested went on to qualify.

One factor that influenced the attitude towards puppy-walked dogs at the training centres was the contrast with approval dogs and the difficulty experienced by some training staff in handling dogs that were 'softer', physically and in temperament, than many of the hardened campaigners they had been used to. The council were aware of the problem and in October 1961 decreed that 'care should be taken in the allocation of which puppy to which trainer.' Freeman began going out with trainers so that he could see what sort of dogs they were best equipped to handle, and then tried to ensure that suitable animals were given to them.

With a misguided concern for economy the Association at first tried to run its puppy-walking scheme with puppies that were either donated or bought very cheaply. Some sorry specimens were offered. Freeman recalls one woman arriving at Leamington with seven puny little puppies, the remnants of a litter that she had not been able to get rid of, thinking that, as a charity, the training centre would welcome them. By now, Freeman had come to the conclusion that good quality pups would have to be paid for and so some days later, for the first time and without higher authority, he offered £10 to a breeder for a nice labrador puppy. Unfortunately this breeder was a friend of the woman whose indifferent pups had just been rejected and when she heard about the purchase she wrote an angry letter to the general manager. Freeman got a rocket for his action but in the process established the principle of being able to buy some good puppies at realistic prices.

Other incidents, such as the occasion he got a phone call asking him to pick up two puppies and arrived to find them, and half the stock of the kennels, suffering from distemper, strengthened Freeman's growing belief that the Association would have to breed its own stock. He and McLean had talked about a breeding programme during their journeys together visiting puppy-walkers, but for some time it was no more than a gleam in their eyes.

A shortage of larger dogs of the right temperament (accentuated by the rejection of males) was another incentive to start breeding. After the war there had been a good deal of indiscriminate breeding of German shepherds as a result of which many of the breed were of uncertain temperament, and attempts to acquire suitable dogs for taller applicants were not very successful.

Although breeding was not yet officially part of his job, Derek Freeman acquired the first brood bitch of what was to become the breeding programme in 1959: a five-year-old German shepherd named Reiner from whom three litters were bred. None of the bitches from these litters was kept as breeding stock, although some became guide dogs, and she never produced any more. However, a male from her first litter was used as a stud and passed on good temperament and physique to his progeny.

It was labrador brood bitches that were acquired in the largest numbers in the coming years. Labradors acquired as adult 'approval' dogs had not been notably successful, possibly because many had come from gun dog lines that had been bred and reared for a very different sort of life. But puppy-walked dogs from other sources soon began to show qualities that were more suited to guide dog work. At the end of 1961 there were five labrador broods to two German shepherds.

McLean urged the council to step up the breeding programme, arguing that the 50 per cent success rate of puppy-walked dogs would not improve until more pups came from the Association's own selected breeding stock. By September 1964 the scheme, although still very small, was beginning to prove itself, with 68 per cent of its output becoming successful guide dogs. A sign of its growing acceptance was Freeman's appointment in February 1966 as breeding and puppy-walking manager (with reception and approval of adult dogs being handed over to the controllers of training centres) and the decision, in principle, taken in July 1967, to move him out of Leamington and into a separate establishment entirely devoted to this operation.

From now on, one might have thought, there would be no looking back. There was certainly no financial need to hesitate. Income continued to exceed expenditure by a generous margin and invested savings were well over £1.5 million. Nevertheless, the council were concerned over rising costs and they did hesitate. Eight months after they declared their intention to set up a separate breeding and puppy-walking establishment they created instead a new sub-committee to discuss still further the methods of procuring dogs ('with special emphasis on the financial

aspect') and consider the possibility of increasing the breeding pro-gramme. In their first report the committee suggested that the high cost of breeding and puppy-walking might make it advisable to scale down the schemes or, alternatively, to consider purchasing adult dogs.

The committee quickly overcame their timidity, however, and in July 1968 persuaded the council to reaffirm the need for a separate breeding and puppy-walking centre. By October a suitable property had been found three and a half miles south of Warwick.

The purchase price of Tollgate House, £27,000, was met entirely by a covenanted donation of £35,000 from The Diamond Corporation – generosity that had its first inspiration in the remarkable farm dog Sweep, whose story was told earlier in this chapter. Sweep's skill in guiding his owner, Mike Tetley, was so admired by one of the Corporation's executives, John Gray, who frequently saw them on the railway station that he used for his daily journeys to work, that he persuaded staff in the office to start collecting for guide dogs. He then asked the Corporation to match the sums raised by staff, but they did better than that and decided

The difficulty in getting enough puppies of the right quality for the puppy-walking scheme led, in the 1960s, to the development of a breeding programme. The first bitch to be acquired was Reiner in 1959, seen here with her first litter.

to fund the new breeding and puppy-walking centre from their Charities Aid Trust.

One of Derek Freeman's first concerns, when he knew that a special breeding and puppy-walking centre was at last to become a reality, was to ensure that he got the best possible kennels. As reception kennel manager at Leamington in the early 1960s he had already had a ding-dong battle with the general manager, Sir Michael Nall, and chief controller, Arthur Phillipson, in order to get kennels that the adult approval dogs and puppies could see out of without having to stand on their hind legs. Although kennels had been considerably improved over the years, and were warm, dry and comfortable by the standards of the time, they did not permit their occupants an unrestricted view, which Freeman believed was essential for animals that were being socialised and groomed for guide dog work. The objection was that the dogs would bark too much, but Freeman insisted that this was a matter of kennel management. He got his way and was allowed to introduce grilles down to ground level.

Freeman had his own ideas about kennel design, but he also solicited ideas from other staff working with the dogs. What he came up with was a novel H-block design that revolutionised kennel management. Each leg of the H had a row of 10 kennels, each pair of kennels having access to a 20ft concrete run via French windows fitted with wired glass. The runs were fenced with strong wire mesh and each could accommodate eight dogs. This arrangement separated brood bitches, stud dogs, boarders and dogs taken in at the end of puppy-walking for assessment prior to allocation to a training centre. In the middle were whelping and hospital blocks and services such as store-rooms, food preparation areas, a surgery, toilets and an office. With everything under one roof, the kennels could be managed a good deal more efficiently than others at that time. Inside corridors gave staff easy access to the dogs; kennels and runs could easily be hosed down to make cleaning quick and effective; and central heating ensured that the place was kept dry and warm.

Three units were built separate from the H-block: an isolation kennel for animals with infectious diseases; a mating room; and a puppy block where litters coming in at six weeks of age, before going to puppy-walkers, could be given special care while being checked, evaluated and given their first inoculation.

The Tollgate kennels are not, of course, permanent homes for any of the animals. The brood bitches all live as pets with families, as do many of the studs (others being attached to members of staff), and only come to the centre for short periods for mating, sometimes for whelping or perhaps when their 'minder' goes on holiday.

It is interesting to compare the modern kennels with those of earlier days, not in order to condemn what went on in the past, because it was accepted practice at the time; but to see how far ideas have advanced and how much was being learnt by experience. Freeman admits that he was not shocked by the kennels of the 1950s: that was the way dogs were kept then.

When the Leamington kennels were first rebuilt immediately after the war they were called 'princely quarters for the dogs who use them . . .' During 1948 these were replaced by extensive new units that the Association's magazine *Forward* described at the time as 'some of the finest kennels in the country'. These were the kennels that were later described by Freeman as 'reminiscent of a maximum security prison'.

> 'They were constructed of concrete slabs with an asbestos roof', he recalled, 'and, being badly insulated, were cold in winter and hot in summer. The windows were small, with frosted glass, and were far too high for the dogs to see out. The same applied to the doors, which were solid wood . . . with a peephole at about four feet high for staff to view the animals.
>
>   'The yards and runs were pack runs and although of extremely generous dimensions their surface was mostly macadam and therefore very time-consuming to clean. The brick or concrete walls surrounding the dog runs at Leamington were a minimum of six and a half feet high and they gave no chance to observe the dogs, or vice versa. In fact, many a dog was accidentally left out in the run during the winter months and it was only through the diligence of very caring staff who lived in at the time, who would go down to the kennels just to check that things were OK, that many were discovered.'

As Freeman pointed out, control of disease was difficult, with straw bedding, wooden bed boards and surface drains running from yard to yard. Others have described the disagreeable task of removing the foul straw and sawdust used on the floor. Arthur Phillipson has memories of cleaning out the kennels early in the morning, before going in to breakfast at eight and starting the day's training programme at nine. John Weeks recalls that 'the debris was brushed out and you had a bucket and very wet mop that you slapped around the walls, the liquid falling down on the floor. You then did the floor and brushed it out. It stayed wet for a very long time and in the winter it was always wet.' The foul, wet straw and sawdust would be taken off to a distant part of the grounds and burnt, not without causing offence, on occasions, to neighbours or incurring a rebuke from the local authority.

The kennels built at Exeter in 1950 were similar to those at Leamington, but much better quarters were provided for the dogs when, in 1959 and the early 1960s, new kennels were built at Edmondscote Manor and, in 1961, the Bolton centre was opened. Proper heating arrangements kept the kennels warm and dry, thus eliminating the need for the straw or wood wool bedding that had been such a disagreeable feature of the earlier kennels, and there were a number of other improvements. The kennels that were unveiled at Tollgate House in 1970 contained a number of features introduced earlier at Leamington and Bolton, but its H-block design was original and set a new standard for kennel management in the future. The design was so successful that it became the pattern for all future kennel construction at the Association's training centres.

9

Building the Breeding Programme

At the beginning of 1969, while work on the newly-purchased Tollgate House was still in its early stages, John Hodgman, who was chairman of the breeding and puppy-walking sub-committee of the council, pleaded for a much greater understanding of the problem of dog supply. At the time that he made his plea there were already some 30 brood bitches, three or four stud dogs, 200 active puppy-walkers and a growing store of research information, records, X-ray photographs and pedigree notes.

The build-up of the programme over such a short period, mainly by trial and error, had inevitably produced some mistakes, Hodgman admitted, and the stresses and strains and personal differences which seemed to be endemic among 'dog people' had not failed to afflict the specialists groping forward in the guide dog world. 'Nevertheless', he continued, 'we have a working organisation which provides, in the only way we know to date, the dogs which we need and it should be regarded as a credit to its manager, Mr Freeman, and a satisfaction to all concerned.'

But the general manager, Dick Forrester, had reservations. The breeding and puppy-walking manager, Derek Freeman, was a 'dedicated perfectionist', he told the council eight months later, and unfortunately had 'the defects of his qualities'. He went on to complain of Freeman's lack of concern for cost and the way he by-passed his superiors in order to get support. Freeman, a resolute, plain-speaking Yorkshireman, changed little over the years, pursuing his strong convictions with a relentless energy that made him careless of the proprieties and frequently led him into battles with his masters and colleagues. Sometimes he emerged with what he wanted, sometimes charged with obstinacy; but he was always respected for his total commitment to the aim of producing better dogs.

The tide was running against the doubters, however. As the statistics showed, puppy-walked dogs had a higher success rate than approval dogs; those from the breeding scheme did even better. Furthermore, not only would it have been difficult, if not impossible, to find increasing numbers of approval dogs, but the Association's expanding resources were drawing in a wider range of clients whose needs could not always be met from the traditional sources of supply. In the pioneering days, demand so outweighed supply that the centres could choose their clients to match the available dogs. In the future they would have to match the dogs to the clients.

Detailed records were the foundation on which success was gradually established: the progress of every litter was followed closely, enabling Freeman and his team gradually to build up the experience and data they needed to make the breeding programme more refined and selective. Over two decades later the scheme maintains some 200 brood bitches and about 30 stud dogs, possessing between them a range of qualities that enables the needs of the most demanding clients to be met. One has to remember, of course, that the success of a guide dog 'unit', as the partnership is usually called, depends as much on the handler as on the dog, but the breeding programme goes as far as it can to produce dogs that will perform adequately with the least proficient blind owner. At the other end of the spectrum it produces dogs that are capable of remarkable achievements with a first-rate handler, but would be disastrous with anything less.

One early product of Freeman's methodical record-keeping was a change of attitude towards the use of male dogs. With rare exceptions all the pre-war guide dogs were bitches. When border collies came in from 1938 onwards, males were used in larger numbers, but in the post-war *melange* of approval dogs bitches were once again preferred. One objection to entire males (castration was not introduced until the mid-1960s) is that they are inclined to fight, which causes problems in kennels, during training and while working with a blind person. They also urinate instinctively, and frequently, for scent marking, which disrupts their work. Nevertheless, some had to be taken because there were not enough bitches to meet the demand.

There was, therefore, a well-established tradition in the training centres of demanding 'bitches only'. Even when castrated dogs from the Association's breeding scheme became available many trainers were reluctant to take them. As long as the numbers remained small, unwanted males could be sold without too much difficulty, but once production increased it was thought unwise to continue this practice, in case breeders protested that the market was being flooded and they were being done out of a living. This left the distressing alternative of having many newly-born male pups put down.

Matters came to a head after Freeman and his staff had been up one night whelping two bitches. In the morning they found themselves with

10 males and three bitches. It was a day on which Tony Clark, who had become general manager in 1972, was visiting Tollgate House. Freeman took him into the whelping block and told him that later that day he would have to take three or four of the puppies down to the vet to be put down. Clark agreed that something had to be done.

Freeman's best ammunition was not sentiment, however; it was figures. He was able to show that in the years between 1960 and 1971, 81 per cent of own-bred males qualified as guide dogs or breeding stock, compared with 76 per cent of bitches. Freeman was no fool, of course, and had sold off the dominant male pups, placing with puppy-walkers only the more sensitive animals. He didn't convert the training staff overnight, but slowly the pattern changed and by 1984 males and females were being used in equal numbers. Today, the balance has swung slightly in favour of males. Males are still physically larger than females, but through selective breeding there is often little to choose between them in temperament.

The problems associated with using males were eased when castration was introduced in the mid-1960s, several years after the spaying of bitches had begun. In the 1950s the neutering of dogs was still frowned on generally, and even when spaying became acceptable, public opinion was against castration. It may have been partly an instinctive hostility to emasculation in a male-dominated world, but it was also argued that the effect of neutering was very different in the two sexes. With bitches, the operation only prevented seasons and had no effect on the dog's nature. A castrated male, however, lost its sex drive and therefore became a different animal, with different behaviour patterns.

An entire bitch was clearly a great liability, and possibly a danger, to its owner when it was in season. The owner had a choice: either to leave the bitch at home or take it out and run the risk of being besieged by any male roaming downwind of them. Amplex tablets or liquid were issued, but they had only a limited effect. Some guide dog owners coped well enough, but others frequently ran into difficulties. One woman had to take refuge in a phone box and call a taxi, telling the driver that he would easily spot the box she was in by the pack of dogs outside.

Derek Freeman admits that he was against spaying when he joined the Association but was converted when he saw a working guide dog in season being harassed and distracted by a male.

The neutering issue appears to have been first taken up in 1953 by Liakhoff, who recognised that castration 'at the right age' would eliminate instinctive urination and the inclination to fight. He also saw the advantage to guide dog owners of spayed bitches. He was in no hurry to adopt either course, however, and told the council that he was pursuing the question with the help of Professor Zuckermann's laboratory in Birmingham University. He also explored it through the short-lived

Runcorn experiment and in May 1954 gave it as his opinion that 'neutralisation' would be a considerable advance to which he could see no objection. Nothing more was heard on the subject, however, until McLean raised it in March 1957 in connection with his new puppy-walking scheme and it was then decided to run a small trial with three pups from a litter of five. Meanwhile, Liakhoff wrote to Hodgman for guidance, received an 'unsatisfactory' reply and declared that he didn't know where else to look for information.

Despite the shortage of expert advice, the council decided in June 1958 that in future all bitches would be spayed after their first season. Several, in fact, died as a result of the operation in the following year but thereafter techniques improved and the practice continued without any significant problems.

The disadvantages of entire males were seen at their worst in kennels, where sexual rivalry and establishing social status often led to fighting. John Weeks remembers that in the late 1940s he and his colleagues would frequently have to abandon a cup of tea they were enjoying in the dog room at Leamington because a fight had suddenly erupted. They would dash to the scene to find a number of dogs bearing the marks of battle and two still locked in combat.

'You whacked them apart, keeping your hands out of the way, and carted them off to the vet for stitches.'

Staff tried to avoid incidents like this by separating dogs as much as possible, but it was clearly an impossible task given the number of dogs and the resources available. It also made great demands on staff, who would often have to let dogs out into the runs individually, a time-consuming job that was particularly unwelcome on a winter's night.

A problem of a different kind was presented by an uncastrated working guide dog, who was always liable to be challenged by another male through whose territory it was passing. It would either turn and fight or, if it was a lower order animal, indicate its submission. Either way, it was going to be distracted from its work. A castrated male, on the other hand, presented no sexual challenge.

Determining the best time to castrate was a problem. In 1954 Zuckermann's laboratory told Liakhoff that they could find no work which bore on the most suitable time for castration – it 'would have to be found out by experiment'. The correct time had to be judged by the behaviour of the dog, Liakhoff declared. If it was done too early the dog was likely to be dull; if it was left too late it would have developed the instincts of a male and would only lack the ability to do anything about it.

Freeman's view is that 'you must castrate them according to their sensitivity and sexual drive, which varies with the individual breeds and animals – usually somewhere between seven months and a year. The nearer a year you are, the softer the dog is going to be. If you were having to do it at six months you should be questioning whether the dog is too dominant for guide dog work.'

*   *   *

One of the most important influences on the breeding programme was the increasing diversity of applicants for guide dogs. What had started, along with puppy-walking, primarily as a means of increasing the supply of dogs and reducing the wastage, gradually developed into a large, complex programme producing endless variations on the basic qualities needed by a successful guide dog. Above all, it produced softer, more sensitive dogs that were easier to handle and better able to cope with the varied demands of the work.

Breeding and puppy-walking are now inseparably linked, because it is recognised that the breeding in itself is of little value unless the pup is properly reared. On the other hand, although good rearing can achieve a great deal, it can never make a good guide dog out of an animal born with all the wrong genes. A third factor that is not always given enough credit, however, is the ability of training staff to spot the qualities of each individual dog and develop them. A trainer's talent for bringing out the best in a dog is every bit as important as a good teacher's ability to motivate a student and uncover qualities that might otherwise lie hidden. If the trainer can also make an inspired choice of partner for the dog – which is almost as difficult as finding the ideal husband or wife – he will have brought the long process of creating a guide dog to a triumphant conclusion.

One dog that came near perfection was a big, handsome golden retriever male called Kendal. 'That dog was special,' recalls Bob Steele, who is now the Association's senior training manager, 'probably the best I've ever handled. He had confidence, tremendous initiative and an appetite for work, yet patient and tolerant with an owner who was rather nervous. The owner's anxiety and apprehension were never reflected in the dog's attitude. It made a decision and stuck to it, despite its owner, but never took advantage of its position.

'Other dogs would try to interfere with him, but he had this noble nature and never allowed them to distract him. He just worked on. And his memory for routes . . .' Sadly, Kendal became ill and died only two years after starting work. He was so outstanding, so adaptable that, in Steele's view, if he could have been cloned there would have been no need to look anywhere else for guide dogs: the clones would have met every possible need.

Few dogs come as close to the ideal as Kendal. The perfect combination of inherited characteristics, sound temperament acquired during puppy-walking and sensitive training does not occur frequently. It is probably an elusive ideal, anyway. Kendal was Bob Steele's idea of perfection; others might have made a different judgement of the dog and advanced their own candidates for the title.

Nevertheless, Kendal possessed the qualities that are found, to a greater or lesser degree, in all good guide dogs: willingness, confidence, patience, intelligence, initiative and the ability to concentrate. Another sought-after quality, which tragically was lacking in Kendal, is longevity. The value of a long working life needs no elaboration.

From the outset of the breeding and puppy-walking programmes the labrador established itself as the most satisfactory general-purpose breed: it was, and still is, a first-class all-rounder. This was becoming apparent even before the schemes adopted the breed as their favourite. The Exeter dog records for 1950–7 show that in those years the centre took in for appraisal about 1,200 dogs (most of whom were rejected, of course). Almost half were alsatians still, but one in five was a labrador. They mostly came from gun dog stock, and had been bred to be rather faster and harder driving than is ideal for guide dog work, but in temperament, and in other ways, they had some advantages over alsatians and collies. They were more solid, reliable dogs, not inclined to be shy of noises and highly adaptable, although these qualities were not fully brought out until it was possible to select individual family lines within the breed. By 1971, the year after Tollgate House opened, there were 34 labrador brood bitches, well outnumbering the 12 alsatians and four golden retrievers.

A labrador thinks nothing of leaving the puppy-walker who has reared it and moving to the training centre where it will transfer its allegiance and affection first to someone in charge of its early training and then to someone else for advanced training, before finally settling down with a blind person. Many a puppy-walker has watched tearfully as her loved one trotted off happily with the supervisor, tail wagging and without a backward glance, clearly quite unconcerned about leaving its foster mother behind. The labrador is an uncomplicated dog, easier to understand and with fewer complexities of temperament than the other guide dog breeds. It responds straightforwardly to praise or correction. It is also a friendly, attractive-looking dog that is welcomed wherever it goes, which is a great advantage socially and in the workplace.

Since the early 1960s, the screening and selection of thousands of dogs has made labradors of Tollgate breeding more sensitive and willing than they used to be. They are almost too easy-going at times. But they are ideal to live with and in temperament are the best-balanced of all guide dogs.

They do, however, have some disadvantages. Their friendliness allows them to be more easily distracted from their work than some dogs or perhaps to attach themselves to a stranger while free running in the park. They can be a bit too boisterous at times and inclined to use their noses too much. But their biggest drawback is that they scavenge. They are greedy dogs, always hungry and will bolt down almost anything they can find or are offered. One of the greatest trials that the owner of a labrador guide dog has to endure is the well-meaning but misguided person who surreptitiously slips tit-bits to the dog on the train or in the pub. It is hard enough controlling its scavenging for discarded food without having to cope with this additional temptation. Even more thoughtless members of the public have been known to stride alongside a *working* guide dog offering a biscuit, thus adding distraction to the dangers of obesity.

Most labradors are guilty of gluttony, but few have sinned on a scale to match Rajah, who was an approval dog in the late 1940s. One day, hearing the dishes of food being put out, he jumped a six-foot fence from one run to another, over another fence into a corridor, then over a barn door to where the food had been placed outside a row of kennels. The kennel maid had gone off to do something else and so Rajah had the field to himself. He rapidly went down the line, scoffing the top eight dinners, then without pause started flipping off the empty top dishes to get at the ones below. He was on his twelfth helping before the kennel maid returned, by which time he was blown up like a balloon. Suddenly, with a great burp, he brought the lot back and managed to consume it again before the kennel girl could intervene. It was two days, we are told, before he could fit into a harness again!

One of Paul Holden's most vivid memories of his days as a trainer in the late '40s and early '50s is of a labrador, one of a pair that had been given as six-month-old pups. It was a huge animal and was given to a correspondingly large, lumbering Yorkshireman, who was partly deaf as well as blind. The dog took to the work like a duck to water. 'It seemed to sense that this great clumsy Yorkshireman was dependent on him and was in his care,' Holden recalled.

He took a number of pictures of the pair working together during their training. One of them shows the dog just as it had stopped at a kerb, bracing itself rigidly while its owner blundered on. Another shows the dog struggling to haul its master clear of a lamp-post which he seemed determined to walk into.

'Perhaps I should never have trained him,' Holden reflected, 'but he had complete faith in this marvellous dog. He lived in Boroughbridge, and they became the talk of the town.'

*   *   *

By 1977, the post-World War I sentiments that led to the German shepherd dog being re-named the alsatian in Britain had disappeared and the original name of the breed was reinstated. It will therefore be referred to as the German shepherd from now on.

It is, perhaps, surprising that the breed which dominated the guide dog field in the 1930s and reappeared as top dog, numerically, after the war should have lost the lead to the labrador and others. Nowadays, only one in every 10 guide dogs is a German shepherd. But a number of factors worked in favour of its rivals. The early age of 10 months at which training started for all breeds placed German shepherds at a disadvantage. They are relatively slow to mature and it is now recognised that they are not ready for training until they are about 14 months old – two or three months later than golden retrievers and labradors.

The German shepherd is also less adaptable than the all-purpose labrador. It is often thought of as a one-man dog but Derek Freeman, who unashamedly champions the breed, thinks this is an over-simplification. They will adapt to change, he believes, but it takes time and sensitive handling to accomplish. They tend to fret more than labradors over the move from a puppy-walker's home into kennels, and take less well to being handled by several different kennel and training staff. They like to establish a close bond with one person and in kennels they easily lose condition and develop behavioural problems.

Bob Steele remembers a German shepherd that was reared in a family and was developing so well, and was so good with the children, that it was being considered for breeding stock. But back in the kennels it lost weight, became noisy and protective and eventually had to be rejected because it became aggressive towards children.

'Had that dog been trained from home, he would have made a superb guide dog, I'm convinced of it,' said Steele. 'The kennel environment just wasn't right.'

Another reason so few German shepherds are used nowadays is that their size and long, striding gait do not suit everyone. Furthermore, they do not take kindly to handlers who are a bit clumsy, so that making a good match is not easy. From the outset of the breeding programme the emphasis was, of course, on supplying larger German shepherds for the taller clients – as well as improving the temperament of the breed. Many of the approval shepherds at that time were quite small, thin, nervous dogs. Freeman achieved this objective but in doing so did little to encourage the greater use of German shepherds.

Enthusiasts for the breed among training staff and guide dog owners often swear that if everything goes right for them and they have a good handler German shepherds make the finest guide dogs. The truth is probably that because only a few of the best get through, their reputation is not diluted by all the average dogs, as it is with labradors. All the breeds now used for guide dog work produce their outstanding individuals, and it

John Bailey in 1970 with Valis, a large male German shepherd that typified the best of the breed. Despite his size, Valis was a gentle, sedate dog who was described by his owner as 'a perfect gentleman'.

would be a brave man who claimed that one was better than the others.

A dog that typified the best in German shepherds was Valis, a large male belonging to John Bailey, who was the Association's appeals manager for the north-east until he moved to the head office in 1984. Derek Freeman was at a large gathering at a hotel in York one day when Bailey and Valis appeared at the far end of the room. The dog steered Bailey through all the tables and chairs to where Freeman was standing at the bar without either of them so much as brushing an obstacle.

'He was like a dog working in carpet slippers,' Freeman recalled. 'He worked so carefully, so sleekly, so adroitly. I remember him as a robust little pup that would knock anything over – coffee table, coffee pot, the lot. John and Valis weaving through that room showed what guide dog work is all about, and what handling dogs is all about.'

Bailey's tribute to Valis was that he was 'a thorough gentleman. He never ran anywhere, but walked sedately and was so kind and gentle one could not believe he was so big.'

*   *   *

John Bailey's next dog, when Valis was retired in 1978, was Regan, a male golden retriever that served him magnificently for 10 years. Another golden retriever, Elgar, followed and Bob Steele explained what led him to make this particular match. 'We had to consider John's personality and the nature of his work. He can spend days in the office and then go out visiting schools, to meetings or social and fund-raising events of various kinds. It's easy enough to find a dog that is quite content to curl up and sleep or keep quiet in the office for most of the day; but difficult to find one that combines these qualities with ambition and drive when working.

'John may be taken to a social event in a town hall and then have to find his own way out again afterwards, along corridors that he met for the first time on the way in. A dog that can remember its way back and make decisions is usually the active, outgoing type that can sometimes be a bit of a handful socially.'

Elgar happened to be a golden retriever, a breed that comprises about one in ten of the guide dog population. They are glamorous, easy to live with and make wonderful guide dogs. So why are so few used? Because for all their virtues, they are less flexible than labradors and more prone to develop problems. Goldens are often thought of as stubborn. They can suddenly decide not to work for a blind owner who is perhaps not very assertive, but will behave perfectly when an instructor turns up to help – someone who can control the dog effectively.

Bob Steele prefers to call them determined, which can be awkward at times but is also a characteristic that can be valuable to, say, a less capable guide dog owner whose travels are limited. Once the limited number of routes – trips to the corner shop, the post office and so on – has been imprinted on the dog (and assuming it is a dog that is content with a small work load) it will show great determination in getting to its destination, no matter how badly it is handled.

Steele confesses to mixed feelings about the breed, but reckons that a high proportion of the better dogs that he has trained were goldens. He is wary of using more, however, because they need more understanding.

Present-day border collies are mostly smaller, lighter-boned animals than those that dominated the guide dog scene in the 1940s. Few are used now. Although they generally have long lives, they have many less desirable qualities. They can be rather sensitive, particularly to noise, their chasing instinct is strong and they are often over-active.

A few curly-coat retrievers are used and other pure breeds contribute a few individuals from time to time; but the big success of recent years has been a cross between the labrador and the golden retriever. In the course of seeking out the best animals from which to breed, and matching studs to broods in the hope of combining their best qualities, it was inevitable that cross breeding would be tried. The retriever breeds were chosen initially because they had the best track records and it was hoped that the labrador's great willingness and generosity would overcome any lack of these qualities in the golden without smothering the latter's gentleness.

Right from the start it was a success. The first litter was, in fact, a product of the Bolton training centre where the controller, Derek Carver, decided to run his own unofficial experiment with the cross. All the centres dabbled in breeding occasional litters as a sideline, and this time Bolton hit on a winner. Thereafter, the lab/golden cross was taken up by the Tollgate team and a succession of lovely litters was born, containing pups that were less exuberant than many labradors, easy to walk and control, and a delight to live with. The males were as good as the bitches, which helped greatly when Freeman was trying to persuade the training centres to use more males. The fruitful blending of qualities in this way was reflected in a higher success rate than any of the pure breeds and the number of crosses increased rapidly. At the time of writing half the guide dogs produced by the training centres are lab/golden crosses.

Other crosses that have been tried on a small scale, and proved successful, are a lab/curly-coat and a golden retriever/collie. The latter was an attempt to find a way round the difficulty of establishing pure collie lines that were suitable for guide dog work. All but one of the first litter of seven made the grade and the cross has now been repeated several times.

It might be supposed that several generations of lab/golden crosses had now been bred and that an identifiable and separate breed was beginning to emerge; that the 'British guide dog' or the 'Leamington leader' was well on the way to recognition by the Kennel Club. Unfortunately, it has not

Derek Freeman, who retired in 1987 after more than a quarter of a century devoted to developing the breeding and puppy-walking programmes, with the legendary stud dog Voss. Between 1974 and 1982 567 of Voss's progeny were placed on the puppy-walking scheme, of which 460 became working dogs and 42 joined the breeding stock: a success rate of nearly 90 per cent.

worked out like that. Second generation crosses, or double crosses, were producing over-sensitive animals and so, for the present, Neil Ewart, who took over the breeding programme after Freeman retired in 1988, is sticking mainly to first generation crosses.

Arguably, if first crosses are producing such good results, there is no point in aspiring to a special guide dog breed. That's fine as long as the successful matching of pure breeds continues. It does not offer quite the same assurance for the future, however, and the hope of a specialised breed is unlikely to be abandoned entirely.

In the meantime, there are still problems to be solved. Artificial insemination is a technique on which much work remains to be done. Freeman experimented with AI in a small way but with only limited success. More recently, better progress has been made. There is clearly great potential in the use of frozen semen from outstanding stud dogs, and some has already been stored to await the development of a reliable inseminating procedure.

The most treasured semen is that obtained from Voss, a yellow labrador with a record that made him the undisputed top dog of the breeding programme. His first litter was born in February 1974 and during the next eight years 567 of his progeny were placed on the puppy-walking scheme. Of these, 460 became working dogs and 42 joined the breeding stock: a success rate of nearly 90 per cent.

Another very special stud dog was Angus, a golden retriever who stamped his remarkable temperament on nearly 200 guide dogs and breeding stock. The 80 per cent success rate of his progeny did not match Voss's but he had a decisive influence on the development and improvement of golden retriever blood lines, and sired many of the early crosses with labradors. His mother, Bonnie, was a fine bitch that Freeman had acquired from an outside source and initially put through for training. But when she was withdrawn after a load of steel rods fell off a lorry alongside her and made her incurably apprehensive of large vehicles and loud noises, Freeman took her on as breeding stock, recognising that although the traumatic incident may have spoiled her for guide dog work, it did not affect the basic qualities of temperament for which he prized her.

Angus was remarkable for his tolerance. He would mix with other studs without ever challenging them and his patience as a baby-sitter was legendary. If there was ever a six-week-old puppy on its own at Tollgate Angus would be summoned. 'He would lie with it, play with it, let it gallop over him while he tried to sleep, it would rag him,' Freeman recalled. 'Some golden retriever mums wouldn't tolerate that.'

There is not the space here to pick out more than a handful of the many fine breeding animals that have made their mark on the regiments of British guide dogs. Among the bitches that stand out in Freeman's memory is Wayfarer, a labrador with an abundance of initiative who was really too much of a handful for several of the people who had looked after her. 'She had a bit of fire in her belly, and that came out in her puppies. It gave them the drive that made them ideal working dogs for piano tuners and other very active people working in busy areas. Guide dogs shouldn't be aggressive in a hostile sense, but they do need a certain type of aggression – call it determination or drive – if they are going to work in busy towns or cities, pushing their way through crowds on the streets and public transport.'

Wayfarer was eventually looked after by a young girl with cerebral palsy. She immediately established a relationship with the bitch that none of her other handlers had been able to achieve. 'The dog respected her, was completely under her control and did everything she wanted. I've seen her discipline that dog more severely than I would have dared to do,' said Freeman.

Tawny was another labrador, but with a temperament that produced pups suitable for less active people. She was usually mated with Voss, but it wasn't his influence alone that made her progeny so good. Of the 41 pups from six litters she had to Voss, 37 became guide dogs or breeding stock. A seventh litter of six to Ben all qualified.

*   *   *

A constant concern of the breeding programme has been the control of inherited physical defects that can affect the work of a guide dog. The condition that has attracted the greatest attention is hip dysplasia, a malformation of the joint that can be crippling. Although the condition had been recognised for a long time, it made no impact on guide dogs until the 1960s, when it began to emerge that a great number of the country's dogs, particularly the large breeds, were affected. Most experts at the time advised against breeding from dogs that were even slightly affected and putting down the more serious cases. For a while, this advice was followed and dogs with desirable qualities but bad hips were discarded while others with good hips but poorer temperaments were kept. If this policy had continued for long it would have had a disastrous effect on the breeding programme and consequently on the quality of the working dogs.

In the end, after much uncertainty and conflicting advice, common-sense prevailed. Guide dogs were not expected to have perfect or near-perfect movement, and as long as they could exercise and move about freely without discomfort they were accepted for training. If they passed this practical test they were not X-rayed, which was reserved for potential breeding stock. In deciding which dogs to keep for breeding, hips were only one of the factors taken into account.

Progressive retinal atrophy, an eye defect which causes night blindness in a small number of dogs, can shorten the working life of a guide dog and has therefore been the subject of much study. A major contribution to reducing its incidence has been the work of Dr Keith Barnett, who started to make regular examinations of all the Association's dogs in 1964 when he was on the staff of Cambridge University. Later, he joined The Animal Health Trust but kept up the programme of eye checks under their auspices. For some years he was also a member of the Association's general council.

If one had to select an achievement of the Tollgate House team led by Derek Freeman to place above all others, it would have to be the breeding of more sensitive guide dogs. Without it guide dog ownership could never have become so widespread, and there would be far fewer dogs able to cope with the traffic and urban conditions of today. In the guide dog world, at least, the younger generation are made of much better stuff than most of their predecessors, and for his part in bringing that about Freeman was awarded the MBE in 1986.

10

Getting into Harness

Until the late 1960s the time allotted for training a guide dog was usually no more than 12 weeks, sometimes less when the pressure was on. John Weeks recalls that on one occasion, when he was still at Leamington in the late 1940s, he walked down to the station to collect a new dog and started its training on the way back to the centre. Today, the training is less intense and takes nearly four times as long.

The crash programme of earlier years was dictated by the limited resources available and the very long waiting list that persisted year after year. It worked largely because expectations were not so high. Guide dog owners knew they were members of a privileged minority and that if they were unsuccessful with their dog they might not get another one, or might have to wait a long time for a replacement. They were therefore prepared to tolerate difficulties and expected to be given imperfect guides whose training they would have to polish up 'on the job'.

One benefit of the large waiting list, however, was that it was possible to select for training only those blind people who had the physical qualities and the temperament needed to cope with hastily-trained dogs that were often quite hard to control; people who were able to overcome the inevitable problems that would arise. Age was one crude method of selection. With few exceptions, no men over 50 or women over 45 were considered. This barrier was gradually raised, and today there is no upper age limit. Not many years ago an 85-year-old man in Kent got a guide dog for the first time and he was still using it in his nineties.

Another factor in the short training programme was the dogs. Because they were usually pretty tough they could be forced through in a way that would have been impossible with more sensitive animals. If they weren't tough enough they didn't survive the course. Even so, the stress on them was considerable and manifested itself from time to time in cases of wet eczema, loss of weight and neurotic behaviour.

'When visitors came round we used to hide them down in the kennels,' recalled Derek Freeman. 'We didn't take them into town with us. We didn't understand fully what was happening to them, but we've learnt since.'

The methods used to push dogs through the 12-week training pro-gramme were sometimes harsh by modern standards. Obedience was the cornerstone of the regime and was used to establish the dominance of the handler over the dog. One exercise that was taught as part of the obedience package, and partly because it was thought to be useful to some blind people, was the retrieve, or *apport* as it was then called (from the French, meaning 'to carry'). Retrieving does not come naturally to many dogs, but nevertheless they were forced to learn it. If a dog refused to pick up the dumb-bell that was used in training the instructor would give a fierce jerk on its check chain and then take a turn round his hand to pull another link through so that the dog started to choke. As soon as it opened its mouth the dumb-bell would be popped in, the chain released and the dog showered with praise. Once the dumb-bell had been mastered, the dog would be taught to retrieve a variety of other items, often very small objects such as coins, marbles or hairpins.

The teaching of *apport* is remembered vividly, and with distaste, by the apprentices who were taken on at the end of the 1939–45 war, but it was soon discontinued. Attitudes were changing and many people thought it was an unnecessary infliction on the dog. It had a value to the guide dog owner in that in almost any situation where he wanted to assert his control he only had to drop something, give the command *apport* and the dog would obey (it had learnt the price of disobedience). But it seemed that few blind people used the command for the practical purpose of getting the dog to bring things to them, and as teaching the technique occupied valuable time in the training programme it was dropped.

Correction seldom went as far as the occasion on which Liakhoff grabbed a dog that was not responding quickly enough to its trainer, lifted it off the ground by its check chain and swung it around several times before returning it to the trainer with the comment that it would obey now. Nevertheless, correction was used a good deal and out of sight of the public dogs would sometimes get a pretty severe whack with a riding crop or cane if, for example, they did not walk fast enough. Time was too short to permit dogs to learn gradually.

For a short period, and on rare occasions only, a special corrector was used that would give the dog a mild electric shock when a remote control button was pushed. The device, which was attached to the harness, was only used when all other ways of teaching or correcting had failed, but it sometimes had unpredictable results. It was being used one day in Bolton on a dog that was persistently distracted by other dogs, to the detriment of its work. Normally the shock brought no dramatic reaction from a dog, but on this occasion when the button was pressed, to everyone's astonishment it leapt about three feet in the air and landed in the fountain it was passing.

On another occasion when the corrector was being used in an attempt to make a dog come when it was called after a run in the park it had exactly the opposite to the desired effect. When the dog felt the jolt from the corrector it stood in stunned amazement for a moment and then took off like a greyhound in the opposite direction. It ran about a mile and was not recovered until two or three hours later.

But slowly the emphasis swung from a great reliance on correction to learning by encouragement, which takes more time, of course. One important influence on the pattern of training was the growing breeding and puppy-walking programme and the reaction from Derek Freeman if a training centre rejected one of his dogs without a cast-iron reason. The more sensitive dogs that were coming through did, of course, need more considerate handling but with Freeman breathing down their necks centres undoubtedly spent more time than they might otherwise have done on some dogs. So keen was Freeman to see his dogs succeed and to establish a solid reputation for his work that he would sometimes give a dog rejected by one centre to another, in the belief that it would fare better under a different instructor.

The pattern of training was changed gradually by the decision, taken in 1958, to engage female training assistants who would be responsible for much of the basic training, leaving the qualified and experienced instructors free to concentrate on the final preparation of the dogs and teaching the blind students how to use them effectively. It was an important step which led to the creation of the early training units that still exist today under the name of dog supply units.

It took time for these innovations to have any appreciable effect on the training regime. As a new boy at Bolton in the mid-1960s Steve Lambert, who is now regional controller for the area, was picking 'absolutely raw dogs' from the approval stock in kennels that were going to be handed over to blind people 12 weeks later. Training staff who came on the scene at the end of the '60s can remember that in their early years dogs were still going through in 12 weeks.

'Occasionally, you would be so desperate for dogs you would look at those in isolation (newly-arrived approval dogs) to find something you could lean on, work hard and knock into shape quickly,' Bob Steele recalled. 'The dog would be tough enough to take it and with the right owner who could carry on where you left off some of them turned out quite well.'

Nowadays a dog is coaxed rather than bullied and although it is bound to experience some stress occasionally it is never pushed too far. If it needs more time to master an exercise it is given it. Praise is a great

motivator, of course, and has always been one of the foundation stones of guide dog training, but its importance is even greater with the modern, more gentle approach.

* * *

Although the way in which the dogs are trained has changed a great deal, what they are taught is still basically the same as it was in the 1930s. The conditions in which the dogs have to work are also very different: crowded pavements with more street 'furniture' and more traffic on the roads present greater challenges and therefore demand more reliable dogs. But their basic tasks are the same.

Far and away the most important role of a guide dog is to lead its owner safely along the centre of the pavement, avoiding any obstacles in its path. There is a popular misconception that crossing the road is a guide dog's greatest achievement, but it is, in fact, most vulnerable when dealing with traffic. The hard bit is the pavement work. Guide dog owners can always get sighted help to cross the road if traffic conditions are difficult, and indeed are strongly advised to do so if they are at all unsure of

When the boys and girls come out to play at the Exeter training centre they mean it. A guide dog, whether in training or during its working life, spends at most only a few hours a day in harness, and at other times enjoys a good run as much as any other dog. (Mike Alsford)

themselves. But they rely absolutely on their guides to prevent them bumping into lamp-posts, falling down holes or tripping over a sack of refuse.

All guide dog work starts with the straight-line concept. The dog must learn to walk in a straight line and to keep going – not to turn or drift round a corner because it thinks it is going that way. Everything is built round keeping the continuity of the straight line. If the dog has to avoid an obstacle, it should return as soon as possible to the original line and keep going straight ahead until it reaches the down kerb or is given a command that over-rides its primary task. At the down kerb it waits for the next instruction, which may be 'Forward', 'Left', 'Right' or 'Back'. A crossing is always made at 90 degrees to the kerb, never diagonally, and always at a junction or pedestrian crossing.

The most common threat to the safety and effectiveness of the team is the development of a 'left tendency', which destroys the straight-line concept. It was more of a problem in the past when so many collies were being used. With their high body sensitivity, they were really only suitable for people who had good balance and were light on their feet. Anyone who was a bit unsteady or clumsy would soon find that his dog was pulling to the left to avoid being knocked or trodden on. Dogs that were sound-shy and pulled also developed a left tendency. The problem was sometimes so bad that harnesses would be worn away on the left-hand side through constant scraping against walls. Pulling to the left becomes dangerous at junctions with a busy road at right angles on the left. Instead of crossing straight the dog will lead its owner out towards the stream of traffic on the left before swinging back in again to reach the kerb.

Although sound-shyness, pulling and body sensitivity are no longer the problems they once were, training staff still have to watch out for a left tendency. A client whose balance is not too good will be given a dog with a low body sensitivity and a forgiving nature; and in the final preparation of the dog the instructor will gradually introduce some of the clumsy handling that is in store for it so that the transition does not come as too much of a shock.

A necessary interruption to the straight-line concept is the avoidance of obstacles. The dog has been avoiding obstacles from the time it started to walk, of course, but it now has to learn to allow for the width and height of the person it is guiding. It is a long process that starts with the trainer ensuring that even on 'straight-line' walks on the lead there is sufficient space for both of them. He never tucks in behind the dog to squeeze through a narrow gap between people, but slows down until the way is clear for them to proceed side by side at a normal speed.

Teaching a dog to avoid a fixed obstacle like a lamp-post is relatively easy. If it does not leave enough room for its handler to clear the obstacle, it is shown the object, then taken back to try again with the trainer encouraging the dog to go wide.

Avoiding the people that surge along the busy pavements of major towns and cities is very much more difficult. A gap that appears one minute closes the next; or a family of four advances in line abreast, taking up three-quarters of the pavement. A trainer can only build up the dog's awareness of width by constant repetition, teach the dog to be patient, give it as much experience as possible and then encourage it to use its initiative.

A good dog and handler in reasonable conditions will weave their way from one kerb to the next avoiding everything in their path with a skill that is delightful to watch. However, in crowded spots, like the centre of London, compromises are inevitable and the occasional bump is bound to occur if any progress is to be made. Getting on a train in the rush hour means heading for the door and squeezing in with everyone else – never mind what you were taught at school.

Another difficult task for a dog is to make allowances for its owner's height. It is no different, in principle, from allowing for width and dogs are quite proficient at it when they leave the training centre. The trouble is they get less practice with height than width and unless training is constantly reinforced it gets rusty.

Turns make few demands on the dog. All it has to do is to react correctly to simple commands. The left turn at a kerb may seem strange to the onlooker, but it is quite straightforward for the dog. In the early days the dog's handler would step down into the road and pivot around his dog. The obvious danger of the movement led, in the 1950s, to the three-quarter turn in which the handler steps back a pace and the dog circles him to the right until they both face to the left of their original position. It is not the most elegant of manoeuvres, perhaps, and can cause some confusion among other pedestrians if the pavement is crowded, but at least it is safe.

The one aspect of guide dog work that has become more risky over the years is dealing with traffic. Despite the improvements in training and in the quality of the dogs there are severe limitations on a unit's ability to deal with many of the conditions that are encountered when crossing a road. The basic problem is that, unless a dog has actually been struck by a vehicle, it does not understand that it is dangerous. Hitting a dog with a car during training is out of the question, partly because it would be inhumane and partly because it would scare sensitive dogs so much that they would never set foot off the pavement again. A variety of other stratagems has been tried, including firing a water pistol at the dog from the car, but none of them has succeeded in producing a dog that could grasp the lethal potential of a vehicle.

A dog is thus taught that an approaching vehicle is a signal to remain stationary or to stop, but it does not know *why* it is doing this. So what? (you may ask) as long as the dog has been thoroughly programmed to recognise and respond to the signal, all should be well. Does it matter that it cannot understand the reason for its actions? The trouble is that away from the ideal conditions created at the training centre it is easy for conflicting influences to affect the quality of the work.

To appreciate what can happen, one has first to understand the basic technique used for crossing a road. The dog will lead its owner straight to the kerb and stop, waiting for further instructions. The blind person will then listen for traffic and when he believes it is safe to cross he will give the command Forward. The dog will then move off *unless* it sees an approaching vehicle within the critical distance that it has learnt to recognise as a signal to remain stationary. If it does pick up that signal – in this case from the 'near traffic' stream coming from the right – it will ignore its owner's command to go forward. The blind person will then reassess the situation and give the command again when he thinks it is safe. If, this time, the dog picks up no warning signal it will set off across the road and turn its attention to the 'far traffic' – vehicles approaching from the left on the other side of the road. A moving vehicle that comes within the critical distance will again be recognised as a signal, this time to stop. When it has passed, the dog and its partner can proceed to the up kerb.

Now consider what happens at a pelican crossing on a busy road. Dog and owner wait at the kerb until the audible signal indicates that it is safe to go. Even though a car may be approaching from the right the handler gives the command Forward, knowing the lights are showing red against the car. A well-trained dog should hesitate but, urged on firmly by its owner, who knows that there are only a few seconds before the lights change, it sets off and is praised for doing so.

A bit further on they are half-way across a zebra crossing when a car approaches from the left. By all rights the dog should stop, but again it is encouraged to continue and is praised for doing so. Before long, if they use pedestrian crossings and traffic lights enough, the dog will learn that the rules have changed – it no longer has to stop for approaching vehicles.

Because of the erosion that can take place in this way traffic training must be constantly reinforced by guide dog owners. Using near traffic only, they choose conditions in which they can be sure of their judgment – a road in which the traffic is light and easily detected – and then, at a junction where they would normally cross, give the command Forward when they know a vehicle is approaching within the danger zone. If the dog starts to move off, because its traffic work has deteriorated, it is checked. If it stays still it is praised. But this reinforcement must be an almost daily routine to maintain a high standard of traffic work, and many working guide dogs are undoubtedly less than perfect at it.

Some drivers who spot a guide dog and its owner waiting at a junction will stop, even though they have the right of way, to allow the unit to cross. This is not encouraged, however, because it breaks the normal traffic pattern, causes confusing signals and does not prevent other drivers continuing on the outside lane to knock the pair down as they emerge from in front of the Good Samaritan's car.

The value of being identified as a guide dog owner is now well recognised and blind people are no longer reluctant, as many were in the early days, to draw attention to their blindness. In the early 1950s, after a fatal accident to a guide dog owner at night, harnesses were changed from brown to white (after a brief experiment with luminous paint). In more recent years, fluorescent sleeves have been added to the harness straps and guide dog owners have been provided with fluorescent arm bands and Sam Browne belts. There is also a short, collapsible white cane that can be quickly assembled and held out as a signal while crossing the road. Measures such as these to make guide dog owners more conspicuous are all designed to improve safety, and during traffic training it is constantly impressed upon students that they should seek sighted assistance on all but the safest road crossings. Strange as it may seem, it is not the areas of most dense traffic that present the greatest dangers. The slow-moving traffic in major towns and cities is nothing like as hazardous as speeding vehicles on many other roads, and guide dog owners can often rely on moving with the crowd to cross safely.

The British practice of driving on the left presents an additional hazard to British guide dog owners. With rare exceptions, a guide dog works on the left of its owner where, as it waits at the kerb, it is largely hidden from the view of a motorist approaching from the right. This should not matter if everything works perfectly, but if the traffic approached from the left, as it does in most other countries, the dog would be much more visible and drivers would be more easily alerted to the need for extra care.

The reinforcement of traffic training is one of the purposes of regular aftercare visits by training staff; but it is not without hazard for the instructors, many of whom have been pulled from their cars by irate onlookers who were convinced that they were driving irresponsibly and endangering the life of the guide dog owner. One instructor recalls a police car arriving at speed and being hauled out of his seat by the collar to explain his apparently reckless driving. On another occasion, a guide dog owner who was out on an aftercare reinforcement exercise was warned by a bystander that there was someone in a car trying to knock him down every time he tried to cross the road.

It is sometimes thought that a guide dog's training to ignore the

Forward command when the traffic conditions demand it is a unique feature of its work. It may well be that seldom, if ever, are other trained animals allowed to exercise their judgment in this way, but with guide dogs it is not confined to traffic. A similar situation may occur when walking along the pavement. An owner may hear a possible distraction for his dog just as it swings off towards the sound. So, it is checked and told to leave it alone. In fact, the dog may have been avoiding a ladder or a hole in the ground. So what does it do? Ignore the correction and continue going round, or carry on walking into danger? Much depends on the amount of initiative the dog possesses and the degree of confidence its handler has in the decisions it makes, and more than one owner who thought he knew best has finished up with egg (or mud) on his face.

Mike Csernovits, regional controller for the north-east, remembers an aftercare visit when he watched a guide dog try to take its owner to the kerb in order to avoid a pile of coal several feet high that had been dumped on the footpath. Instead of allowing the dog to proceed, the woman checked it sharply and ordered it to go straight on. The dog tried again and received another sharp correction. After a third attempt, and an even more severe reprimand, it gave up and led its obstinate handler on an undignified scramble over the top.

A complete contrast to this stifling of initiative was shown by another guide dog owner who allowed her dog to continue walking in the road despite her gentle urging to return to the pavement. She had not gone many yards before she was approached by an onlooker who told her that the dog was avoiding a sheet of ice on which it would have been impossible to stand.

'That was initiative,' Csernovits observed, 'but it only develops when the dog and its handler trust each other.'

*   *   *

One of the more intriguing aspects of guide dog work is the dog's ability to 'find' places and remember routes. During its training the dog is taught to recognise a number of useful objectives, such as doors, pedestrian crossings and steps. A blind person can therefore ask his dog to 'find the crossing' when he knows he is in the vicinity of it and the dog will lead him there. Many guide dog owners develop this skill a good deal further. One undergraduate at Manchester University could ask his dog to lead him to any one of about 40 rooms that he used regularly.

A piano tuner will employ a dog's route memory more than most. He may have dozens of clients that he visits perhaps only once or twice a year and a dog with plenty of initiative will quickly remember most of the destinations. Once the owner gets them both in the neighbourhood of one of their regular calls the dog will lead the rest of the way with little or no direction.

This ability can have unforeseen consequences. One guide dog owner was walking down the street with his wife when his dog suddenly turned in at a gate that it recognised as a regular port of call. It was, in fact, the house of the man's mistress, a liaison that his wife had suspected for some time but he had vigorously denied. Unfortunately for him, his dog provided the evidence she needed.

One woman told her dog to 'find the door' when she knew she was near a large store in which she wanted to do some shopping. It was a warm summer's day and the shop had its doors fixed open, so that the woman kept on urging her guide to 'find the door' after she was actually inside. Looking around for the nearest door, the dog stopped in front of a display of shower cabinets. Although the door seemed a bit strange to her, the woman nevertheless opened it and went inside, only to have the unit collapse around her.

Mike Tetley taught his dog Sweep to 'find the lavatory' but decided to stop using the command after being taken into the women's side of a public loo on more than one occasion. Once when he was in a public lavatory (the men's side) he knew that Sweep must have been bursting so he stepped aside and invited the dog to 'get busy'. Sweep moved forward, cocked his leg and aimed as if he had been using the place all his life. As they left, Tetley heard the attendant say in wonder to another onlooker, 'Did you see that dog?'

A dog's talent for finding locations and remembering routes will depend largely on its initiative and the extent to which this has been developed during training and working. But it will also depend greatly on what incentive it has to extend itself. That incentive can sometimes be simply food, but more often it is praise. Most dogs will go through fire to earn their master's praise and a handler who knows how to show his pleasure will be the one whose guide will most enjoy its work and be most anxious to please.

Obedience exercises, such as sit, down, stay and come, are basic elements in guide dog training and are relatively uncontroversial, one would have thought. Nevertheless, a storm once blew up over recall training. Free-running in a park or open ground is an important and enjoyable part of a guide dog's life, as it is for any dog, but it is vital that the blind owner should be able to recall his dog easily. Many people can get an immediate response to their call, but others are unable to use their voices so effectively, and so in 1966 it was decided to introduce whistle recall, a technique widely used by shepherds and gun-dog handlers.

In retrospect, it is hard to see why passions should have been roused by such an apparently sensible move; but it was met by fierce objections from Michael Tucker, an instructor at Leamington, when he was asked to employ it with his class. He flatly refused to do so and was promptly suspended. Three of the remaining four qualified training staff then resigned in sympathy, a number of guide dog owners took up the cudgels and the media had several field days. Some weeks later, after a good deal of investigation and discussion on the issue, Tucker's suspension became dismissal.

It would take a complete chapter to examine the episode fully, and that would exaggerate its importance. Its substance can be put fairly briefly. Although use of the whistle was the immediate cause of the dispute, unrest had been building up for other reasons. Some of it is explained by personality clashes and indifferent management, but Tucker would never have been suspended or dismissed if he had not challenged authority too often already. By 1966 he was regarded as a nuisance.

There was also another training technique at issue: the use of meat to try to distract the dog while it was working. Tucker claimed it was cruel, others maintained it was a good way to reinforce a dog's training and test its concentration. The conclusion of an independent investigating team from the Kennel Club was that 'not only was there no vestige of cruelty involved, but that in the worsening traffic and pedestrian congestion every fair means of ensuring the safety of blind people through their guide dogs was highly desirable.' They were less convinced of the value of the whistle.

Tucker was dismissed at the end of September 1966, but it was not the end of the affair. The Kennel Club report put the technical issues in perspective but other question marks remained and in March 1967 the general manager, Paul McConnell, resigned.

*   *   *

Most trainers could fill a book with stories of the dogs they have trained. Steve Lambert, regional controller for the north-west, remembers one big, black woolly dog – one of the old approval stock of unknown parentage – that was returned to the centre after working for six years because its owner had lost a leg and the dog was too fast for him now that he had an artificial limb. Lambert was re-training it to walk more slowly and was waiting at a crossing beside a pram in which there was a child with a toy bugle. The first time the child blew the bugle in its ear the dog just shook its head. On the second occasion it reacted similarly. But as the child raised the bugle for the third time the dog decided that it had been patient for long enough. It turned its head, took the end of the instrument into its mouth and squeezed, silencing it forever.

After many weeks of daily training sessions the instructors know their dogs inside out. The dogs also know them and have got used to the expert

Dr Julia Schofield runs her own computer business in south-west London and depends on her guide dog Yates for visiting clients throughout Britain. Dr Schofield often uses British Airways' domestic flights and so Yates received special training to prepare him for air travel.

As part of their conditioning for the noisy world in which they will be working, guide dogs in training at the Wokingham centre are taken to the nearby army camp at Arborfield where, as this picture demonstrates, they take band practice in their stride. (Paul Haley for Soldier Magazine)

ways of their handlers. It is important, therefore, that they should be prepared for the unsettling effect of being taken over by a stranger who may never have handled a dog before and is, in effect, a learner driver. This can be achieved to some extent by the instructors deliberately handling their dogs rather more clumsily in the final weeks. They also wear blindfolds while out on training walks in order to simulate for the dog the feel of leading a blind person and to test it under conditions that are as nearly realistic as possible. On one occasion Steve Lambert was working in blindfold through a shopping area in Bolton when he heard someone say, 'It's got my cakes!' He stopped and removed his blindfold to find the dog gently holding a bag of cakes in its mouth. They were quite untouched and were swiftly returned, with apologies, to the somewhat astonished owner.

As the final stages of the training are reached, instructors have the crucial task of choosing the best partner for each dog. It is a selection which must be done well if the long programme of breeding, rearing and training is to reach a successful conclusion, and the current balance between supply and demand does not make the task any easier. With shorter waiting lists there are fewer people to choose from and therefore not so many options available in trying to create ideal partnerships.

Once the pairings have been decided the dogs are given any special preparation that may be necessary. One instructor used shuttle flights from London's Heathrow airport to give a final polish to the training because it was a journey that the dog's prospective owner would be making frequently. A dog intended for a commuter into central London will be thoroughly conditioned to the Underground and the crowded pavements.

With the finishing touches complete, the dogs are ready for their blind partners. All that remains are the final weeks – usually three or four – during which the new owners learn how to use their highly-trained guides effectively. In this, as in the years of working life ahead, much will depend on whether the individual can develop that special relationship with his dog which will encourage it to develop its potential to the full. Dogs are no longer only partly-trained when they leave the training centre, but there is still enormous scope for the development of their abilities with experience, encouragement and skilful handling. Brian Moody, who is currently director of operations, once trained a man who had lost his speech following a stroke. He had such an instinctive feeling for dogs, however, that he was able to communicate with his guide without difficulty and used it very effectively. Few people can achieve that degree of rapport with an animal, but many can, and do, inspire their dogs to become outstanding guides.

11

Creating a Partnership

Training staff will tell you that preparing the dogs is easy compared with teaching blind people how to use them effectively. It is an assertion that should cause little surprise: people, whether blind or sighted, are seldom as anxious to please as dogs and often have their own ideas about how things should be done.

There are also other problems. Guide dogs are young, fit, sighted and carefully selected for the job. Blind people, when they apply for a dog, are often unfit and a poor match physically for their guides. The effects of blindness can be devastating, not least on an individual's health. Active people suddenly find themselves unable to get out and about in the way they used to, with the result that they easily become overweight and debilitated through lack of exercise.

The first task for a prospective guide dog owner, therefore, is to get fit. The tolerances are very much greater than they used to be, of course. It is now common to give guide dogs to elderly people with limited mobility needs, but even they must be able to walk at an adequate pace for a reasonable distance in order to learn how to use their dogs.

Some blind people suffer from poor balance or a shuffling step, others have a poor sense of direction. In these cases, some prior instruction in orientation and mobility is invaluable. Often this is available from local authority social workers, but in many areas the provision is inadequate. For this reason, the Association now has instructors with these skills who can give blind people the necessary preparatory training.

A problem for which there is no easy solution is the person who lacks confidence or motivation. In the early years motivation was seldom lacking. With few exceptions the pioneers were determined people who were going to succeed no matter how inadequate their dogs were. Nowadays, some people apply for a guide dog with the attitude that since it is available they might as well have one, but many of these applicants lack the determination of the early guide dog owners. The effort required to be successful is sometimes greater than they are prepared to make.

The person who lacks confidence can be helped to some extent by being given a dog with plenty of self-confidence and initiative. The dog has to be selected very carefully, however. A confident dog probably needs firm control, something the hesitant individual may not be able to give adequately, so the balance has to be just right.

This balance between a dog's need for control and an individual's ability to provide it is one of the key factors in matching dog and blind person. Give a dog with too much initiative to a timid handler and it will start taking advantage of its owner. On the other hand, a dominating handler with a dog of low initiative could inhibit it to such an extent that it stopped taking decisions.

The factors which determine whether a match is going to be successful are too numerous to explore here. It will be apparent, however, that the task is far from easy. Not only is there a great variety of people and dogs to be matched, with nuances of temperament and ability on both sides that complicate the issue, but expectations are now so much higher than they used to be, and people are more ready to hand a dog back and demand another one if they experience difficulties that an earlier generation of guide dog owners would have taken in its stride.

A thorough assessment of each applicant's physical condition, temperament and circumstances is obviously necessary before staff can decide whether he is likely to succeed with a guide dog and begin to look for a dog that will suit him. Until the late 1950s the only information on which to base these judgments was an application form and a report from the applicant's doctor. Today, there are not only reports from a social worker as well as a doctor, but an interview at the applicant's home by an instructor. During the visit they will go out for a short walk together, the instructor leading the applicant with a 'short handle' that simulates the feel of being guided by a dog. In this way, the instructor can gain a fairly good idea of the applicant's balance, gait and ability to control a dog. If he is still uncertain, the applicant is invited to attend a short assessment course at a training centre.

*   *   *

The training of congenitally blind people presents special problems, mainly because they have never seen and therefore have no visual memory. They have a perception of the world which is very different from that of sighted people or those who have gone blind later in life. One instructor remembers a congenitally blind child asking how many walls there were in a large room if there were four in a small room. On another occasion he was asked what colour the wind was. Steve Lambert once trained a young woman who had led a very protected life at home until she came to the centre. Waiting to cross a road with her one day, Lambert explained that a big bus was coming. 'Mr Lambert, what is big?' she asked him. Later that day, he arranged to take her to the bus depot where she was able to explore the bus with her hands, feel the tyres, go upstairs and in this way get some appreciation of its size.

People who have never seen streets or buildings cannot perceive distance, perspective and size in the way that sighted people can. It is much more difficult for them to follow a route because they cannot visualise it, and instructors have to use a good deal of imagination to overcome the problem. Understanding traffic is not always easy.

At one time many congenitally blind people grew up with mannerisms that were an obstacle to success with a guide dog. A sighted child learns gestures and body language from watching its parents or other people, but someone blind from birth is deprived of this opportunity and can develop habits, such as shuffling, body-rocking, eye-poking and uncoordinated movements of arms and legs that will be unfamiliar and perhaps frightening to a dog. There have been occasions in the past when a dog that was being taken in to meet its new owner for the first time refused to cross the threshold of the room because it was frightened by the mannerisms that were being displayed.

The problem is rarely encountered now because schools for the blind teach children to adopt the ways of the sighted world. Other aspects of the narrow way in which the congenitally blind were often brought up in institutions or at home have also disappeared. One member of the training staff recalls going into the dining room at a training centre for his first meal after joining as an apprentice in 1962, having a spoon thrust into his hand by the training manager and being told to teach one of the students how to use it. Sitting at one of the tables was a blind man eating his meal with his hands. It would be difficult, if not impossible, to find that situation today. Blind welfare has made enormous strides in recent years, encouraging far more integration with the sighted world and opening up the old, closed world of the workshops and other blind institutions.

The ability to 'hear' objects such as lamp-posts by picking up reflected sounds or sensing their presence in some other way is possessed by many blind people, and it is often developed to a very high degree among the congenitally blind. This has obvious advantages, but it can also cause a guide dog owner to override his dog's decisions. If this happens frequently the dog's work will soon deteriorate. It is a danger to which people with some sight are also exposed and an important part of their training is learning to use it in a constructive way without hindering the dog. At one time people with some residual vision were discouraged from using it at all, often wearing a blindfold to ensure that they could not see anything, but nowadays it is recognised that, used correctly, it can complement the dog's work.

It comes as a surprise to many people to learn that guide dogs are offered to applicants who are not totally blind. Blindness, however, is not a clear-cut matter of being totally without sight. There are many ways in which vision can be affected and varying degrees of impairment. Only a small proportion of the 150,000 or so people who are 'registered blind' in Britain are unable to see anything at all. The important consideration is the usefulness of the vision. A person may be able to see something in a shop window or identify an approaching bus, but be quite incapable of getting about freely without help. This 'tunnel vision' can cause misunderstandings at times, when members of the public see someone with a guide dog reading a notice or admiring the latest fashions. Vision that is restricted to a very small, central field is very little help in travelling about, however. One needs peripheral vision as well to pick up all the information necessary to dodge obstacles and steer a safe course. Anyone who wants to find out for himself what it is like has only to place two tubes of rolled-up newspaper to his eyes and try moving around the room without tripping over a stool or knocking over a standard lamp.

Far and away the biggest cause of blindness is old age, but many elderly people have no real use for a guide dog or would be unable to use it successfully. Nevertheless, there is among guide dog owners an increasing number of over-60s who may need special consideration.

Diabetics may lose their sight while still young or in their middle years, and are a small but significant proportion of applicants for guide dogs. They can present special problems because the amount of exercise they have to take during training can upset the insulin balance in their bodies. If this does happen, it can produce physical reactions which, although seldom dangerous, can affect the training programme. Many diabetics also suffer from poor circulation and loss of feeling in feet and hands. Healing powers and resistance to infection are often low in these parts and great care must therefore be taken to ensure that all the walking that is necessary does not produce blisters or other lesions that might become infected.

From time to time, but only in special circumstances, someone who is deaf as well as blind is trained to use a guide dog. Deafness, like blindness, occurs in varying degrees, and it would be impossible to train someone who was profoundly deaf unless he had enough residual vision to pick up the information that was necessary to deal with direction and traffic, for example.

Clark Steven, who is totally deaf and mute, was successfully trained with a guide dog in 1986. He did, however, have a useful amount of tunnel

Clark Steven, who is totally deaf and mute, but has some tunnel vision, at the Forfar training centre where a special programme was devised to provide him with a guide dog. Staff communicated with him using deaf/blind sign language and ingenious improvisations such as the one being used here by instructor Syd Duncan to refer to the dog, which was named Nelson after the hero of Trafalgar who lost an eye in battle.

vision. A male labrador called Nelson was prepared for him, using specially-devised non-verbal signals to direct the dog and giving exaggerated physical encouragement and material reward instead of verbal praise. Training staff learned deaf/blind sign language in order to communicate with Steven and special code signs emerged. Remembering the hero of Trafalgar, Nelson was signed by putting a hand over one eye.

Clark Steven's success was a triumph of determination for him and a great achievement for the staff at Forfar training centre who devised and implemented his special programme. He was not the first deaf/blind person to have a guide dog, and others will come after him. Making provision for people with additional handicaps has been given increasing attention in recent years. But the numbers of people in this category that can be helped will always be limited by the need to ensure that a guide dog can be used safely.

*   *   *

This brief review of some of the special human problems that have to be taken into account when trying to create successful guide dog 'units' will have indicated how infinitely complex and subtle is the final stage of the long process: training the students. Although in special circumstances some students remain at home while being trained to use their dogs, most attend a residential course at a training centre that normally lasts three to four weeks.

There are now seven major centres around the country – at Leamington, Exeter, Bolton, Forfar, Wokingham, Middlesbrough and Redbridge (NE London). Each has a staff of about 80 to conduct the training programme, run the kennels for 100 or more dogs, supervise the puppy-walking, and look after fund-raising and administration. They are both mini-hotels in terms of the accommodation and catering they provide for the blind students and resident staff, and regional centres for the Association's work. In addition, there are four very much smaller establishments at Belfast, Cardiff, Maidstone and Glasgow that draw their trained dogs from one of the major centres and offer a training and aftercare service in areas that are some distance from the main centres.

There are usually between eight and 12 blind people in each class, with one trained instructor and one or two apprentices to every four students. Before they are joined by their dogs, the students are given a few walks with instructors leading them on the 'short handle' so that they get some feel for the experience ahead. There will also be some discussion about the choice of the 'real' handle that will be their link with the leather harness worn by the dog. It can either be straight or curved, so that the top is offset a few inches to help the handler keep clear of his dog.

Since 1989 there has been another decision to make – where the handle is to be fixed to the harness. In the 1930s the handle was fastened at shoulder level, coming up through a loop on each side higher up on the harness. At some point, after the smaller, more sensitive collies started to come in at the end of the 1930s, a shorter handle that was attached to the back of the harness was introduced. This pattern remained in use until 1989 when the 'combi-harness' was designed. As its name implies, it allows a handle to be attached either in the old '30s style or higher up in the newer position.

The main advantage of the lower fixing is that it gives more positive guidance. The handler can feel the dog turn more easily. On the other hand, because the fixing is more solid, a clumsy handler can easily upset his dog. It is not suitable for a dog with a high body sensitivity, but there are few in that category nowadays.

An advantage of the higher fixing is that it permits the dog to be checked more effectively. A dog that is easily distracted can be reproved with a flick on the handle that is possible with the loose fitting on the dog's back but not with the more rigid shoulder fitting.

There are arguments for both positions, and with the combi-harness trainers can discuss with each blind person the arrangement that is best for him and his dog. Nearly every other guide dog school around the world uses the shoulder fitting, and it is logical, therefore, for it to be offered as an option in Britain.

The arrival of the dogs on the second or third day is usually an emotional occasion. Because of its importance in getting the new partners off to a good start together, each student meets his new guide for the first time in the privacy of his room. An instructor brings the dog to him and leaves them together to start forming the bond that is so important to their future relationship. The temperament of most guide dogs these days makes this an easier task than it was sometimes in earlier days, but even so the new owner has to win the dog's allegiance from the instructor with whom it has been working for some months. The ease with which he can demonstrate affection and assert his authority will determine how well and how quickly he gains the dog's loyalty, but he will be helped by being in total command of it from now on – its new pack leader in effect. He will feed it, groom it and have it with him night and day. The kennel days are over; in future the dog will always be at its master's side and will sleep in his room at night.

On occasions, training staff have had a bit of fun when introducing a student to his new guide. A goat that was kept at one of the training centres would sometimes be handed over instead of a dog, with some highly implausible explanation about it being a new breed that was being tried. A pet whippet kept by one of the staff was also used in a similar fashion. Needless to say, these pranks were only played on students who would enjoy the practical joke as much as the staff.

The training now starts in earnest, with walks on artificial pavements and through an obstacle course in the grounds of the training centre. Students are also taught how to deal with 'off-kerb obstacles', when the pavement is completely blocked and it is necessary for dog and handler to step off the kerb and walk in the road to get round the obstruction.

At first, an instructor is in close attendance, sometimes holding the dog's leash, in order to give detailed instructions and guide the early, hesitant steps. As time goes on he keeps at a greater distance in order to reduce his influence on the dog.

Once a degree of expertise has been acquired in the grounds of the centre the new partners can begin to take on the outside world. Still watched carefully by an instructor they go out into busy town streets to deal with 'real' obstacles. Traffic skills will be acquired initially on quiet roads using one of the centre's vehicles, followed by experience in the town centre.

The course is seldom easy for students. There is the sheer physical stress to which many of them are unaccustomed; and then there are the

David Blunkett, Labour MP for Sheffield Brightside, with his guide dog Teddy in the House of Commons in June 1987. The liver labrador crossed with a curly-coat became a nationally-known character and died in 1988 at the age of 11. The Sheffield MP is now being guided by Offa, a black and tan golden retriever × German shepherd.
(Press Association)

psychological factors. The euphoria of the meeting with the dog and the early days of the developing partnership are often followed by a low in the middle of the course when problems arise and nothing seems to go right.

About 60 per cent of the places on courses are taken by students training with replacements, a proportion that has risen steadily over the years, and for them there can be additional problems. It can be very difficult giving your heart to a new dog when it has already been given to the one that has been left at home – or died unexpectedly. It is difficult, too, to avoid making comparisons with the guide that you had come to regard as nearly faultless and had served you so faithfully for many years.

One hurdle that has to be overcome by those training with replacements is the age difference. A sedate, middle-aged guide is being replaced by a bouncy, energetic youngster; and its handler is perhaps 10 years older than he was when he got his previous dog. He may also have developed a few bad habits in handling his old dog which he has to overcome. His previous experience can be a great advantage in some ways, but it can also have its drawbacks.

Occasionally, old hands in a class can be a bit exasperating because they have done it all before and know just how it should be done this time. But far more often they are a help and comfort to the new students in the crises they are experiencing for the first time.

Apart from acquiring the skill to handle their dogs well, the students also learn how to care for them properly, with practical lessons in grooming and talks about diet, health and the temperamental and physical characteristics of dogs. Arrangements for free half-yearly veterinary check-ups are explained.

As the course draws to an end each student signs an agreement which transfers the ownership of the dog to him for a nominal 50p. No other charge is made, and in addition he is offered a generous allowance to help with feeding costs. The intention is that there should be no financial obstacle to anyone having a guide dog. If he needs help to provide fencing for a garden so that the dog cannot wander off, that too will be given. And if there are problems about accommodating a dog at work, employers will be offered a secure kennel and run in which it can be kept during the day.

The course finishes with a 'christening' party and the students depart for home. That is not the end of the matter, however. It is only, in Churchill's famous phrase, the end of the beginning. Within two or three days an instructor visits the new guide dog owner to go over regular routes and journeys with him. Advice is offered on how to tackle any difficult local crossings and any other problems are discussed. This immediate aftercare visit is now regarded as a vital part of the training process, an opportunity to ensure that the months of preparation can be

George Cole and Ula on the road from Land's End to John O'Groats in June 1985. The 69-year-old guide dog owner slept at night in a tent that he carried with other basic necessities on a specially-constructed trolley that he pulled behind him. Unfortunately he had to abandon the journey shortly before reaching his goal.

applied successfully in the circumstances of the individual's everyday life. And yet, as a regular routine, an essential final stage of the training, it is a relatively recent innovation: a product of the 1970s when people began to have more time for concerns other than the volume of production. Prior to this, post-class aftercare had been a rather intermittent activity, undertaken only when it was thought necessary, but under Derek Carver, who was director of training from 1974 to 1985, it was given greater emphasis, the immediate visit being followed by another six weeks later.

*   *   *

References to aftercare do not occur in annual training reports until 1951. 'Only one visit had to be made during the year', Liakhoff reported at that time, '... owing to geographical peculiarities of the town.' Three other units were called in for checks, which were made, Liakhoff explained, 'whenever a report is received (sometimes from the guide dog owner, sometimes from an onlooker) which questions the safety of the work.' The check lasted two or three days and determined whether any retraining was needed. 'In none of these three cases was any dangerous fault found to exist.'

One refresher course lasting four weeks was given to a pair whose work had deteriorated. The only other cases referred to as aftercare were three dogs withdrawn completely from work and two that were withdrawn and successfully re-used.

If a guide dog owner had a problem that he could not deal with himself he was expected to write for advice. The response was not always very helpful or sympathetic. One man who complained that his dog was dirty in the house, destructive, howled when left, stole food, dug up the garden and had killed the neighbour's cat was given little comfort. 'You wanted a dog,' he was told. 'Dogs do these things.'

John Weeks recalled that at first the need for an aftercare visit was regarded as something of a reproach. It was a black mark in the instructor's record that the training had not turned out as well as it should have done.

It is hardly surprising that aftercare was given such a low priority at the time. As the annual report for 1951 shows, there was a huge backlog of people waiting for a guide dog. At the beginning of October 1950 329 applicants had been accepted and were waiting. During the next 12 months only 24 were called for training (although 15 replacement dogs were also provided), but 63 more applicants were accepted. Allowing for 12 that withdrew for various reasons there was still a net increase of 27, giving a waiting list that, at the prevailing rate of training, would have taken 15 years to clear, even if no more applications had been accepted. The wonder of it is that more did not drop out faced with such a long

Bertie McConnell, who in March 1946 became the first guide dog owner in Northern Ireland, with his sixth dog Solyman in 1985. He was active in local and national politics, becoming Mayor of Bangor in 1976 and holding a seat in the Northern Ireland parliament from 1969 until 1972, when direct rule from Westminster was introduced. One day when the parliament building suffered a power failure McConnell and his guide dog led the deputy speaker and members out of the pitch-black chamber and thereafter he was able to claim that he had been leader of the house for a day.

wait, although it is clear that at times it was a major deterrent to applicants that was still having an effect in the early 1980s.

Liakhoff started what he called 'my plan of general aftercare for guide dog owners at home' after handing over control of the Leamington centre to Bibikoff on 1 January 1954. He was always accompanied on these aftercare visits either by his daughter, Abou, or by a member of the training staff, who acted as his chauffeur and assistant. He saw 39 people in the year to the end of September 1954 and 73 in the following 12 months. It was while touring Glamorgan on aftercare during February

1956 that he saw a guide dog owner in Cardiff with 'a collapsible white stick, now issued by the RNIB'. On complicated crossings the man took it from his pocket, extended it to its full length and gave 'the sign used by blind people who are not guide dog owners'.

'Mr Blackmore's use of the collapsible white stick is original', Liakhoff commented, 'and might be adopted with advantage by other guide dog owners on busy crossings where it is inconvenient to ask for assistance or (as in many cases) when guide dog owners resent asking'. A collapsible cane is, in fact, now offered to all students during their training and many make frequent use of it.

By the middle of 1956 Liakhoff's health was seriously affecting his work and for some months, until he left in January 1957, George Sheppard, who was deputy director of training as well as controller of the Exeter centre, took over the aftercare visits. Between July and December he visited 66 clients in Scotland, Ireland, the Liverpool area and the north of England, concluding in his final report that general aftercare was not only beneficial for the guide dog owners but also a further improvement of the training. Problems that had arisen with some of the dogs led him to recommend that all bitches should be neutered before they were given to their future blind owners: a practice that was adopted 18 months later.

The value of routine aftercare was by now generally acknowledged and visits became part of the duties of qualified training staff. Reviewing the training situation in February 1957, Liakhoff noted that 'two members of the training staff will be engaged on aftercare work for two or three weeks in each month.' The instructor or senior trainer finishing a class would have a rest and then go on aftercare work. 'If no instructor or trainer should be free . . . I am always available to fill the gap.'

The programme developed rapidly, the 1963 report recording visits to 769 guide dog owners that occupied 560 training days and involved travelling an estimated distance of 70,000 miles. 'The importance of this aspect of the work must be emphasised,' wrote Arthur Phillipson, who as chief controller submitted the report. By the end of the decade the number of visits had doubled and 10 years later had nearly doubled again: a reflection of the Association's growing prosperity and ability to devote increasing resources to activities complementary to the main aim of producing more guide dogs. During the 1980s the continuation of this comfortable financial position gave further impetus to the aftercare programme and by 1989 guide dog owners were being visited, on average, every 28 weeks – a total of about 7,300 annual visits. Further improvements in the service are planned, the target being three visits a year.

One of the benefits of frequent aftercare visits is that instructors can keep an eye on an ageing dog and plan its replacement. A guide dog's working life varies in length. Some carry on to a ripe old age, but most are

slowing down significantly by nine or ten. When a dog does retire, it usually stays on as a pet in the family, but if this is not possible there is never any difficulty finding another loving home for it.

One retired guide dog that could never quite reconcile himself to staying at home was Shep, a border collie that carried on working to a good age and lived until he was well over 16. Shep spent the first winter of his retirement by the fire but when spring came round he started getting restless. One day, when his owner had gone off to work as usual with his new guide, Shep disappeared from the garden where he had been let out for his mid-morning run. About an hour later he turned up at his master's workplace.

After that, he would take it into his head from time to time to follow his old routine, so he would head for the bus stop, sit at the front of the queue, jump on board and sit under the stairs until he got to the bus station. There, he would trot across to another bus for the final leg of the journey. He always knew which stop to get off at.

Many dogs have this ability to recognise a regular stop and some guide dog owners have used it to their advantage. One man who had a long journey on the London Underground taught his dog to bark for a biscuit one stop before the station at which he always got off. Thereafter, he was

Basil Parsons, a Kent farmer, with his guide dog Sally shortly before she retired in 1980 after eight years' work. For farm work he often found it more convenient to use the dog on a leash rather than with the conventional harness and rigid handle. (Farmers Weekly)

able to go to sleep knowing that his dog would never let him miss his destination.

*   *   *

The effectiveness of guide dogs in giving blind people more independence is now taken for granted. They have revolutionised thousands of lives. But when they first came on the scene their impact was, if anything, greater than it is now. They entered a world in which a blind person was given no formal mobility training of any kind, and although many individuals became very good at tapping their way about with a white walking stick, it was only the more enterprising and determined who developed the skill to any degree. To be trained in the use of a guide dog was to be given a passport into another world that was beyond the reach of most blind people.

The history of blind welfare is beyond the scope of this book, but it helps to put guide dogs in perspective when one reflects that in the 1930s blind people were generally not expected to live and work side-by-side with the sighted. The Blind Persons Act of 1920, important though it was in making local authorities responsible for keeping a register of the blind and for providing welfare services for them, included employment within the welfare framework. Over the next two decades the workshops, which provided just about the only hope of employment for most blind people, were greatly expanded and by the time of the Second World War there were more than 60 providing employment for about 4,500 blind workers in traditional crafts such as basket-making and upholstery. The few blind people to be found working in the sighted world were usually either typists or telephonists, who were largely newly-blind rather than con-genitally blind, or the lucky ones who had come from middle-class homes, received a decent education and joined one of the professions. As June Rose put it in her excellent survey of blind welfare in Britain, published in 1970, there was 'a meritocracy of top people – the graduates of Worcester and Chorleywood and the Royal Normal College – destined for good jobs in the professions, and the workshop blind – almost the write-offs who would remain, to a greater or lesser extent, dependent on charity all their lives.'

It would be wrong to claim that guide dogs made a significant impact on more than a few of these people's lives. In 1939 there were only 76 blind people using guide dogs. Nevertheless, their example must have encour-aged the aspirations of countless others and helped to build a bridge to the sighted world.

It was not only by dramatically improving mobility that a guide dog helped to bridge the gap between the two worlds. The blind were regarded – and still are very often – by the sighted with a mixture of

emotions ranging from embarrassment to sentimentality. Sighted people frequently avoid them, treat them condescendingly or find it difficult to talk to them. Use of the third person – 'Does he take sugar?' – is the classic example of this behaviour. Guide dogs have helped to remove these obstacles by providing openings for conversations and contacts that blind people on their own would never attract.

The biggest breakthrough in the barrier between the blind and the sighted worlds was brought about by the 1939–45 war, and it is perhaps some compensation for the slaughter and suffering of those terrible years that out of them there also came many beneficial changes in society. The acute manpower shortage led to the employment of hundreds of blind people in factories and offices, and sighted workers realised that their new colleagues were ordinary people like themselves who were just as capable as they were of doing many jobs.

In the post-war years a steadily-increasing number of blind people have found a place in the world outside of the sheltered environment of the

Michael and Jennifer Hall from Abergele in North Wales with their four children and two guide dogs in 1984, the year she won the Variety Club of Great Britain's 'Mother of the Year' award. (Syndication International)

workshops, helped by better education of those who lose their sight at birth or soon after and greater provision for the rehabilitation of the many who become blind later in life. Until 1939 St Dunstan's provided the only comprehensive rehabilitation facilities for the newly-blind, but they were, of course, available only to servicemen. Others were served by home teachers, who had been the focus of welfare for all blind people since the 19th century. As specialists in blind welfare, they were often very effective in catering for the needs of their clients and teaching them daily living skills, but job training was no part of their function.

The RNIB had already been considering the need for rehabilitation of the civilian blind when the Second World War broke out. The Institute's blind chairman, Captain Sir Beachcroft Towse VC, promptly offered his home at Goring-on-Thames as a rehabilitation centre. Two years later, in 1941, another centre for the civilian blind was opened in Torquay. At first it was primarily a convalescent home for blinded war casualties, but it later offered employment retraining as well as teaching daily living skills.

Two post-war developments that affected the course of blind welfare were the reorganisation of social work following the Younghusband and Seebohm reports of 1959 and 1968, respectively, and the introduction of the long cane technique to improve mobility. The changes introduced after the Seebohm report abolished the specialised home teachers for the blind and gave all qualified social workers a mixed caseload. Many blind people and members of voluntary societies or charities serving the blind deplore the change, which they see as an erosion of a valuable service. Whatever the gains may have been in other areas of social work there can be little doubt that local authority provision for blind welfare at present is very patchy and often leaves a great deal to be done by the voluntary agencies and charities.

The long cane is nothing like as effective as a guide dog as an aid to mobility, but it is a considerable improvement on the white stick and can be very useful to people who for one reason or another may not want or are not able to use a guide dog. It was developed in America during the Second World War for use by blinded veterans and adopted in Britain in the late 1960s following reports by Dr Alfred Leonard of Nottingham University and Walter Thornton, who was blind himself and had a special interest in mobility. Trials were also conducted by the RNIB and St Dunstan's. The Association became interested in the new technique and in 1971, after its offer of co-operation with the RNIB came to nothing, explored the possibility of introducing a scheme for long cane training at Forfar, where the productive capacity was not being fully used. However, the council decided that 'it was not considered advisable to proceed with this project at this juncture.'

The advantage of the long cane over the old white walking stick is that

the cane, which is actually made of aluminium alloy, warns the user of obstacles ahead. The walking stick can only be used to tap along a wall or pavement edge and therefore provides little or no help in avoiding hazards. The long cane, on the other hand, has a greater reach and is swung in a narrow arc just above the ground ahead of the user so that he has a warning of any obstacles in his path.

It takes time and expert tuition to become proficient in the use of the long cane. Once its superiority to the white stick had been established the National Mobility Centre was therefore created to train instructors, and local authorities began to employ mobility officers as members of their social work teams. However, some authorities have not fulfilled their responsibility for mobility as well as others, and parts of the country are poorly provided with teachers of the long cane technique.

Blind golfer Terry Wallace walks jubilantly down the fairway with friend and caddy Tony Middlebrook and guide dog Zeus after driving 127 yards for a hole-in-one at Pickett's Lock golf course in north London in September 1986. (The Observer)

Nowadays, use of the long cane is taught as part of an orientation and mobility package. With the development of the new device, it was recognised that users also needed to have a good spatial awareness: the ability to orient themselves accurately in relationship to their surroundings. It is an ability blind people have always needed, of course, and many of them developed it quite well for themselves or with the help of a home teacher. But orientation and mobility training develops it in a more organised way.

Many people who apply for guide dogs have already received this training. As a preparation for working with a guide dog its value was recognised as early as September 1972 when it was recorded by the general council that 60 students who had received prior orientation and mobility training had found guide dog training easier. Eight months later, after 50 more long cane graduates had proved themselves in guide dog training, the council recommended that there should be at least one trainer at each centre who had qualified in the long cane technique. It was another two years before anything was done about the proposal, but in July 1975 the new director of training, Derek Carver, proposed that a trial orientation and mobility officer should be installed at the Exeter centre. Early in 1976 one of their instructors was sent to the National Mobility Centre for a six-month course, but not long after completing it he left the Association. When a council member enquired in October 1978 whether the post had yet been filled he was told that staff could not be spared, and it was the late 1980s before the centres were able to offer orientation and mobility training to appropriate applicants.

Although there are many satisfied users of the long cane who have no wish to apply for a guide dog, those who have made the change are unanimous in proclaiming the superiority of their dogs as a mobility aid. Above all, they claim, the dog removes the constant stress which accompanies the use of the long cane.

At the end of 1989 there were some 4,000 working guide dogs in Britain and the number of users is still rising. Where the peak will occur is a matter of speculation that surveys have done little to resolve. Some say 5,000 is the limit, others think 6,000 is possible. Neither figure is a large proportion of the total blind population, but if one sets aside the elderly and those with other handicaps who would be unable to use a dog it becomes substantial in relation to the younger, more active members of the blind community. To them, however, the value of 'another pair of eyes' is quite simply immeasurable.

12

Which Way Forward?

The Association's first 30 years were punctuated with crises over funding, dog supply, premises and relationships between Liakhoff and his associates. Nevertheless, at the end of 1961 there were 738 working guide dogs in the country, the annual output of new dogs had reached 146 and the financial position was strong. The 30 years since 1961 have been spent getting more order into the enterprise, learning to manage it successfully and adapting to life as a large, fast-growing service with substantial assets but an unfulfilled potential.

Coming to terms with the expanding scale of operations was not easy for an organisation conditioned by years of penny-pinching struggle and by the whole ethos of charitable work to a cautious approach to new ideas and development. In the early 1960s the council began to reconcile itself to the success of the fund-raising operation. The 1961/2 financial year yielded an income of £180,000, while running costs, including depreciation, amounted to only £117,000. That left an excess of £63,000 which was transferred to the building reserve or general fund in the balance sheet. Legacies added another £105,000 to the reserves, so that by September 1962 the balance sheet stood at £784,000, of which £502,000 was investments. It was altogether a very satisfactory financial position that was not the product of a sudden windfall. For several years income had exceeded expenditure by a generous margin and the trend looked set to continue.

Some members of the council were clearly uncomfortable with the wealth that the Association was accumulating and their anxieties surfaced at a meeting of the finance and general purposes committee in March 1963. The time was approaching, Askew suggested, when the Association 'would have to consider whether it was justified in continuing to appeal for money, having regard to what it does at a relatively high cost, when a lot of other blind organisations are virtually scraping the barrel in order to maintain their assistance to the blind.' That the issue was raised by Askew, who was regarded as one of the ablest and wisest members of the council, suggests that this was no casual or passing concern.

As McLean pointed out, however, the Association's stance on appeals should be determined by the potential demand for guide dogs, and he urged that steps should be taken to find this out. Concern had been expressed for some time that demand was apparently falling, but the council had very little to go on in planning ahead. The long waiting lists of the early 1950s had been reduced by increased production, and possibly by disillusionment at the years of waiting between applying for and getting a dog, into a trickle of applications that was barely keeping pace with production, but no-one had any idea whether this was a temporary phenomenon or a signal that guide dog ownership was reaching a plateau.

Askew's anxieties and McLean's promptings led the council to propose a survey of home teachers, in the hope that it would throw some light on the likely demand for dogs in the future, and the Southern Regional Association for the Blind was asked to send out a questionnaire. That, however, appeared to be the end of the matter. Whatever result was obtained from the survey, there is no further reference to it in the council's minutes. Demand began to pick up again, perhaps as word got round that there was no longer a big queue for dogs, but also, no doubt, because the Association had started wooing the blind welfare societies in order to overcome the hostility towards guide dogs still found in some quarters. It is remarkable, for example, to find that in 1960 the head-master of Worcester College for the Blind considered guide dogs as an asset only to old people 'or those who for one reason or another cannot acquire the ability to move about by themselves'. Writing to the RNIB's secretary general regarding a forthcoming visit by the Association's general manager, he declared that while he did not mind Maton talking to the older boys informally, he did not want to lay on anything formal because that would appear to support his message, which he could not do.

'My job', he insisted, '. . . is to encourage the boys to aim at independence, realising that independence consists in the ability to go about by themselves, using, where sensible, a collapsible white stick.' Maton might well have made little headway against such strongly held views but he appeared to be pleased with his visit and even persuaded the headmaster to welcome the idea of a guide dog owner addressing the boys at the end of the term.

Askew's heart-searching about the justification for continued fund-raising had referred to 'the relatively high cost' of guide dogs, and towards the end of 1963 he returned to this issue. Opposing the appointment of a veterinary officer to provide advice on dog care and co-ordinate veterinary services, he expressed alarm at rising costs 'without any recommendation to effect economies'. The organisation, he believed, was becoming top heavy.

Another member of the council, R.W. Pilkington, also took up the cry. The appointment was a waste of money, he declared, and when the council decided, by a small majority, to proceed with it he promptly resigned, saying he could no longer lend his name to the continued increase in expenditure. In the event, the appointment lasted only a year, after which an arrangement was made for the training centres and their local vets to be supported with veterinary advice and services from the Animal Health Trust.

Pilkington and Askew were, of course, quite right to be concerned about costs, although they were bound to rise when it was no longer possible to continue running the Association on a shoestring and it became necessary to provide better conditions for students, staff and dogs, as well as higher standards of administration. The issue was whether costs were rising too fast and whether the more comfortable financial position was leading to extravagance.

Askew was also concerned that the figure of £250 which was given in the Association's literature as the cost of a guide dog was no longer accurate. In reality it was more than twice that figure, leaving aside all central overheads. The subsequent agonising over what should be included in the 'cost of a guide dog', and whether the figure should be used in publicity material, was the forerunner of many anguished discussions on this subject over the years. A high figure might discourage support, it was feared, but on the other hand it was not easy to agree on the basis for a lower figure.

The solution hit on early in 1964 – to set a 'target' figure for fund-raising purposes that did not claim to be the actual production cost – is one that has been employed ever since. It has the merit of providing the many groups or individuals who set out on fund-raising projects with a means of sponsoring a guide dog at a cost that seems attainable, without the Association constantly having to worry over the justification for a more precise figure. The original target figure of £250 to sponsor a guide dog has, of course, risen since 1964 and now stands at £1,000. There are also two subsidiary targets: £500, which sponsors the early training, and £250, which sponsors a puppy.

The difficulty over the 'cost of a guide dog' can be illustrated by reference to the published accounts for 1989. The total operating costs for that year were £15.6 million (£11.9 million if you remove fund-raising and general administrative costs) and 674 dogs were trained. A unit cost based on these figures, however, would be misleading because it would include the maintenance and aftercare of some 4,000 working guide dogs, as well as the cost of hundreds of breeding stock and puppies at walk. Trying to isolate the costs that apply only to the 674 new dogs leads to endless problems about which expenses are relevant and, as always, the figures can be juggled to produce a variety of results.

*   *   *

At the end of 1963, the Earl of Lanesborough, having led the Association for 11 years, declared his intention to retire, and at the AGM in May 1964 it was announced that he would be succeeded by Major General Sir John Kennedy. Sir John withdrew, however, when he learned that Lord Lanesborough had been elected to the non-executive post of president, a situation that he felt could produce a conflict of loyalties and responsibilities. Sir Joseph Napier was thereupon approached, but he too had some misgivings about the role and influence Lord Lanesborough might continue to have after his many years as chairman, and it was not until these were settled that he accepted.

In his new role Lord Lanesborough travelled tirelessly from one end of the country to the other, enthusiastically representing guide dogs at fund-raising events and branch functions. With his genial personality and easy manner he was a popular ambassador for guide dogs for over 20 years, and there was widespread sorrow when he decided to retire from the presidency in 1986.

The new chairman had a commercial and financial background which he promptly put to good use. He was a strong leader and lost no time in reviewing policy and improving the administration and management. Among the major achievements of his 10 years as chairman were the establishment of better conditions of employment for staff and a clear definition of the separate roles of council and management. One of his first acts, however, was to identify eight matters that called for attention and to set these down in a memorandum with proposals for action. Production planning, the financial position and strengthening the management were at the top of the list, together with a re-structuring of the finance and general purposes committee to make it more effective and put him at its head.

As no policy had yet been agreed by the council to deal with the continuing excess of income over expenditure Sir Joseph asked a special sub-committee, chaired by Askew, to consider the matter. Nine months later, in July 1965, they came up with the hardly startling pronouncement that revenue considerably exceeded costs, even after capitalisation of legacies. They were therefore asked to consider whether there should be any expansion in the Association's services to the blind, and to look into appeals and fund-raising activities. Meanwhile, 'the appeals effort will continue but will not be increased.'

There was only one further report from the appeals sub-committee. In January 1966 Askew told the council that he had advised area fund-raising organisers to discontinue any activities that could be interpreted as unnecessary competition with local blind welfare charities. He was also exploring giving greater assistance to guide dog owners in order to make possession of a dog more attractive. Thereafter, the record is silent, and in May 1967 ill-health forced Askew to resign from the council.

It is clear, from correspondence with the Association's lawyers, Joynson-Hicks, that additional ways of helping guide dog owners were being examined during 1966, in particular by the establishment of a welfare or social service department that would help with holidays, medical fees and grants during convalescence from illness, to widowed guide dog owners and in other cases where hardship existed. Enthusiasm for the idea was limited, however, and it got no further, although a proposal for a holiday and aftercare centre was seriously studied, and rejected, during 1968.

Despite the new chairman's good intentions when he assumed office in 1964, no inspired solution to the financial dilemma was forthcoming. Instead, it was decided 'to continue fund-raising until such time as our reserves are such that we could almost run our affairs on the income from this fund'.

Paul McConnell, the general manager, gave this rather inelegant definition of current appeals policy in a report to the council on 23 January 1967, and it has remained the basis of fund-raising ever since. The prospect of funding the Association entirely from reserves is still distant, however. In 1989 investment income provided only 43 per cent of the funds needed to run the Association, and although this percentage could well increase if substantial legacies and a rising stock market continue to boost the value of the portfolio, the time when it could provide *all* the funds needed is very far off. The Association is still growing, it needs a rising income to support its services to the blind and it will continue to depend on its fund-raisers and appeals staff for the foreseeable future.

During the 1960s the Association had five general managers. The decade opened with Charles Maton in the post and when he died suddenly in April 1961 there followed an unusual arrangement under which, for some months, the Earl of Lanesborough acted as general manager as well as chairman of the council. This ended when Sir Michael Nall, who was taken on as general secretary in November 1961, became general manager in the middle of 1962, but he moved on to a job in the City of London in 1964.

Paul McConnell, who as secretary had been waiting hopefully in the wings since December 1959, then took over the post, but he resigned in 1967 and Dick Forrester, a member of the council for some years, stepped into the breach. He saw out the decade, but only just, stepping aside, in 1972, to allow the chairman to make another appointment.

Despite this rapid succession of general managers the decade was remarkably successful and productive for the Association. Progress was made, a little unsteadily at times, on dog supply, training methods and aftercare. Furthermore, the Association slowly began to think and behave in a more businesslike way. It had acquired an income, a productive capacity, assets and responsibilities comparable to a small or medium-size business and was gradually learning to manage its affairs more professionally.

The training scene was transformed by the opening of new centres at Bolton in 1961 and Forfar in 1965. Leamington was also given a complete facelift, so that by the mid-60s productive capacity was well able to meet any immediate increase in demand. In fact, production rose by 51 per cent between 1965 and 1970, despite disruption and staff losses caused by the Tucker affair in 1966. The biggest jump occurred in 1969 when output went up from 224 to 273.

Similar improvements occurred in aftercare and dog supply, and the decade closed with Tollgate House about to open as a permanent base from which to expand the breeding and puppy-walking programmes.

A welcome feature of the closing months of the decade was that for the first time in years the training staff was at full strength. This may have been due, in part, to the introduction in 1965 of a new salary structure which, three years later, was linked to the Burnham scale for teachers. But it is more likely to have been a chance occurrence because it was not long before staff shortages were again causing problems.

The loss of skilled instructors has plagued the Association throughout its history. Low pay may at one time have contributed to the wastage, but it has not been the only factor. Guide dog work may seem attractive in decent weather, but it can lose its appeal when it has to be kept up throughout the winter, no matter what the conditions. Some people drop out because they are less good at training blind people than dogs – although it happens the other way round, too. Others leave because they get more attractive offers of employment and a number of training staff have been tempted into accepting jobs in guide dog schools elsewhere in the world.

It is also possible that the qualities needed by a good instructor easily lead to discontent. He works on his own much of the time, basing his response to the dogs and blind people in his care on his own judgment and experience. Moulding personalities like this into a team is not always successful.

Keeping the turnover of instructors to a tolerable level clearly depends on selecting as apprentices people who are most likely to be suited to the work. Staff selection is notoriously difficult, particularly when it depends on little more than the gut feeling of unskilled interviewers, and in the 1960s and later the Association was no better at it than most other employers. Not surprisingly, therefore, it has had its share of misfits, and staff shortages have reappeared from time to time. It is not a problem that can be solved quickly by going out and hiring replacements 'off the shelf', because there is no shelf. The only guide dog schools in Britain are run by the Association and it therefore has to train all its own instructors, which entails a three-year apprenticeship.

During the 1980s a more professional approach to the recruitment of training staff has been developed. Applicants for apprenticeship are now invited in a group to spend two and a half days on special assessment courses at one of the training centres. This allows them to handle dogs, go through various exercises to test their aptitude for the work and get a feel of the job. It tells recruitment staff a good deal more about the applicants than they would learn from interviews alone, and the result has been a considerable improvement in the quality and performance of apprentices.

The successful candidates are now given far better job training than their predecessors ever had. Immediately after the war and for another 30 years new boys picked up what they could from qualified staff and learnt the rest by experience. It was a haphazard process that was no doubt hard at times on dogs and blind students. Some improvements occurred in later years but it was not until the 1980s that a staff training department was formed which developed the structured programme that exists today.

During the 1950s and '60s no women were recruited as instructors, although many were engaged in more junior positions as training assistants and kennel staff. By the early 1970s, however, necessity prompted a reappraisal of this policy. 'In view of the very poor response to our advertisements for apprentices, would it be worth considering taking on women?' enquired one council member of the director general in October 1972. 'I know the drawbacks and objections', she continued, 'but it might be worth a try.' She also questioned whether it was 'really necessary or desirable to dismiss our female staff automatically just because they are rash enough to get married.'

In fact, a female training assistant had been transferred to an apprenticeship in 1970, but this was an isolated occurrence. She qualified as an instructor in 1973 and left two years later after getting married. In 1975, the year Parliament passed the Sex Discrimination Act, three of the seven apprentices engaged were women and as the '70s advanced women were taken on in increasing numbers. The council had, perhaps, overlooked the new legislation when, in June 1978, it noted that the 'enforced engagement of a proportion of female apprentices' was due to the difficulty of recruiting male mobility instructors, but by then there was, of course, no going back.

*   *   *

In 1969 Sir Joseph Napier decreed that new members elected to the general council should either have business experience or a wide knowledge of dogs, thus giving the Association less of the Lady Bountiful image of charitable work and encouraging a more professional outlook. He also issued, in 1972, a memorandum in which the roles of council and staff were clearly defined.

'The overall responsibility for the day-to-day management and conduct of the affairs of the Association rests on the general manager and the staff under him,' he asserted. He reminded council members that they met only six times a year and that their sub-committees on special subjects were there to help or advise management, not to usurp management's authority in any way.

The proclamation of this sound principle did not immediately transform the Association's administration. Old habits die hard, and personalities have more influence than declarations of principle. Sir Joseph's attempt to distinguish clearly between the roles of council and management coincided with the appointment of a new general manager, Tony Clark, who achieved a great deal during his 10 years as chief executive, but it needed a more ruthless personality than his to wrench power from the hands of assertive, and in some cases, titled, council members who had been dominating affairs for many years. He ushered in a long period of steady growth and sound management, and inspired great respect and affection, but he had less authority than Sir Joseph intended when he followed up his 1972 statement by changing the general manager's title to director general in 1974.

Despite a further re-statement of responsibilities by Sir Joseph's successor, Ken Butler, who declared in 1977 that little move had been made to give the additional powers normally associated with the title of director general, the council continued to dabble in day-to-day business and Butler returned to the subject again in 1979. Pointing to 'an experienced professional team of executives which includes the director general, secretary, directors of training and appeals, chief accountant and public relations officer', he told the council they should 'allow management greater licence to act...' There had been occasions, regrettably, when 'management's competence had been brought into question by the serious doubts expressed on their proposals', and this had led to the inhibiting of initiative. He suggested that greater confidence should be placed in management's ability to manage.

The council still yielded little ground and it was not until a more pugnacious man took on the top management job in 1983 that the issue was more clearly resolved.

*   *   *

The appeal of the dog, which had been recognised with a degree of apprehension in some parts of the NIB as far back as the early 1930s, had by 1972 produced such a 'satisfactory financial position', as the flourishing income was modestly called in the council minutes, that it was decided to offer all guide dog owners an allowance to help with the cost of feeding their guides. In the same year a standard, nominal contribution of 50p towards the cost of the dog was introduced to replace the open-ended, voluntary contribution that had previously applied, although some people still choose to give more than the nominal sum.

The appeal of the dog would have yielded little, however, without the efforts of many thousands of voluntary supporters, most of them working together with energy and goodwill through hundreds of fund-raising branches. It was these dedicated enthusiasts who gave the Association its financial security. They have made it independent of special appeals,

Mrs Phyllis Pask of Leeds had sponsored 56 guide dogs, each one acknowledged with a framed photograph, when this picture was taken in 1985. Her enthusiasm is typical of the hundreds of supporters who have organised fetes, sponsored events, flag days and countless other activities in order to fund the Association's work. (Yorkshire Post Studios)

Richard Spencer and Tina Saxby were among the many children at Mistley Norman primary school in Colchester who collected 1,440 end labels from packets of toilet tissue for the £100,000 Andrex appeal in 1982. Other businesses that have organised marketing promotions such as this include Pedigree Petfoods, who also make special arrangements for supplying guide dog owners with dog food at special rates. (Essex County Newspapers)

marketing promotions and high-profile events, which give unpredictable returns, and ensured the dependable income on which long-term commitments to blind people can be made with confidence. Their story is one of fetes, sponsored events, milk bottle tops, flag days and individual enterprise on a vast scale. There are now over 400 branches, many with long histories, backed up by a network of regional appeals managers who are constantly on the look-out for opportunities to create more branches and strengthen the support in new areas.

The achievements of these supporters are recorded in thousands of

When this public house in Southampton was reopened in February 1984 it was named The Guide Dog *in memory of its former tenant. Between 1967 and her death in 1981 Mrs Marjorie Beckett raised nearly £18,000 for the Association in the small pub that was then known as The Valley Inn. Many other public houses, and many breweries, support guide dogs generously.* (Southern Newspapers)

column inches in local newspapers, and in the pages of the Association's own journal, *Forward*. The annual accounts also bear testimony to their success. In 1989 £8.4 million came largely from the voluntary branches. In the same year £14.3 million was received in legacies. Who knows what inspired these generous bequests – the dogs mostly, no doubt – but branch activity must have encouraged much of it as well.

In the end, of course, the best testament to the branches lies in the whole edifice that ample funding has made possible: some 4,000 working guide dogs, a strikingly successful breeding and puppy-walking

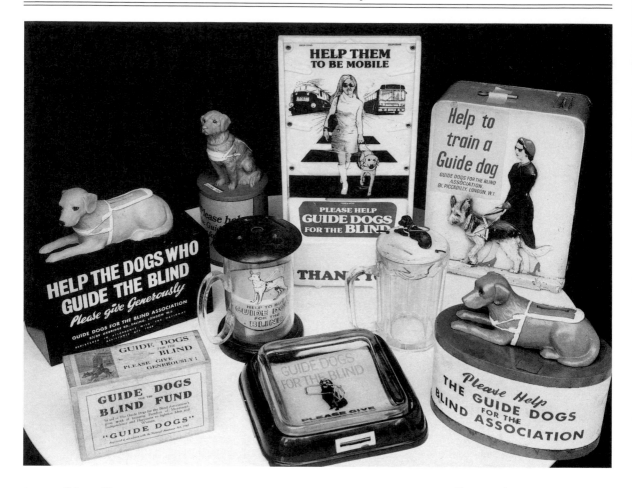

Some of the collecting devices that have been used over the years. It is difficult to establish the dates when they were first used, but the earliest in this group were certainly in use during the 1940s.

programme, training centres turning out annually nearly 700 new dogs, comprehensive aftercare and, more recently, other complementary services to help blind people. It would take another book to do justice to all the fund-raising efforts, and picking out a few examples from the thousands that deserve recognition is inadequate. But some reference must be made to *Blue Peter*, the long-running BBC children's television programme that has introduced guide dogs to hundreds of thousands of young people.

The Association's connection with the programme started in March 1965, when Derek Freeman, the breeding and puppy-walking manager, appeared on the show with a seven-week-old yellow labrador puppy named Honey. She was the first puppy to be 'adopted' by the programme team and followed throughout its puppy-walking by *Blue Peter's* young viewers. Freeman's regular appearances and expert comments not only showed the children how a puppy is raised but also told them (and their parents) more about guide dogs than they would ever have learned otherwise. Apart from the educational and publicity value of the strong

link that was built up and maintained over many years, there were other more tangible benefits. The Three B's Appeal (buttons, badges and buckles) run by the programme during 1974 and '75 raised over £40,000 for the Association. Appearances on the programme also enabled Freeman to appeal for puppy-walkers at times when he needed them.

Four years after the Three B's appeal and the rearing of Buttons, a puppy named after the appeal, Freeman was asked by Biddy Baxter, then the programme's producer, if he would find them a golden retriever to become their permanent dog. He had just picked a puppy from a good litter to place with one of his walkers, so he went back to the breeder for another. This was Goldie, who was mated twice with a stud dog from Tollgate and produced litters that, naturally, featured on the programme. From the first litter of four in 1981, two became guide dogs. Goldie was only rehearsing on that occasion, however. In 1986 she had a fine litter of eight pups, of which six qualified as guide dogs and one became a stud dog. The eighth, Bonnie, kept up the family connection by becoming the *Blue Peter* dog.

Simon Groom and Derek Freeman in the BBC TV Blue Peter studio with Goldie after she had had her first litter of five puppies. This and a subsequent litter were born in the home of Diana Wyndham-Smith, who is one of the most experienced of about 200 highly-valued supporters who keep the Association's brood bitches as pets in their homes.

Blue Peter, *BBC television's popular children's programme, has introduced tens of thousands of young people to guide dogs and supported the Association's work over many years. Here, at the opening of the Wokingham centre in 1977, Princess Alexandra unveils a plaque acknowledging the programme's 3Bs appeal (buttons, badges and buckles) which raised over £40,000.*

*   *   *

In 1971, with replacements rising as a proportion of total output, and *new* demand apparently stable, the general manager and the council concluded that there was little likelihood of any great increase in demand or production in the future without a change of policy. Some progress had been made in training older or more difficult students, but, as the council observed, 'the very large market among the elderly blind remains largely untapped'. They recommended closer liaison with local authorities to stimulate demand generally.

One member of the council who urged positive action was Ted Harte, chairman of the building committee. His review of the available evidence convinced him that there was a pool of potential guide dog users sufficiently large to require another training centre, which should be built

as soon as possible because 'we have an obligation to provide guide dogs for all who can make use of them'.

Part of Harte's evidence was the increasing interest and activity being taken by local authorities in the provision of social services. He had also been talking to controllers of the training centres. One was 'in touch with local home teachers, but not actively so.' Another had no active liaison but 'suspects he would be flooded with applications if he weren't careful.' A third was 'terrified' of any suggestion of a new centre, which 'couldn't possibly be staffed'.

Despite these reservations, the general manager was asked to explore the need for a new centre and in March 1972 provisional approval was given to look for a site. Folly Court outside Wokingham was found later in the year, but the negotiations were protracted and it was another two

Princess Alexandra with guests at the opening of the Middlesbrough centre on 4 May 1983.

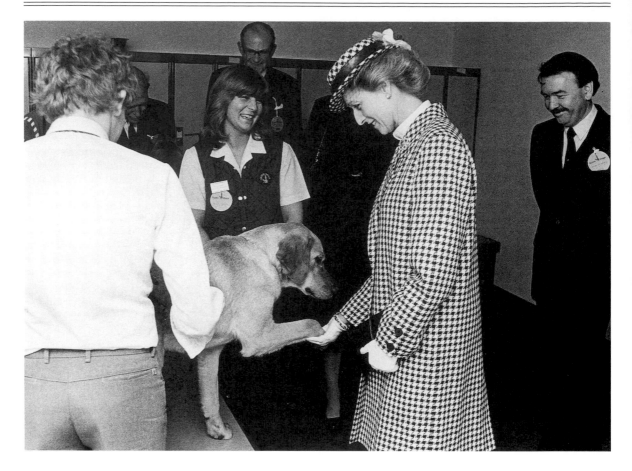

Guide dog Warren extends a welcoming paw during Princess Alexandra's tour of the new training centre at Redbridge, in north-east London, which she officially opened on 7 May 1986. The amused onlooker is deputy kennel manager Ali Firbank. Regional controller Brian Humphreys is on the right.

years before an offer of £100,000 was accepted. Demand was now booming again and although the existing centres raised their output by over one-third in the early 1970s, by the time the Wokingham centre was officially opened by the Association's patron, Princess Alexandra, in May 1977 the waiting time for a guide dog had risen to well over 12 months.

The applications continued to pour in, however, and the loss of an unusually large number of experienced training staff in 1978/9 added to the difficulties. Three years after the opening of the fifth centre, annual production had risen only 15 per cent, from 395 to 457. In 1981, despite a welcome 16 per cent increase in output during the year, new applicants were having to wait 18 months for a guide dog.

The strength of demand in the late 1970s was such that no sooner was Wokingham opened than there was talk of new centres on the north-eastern fringe of London and in the Tyne/Tees area. The latter became a reality in Middlesbrough in 1983, and a London centre serving parts of the capital and East Anglia opened at Redbridge in 1986.

*   *   *

In 1975 Sir Joseph Napier, who was then 80, was succeeded as chairman by Ken Butler, a retired businessman and member of the Kennel Club. Soon after he took over, the secretary, David Greenwood, was taken ill and died later in the year.

During this period an extra burden fell on Tony Clark, the director general, who himself fell ill in November. He made a good recovery, but was advised to reduce his working hours and avoid stress. It was advice that he found difficult to follow, and the long hours that he put in at his desk and travelling to visit centres or attend functions must have contributed to his subsequent illness and stroke in September 1982, which forced him to retire.

One of Butler's first acts as chairman was to set up a liaison committee as a forum in which representatives of the National Federation of the Blind, the Circle of Guide Dog Owners and the Scottish Association of Guide Dog Owners could meet and discuss issues with the chairman and management of the Association. The new committee was a response to requests going back many years from the National Federation of the Blind for representation on the general council. These requests had always been resisted, largely on the grounds that the presence of representatives of a lobby on the council would change its character and inhibit its debates.

There was no objection to the election of blind people as such. Captain Deane, who was blind, was a NIB representative on the council for many years and chairman in the late 1940s. A blind man, J.M.O. Barstow, was elected in 1968 and there are currently two blind members. But the council was not prepared to take in nominees of pressure groups. The liaison committee did not entirely satisfy the Federation, which has continued from time to time to press for representation on the council, but it has met regularly since 1975 and serves as a useful channel of communication.

Another of the new chairman's early concerns was to ensure that there was adequate consultation and communication with staff, of whom there were now over 300 in seven different locations. He therefore encouraged the establishment of a staff consultative committee, which met for the first time in November 1978 and has continued to do so at regular intervals since.

Like his predecessor, Ken Butler strove for a clear distinction between the roles of management and council, and he reminded the latter in 1977 and again in 1979 that its proper function was to give 'broad direction'. On this issue change was slow to occur, but he was more successful with another long overdue reform. Worried by the age of some council members, he asked Lady Freda Valentine, who was then over 80, to hand over the treasurership that she had held for nearly 39 years to a younger person; and Ted Harte, who was nearing 80, to relinquish the chair of the building committee. Believing firmly that people should not hang on too long, in 1980 he persuaded his colleagues that there should be an upper age limit of 75 for members of council and of 70 for its chairman, a decision endorsed at the AGM in 1982. Butler himself reached 70 in 1980 and retired at the end of that year.

Within two years of Ken Butler's retirement Tony Clark suffered the stroke that effectively ended his fruitful term as director general, although it was nearly 12 months before his successor took over at the beginning of August 1983. It also ended a decade of which he could be proud. Output had nearly doubled, aftercare visits had risen by 150 per cent and there were 1,200 more guide dog owners in 1982 than 10 years earlier. Branch income was up fivefold, a remarkable record even allowing for the high inflation that occurred during part of that time. The Wokingham and Middlesbrough centres were built during his time and a site had been found in north-east London for a seventh centre.

The period was not without frustrations and problems, notably the big loss of skilled training staff at the end of the 1970s, but their occurrence makes the achievements all the greater. Tony Clark was a generous, compassionate and kindly man, as well as being an able director general, and his death in January 1990 saddened his many former colleagues and friends.

During 1981 the Association celebrated its golden jubilee and it was fitting that the occasion should occur during the years as chief executive of a man who had held the post for longer than anyone else. The outstanding event of the year's celebrations was a Thanksgiving Service in Westminster Abbey, followed by a parade down Birdcage Walk to the Royal Mews, where the Association's patron, Princess Alexandra, joined guide dog owners, supporters and staff at tea. The service, on 18 July, was an historic occasion in every sense of the phrase. Over 600 guide dogs and their owners were present in the congregation: a moving sight and a remarkable demonstration of the dogs' qualities. Throughout the service the dogs sat quietly beside their owners, ignoring trumpet fanfares, the roar of the organ and 2,000 voices raised in song. There were, perhaps, half a dozen isolated barks; otherwise their only sounds were the occasional yawn and the tinkling of chain leads when the dogs moved.

The parade that followed the service was equally stirring. All 2,000 of the congregation, including dogs, together with people who could not get into the packed Abbey, formed a huge column stretching across and down Birdcage Walk, and marched behind the band of the Irish Guards to the Royal Mews for tea. It was a memorable celebration of half a century of British guide dogs and of the independence they have brought to tens of thousands of blind people.

*   *   *

When the Association celebrated its 50th anniversary it could, with some justification, have paraphrased Dr Johnson and claimed that it knew very well what it was doing, and how to do it, and was doing it very well. Not that it was complacent. But the council and management had a clear vision of their role in blind welfare and pursued it with the confidence born of long experience and financial security. Things might have continued in this way had not Tony Clark's enforced retirement brought on to the scene a man who was suspicious of long-established ways and quickly bored by routine.

Major-General John Groom took over as director general at the beginning of August 1983, on retiring from the army. He immediately made it clear that he regarded the organisation as moribund and embarked with abrasive zeal on a thorough shake-up. Groom may not have been the most popular occupant of the director general's chair, but he brought about a valuable reorganisation of the management and opened up areas of activity that have already become useful features of the Association's work. The programme was launched in 1984 with a number of re-structuring measures, the most far-reaching of which was to decentralise authority to some extent by creating seven regions, based on the training centres, each headed by a regional controller. Appeals offices, which had sprung up over the years wherever it was convenient, were found accommodation at the centres, thus creating seven regional headquarters for the Association's activities.

At the same time an extra tier of management was created at the head office by the appointment of two new directors, one to head an 'operations' group of departments, the other to look after administration. Nick Walters arrived as director of operations in April 1984 and Julian Oxley as administration director in July. This division of responsibilities was not entirely satisfactory and Nick Walters's large portfolio was split at the beginning of 1987. Brian Moody came in from running the Midlands region to take over responsibility for all training, breeding and puppy-walking, with the title of director of operations, and Walters became director of publicity, fund-raising and special projects.

John Groom's early moves to strengthen the management and to assert his authority as director general were necessary and important developments. So, too, were changes which resulted in an improved salary structure and a better career path for those wishing to pursue it. Recruitment of apprentices was stepped up, partly to replace training staff lost from the production line in the reorganisation or moved to other activities, and partly to man new training centres that were in the pipeline. By 1989 a regular annual intake of 25 apprentices had been established and their three-year training was being organised with professional polish. Other staff training, particularly programmes associated with management development, was also being developed.

Groom took the view that previous inhibitions about making vigorous appeals for funds were misplaced and stepped up PR support for the fund-raising effort. As part of an effort to 'raise the profile' and give the public a better appreciation of the Association's work, training staff were often sent to man exhibition stands with trainee guide dogs. The advertising budget was increased and an annual Guide Dog Week was introduced, backed by special posters and leaflets, strong regional advertising and a postal franking campaign. The Association's journal *Forward* was given a face-lift and other publicity programmes were strengthened. A marketing manager was taken on, primarily to develop the trading company, and a drive to increase the number of fund-raising branches was started. There were already 304 in 1983, 40 more than three years before, and over the next two years 100 new branches were formed. Thereafter growth flattened out but the anticipated rise in income started to come through. Legacies continued to rise and in 1989 amounted to over £14 million.

The introduction of new structures and priorities was not achieved without short-term sacrifices in production. After reaching a peak of 645 in 1985, output of guide dogs declined in the next three years and was only 597 in 1988. However, it recovered to reach a new peak of 674 in 1989. Aftercare was another victim of the changes, although in 1988 the number of visits was nearly back to the 1985 level of 7,000 and in 1989 reached 7,300.

Output was also sacrificed for the long-term benefit of having guide dog instructors with an additional qualification in long cane techniques. The value to prospective guide dog owners of orientation and mobility training had, of course, been recognised during the 1970s, although moves to provide instruction in these skills at that time were frustrated by staff problems and the pressure of demand for guide dogs. In 1984, however, the Association began sending its training staff to the National Mobility Centre to become additionally qualified as O & M instructors. The justification for the move was only in part to allow long cane training to be offered to applicants and to guide dog owners who, for perhaps health or social reasons, were no longer able to use a guide dog. There was also the expectation, which turned out to be well-founded, that staff would gain a greater understanding of blindness and the mobility needs of blind people.

Although the Association's interest in orientation and mobility goes back some years there is little doubt that the recent revival of activity in this area has been encouraged by the failure of some local authorities to fulfil their statutory obligation to provide adequate mobility training. Financial constraints and the reorganisation of social services have led to a shortage of mobility officers in the community and there is little prospect that the situation will improve much in the foreseeable future. The trend is now for local authorities to employ rehabilitation officers who can teach mobility as well as daily living skills, their training being provided by the three agencies that have traditionally run courses for mobility officers – the National Mobility Centre and the Southern and Northern Regional Associations for the Blind. The Guide Dogs for the Blind Association began in 1990 to complement the work of these agencies by opening its own school to train a small number of orientation and mobility officers.

The broadening of the Association's horizons soon led to other developments. Better contact with local authorities, voluntary associations and potential guide dog owners was needed, and so during 1989 regional controllers began recruiting liaison teams, each headed by a qualified social worker and staffed by up to three mobility officers and a guide dog owner to improve the counselling and help offered to applicants. Other aspects of the broader outlook taken by the Association during the latter part of the 1980s can be seen in the provision of a number of services and facilities outside of the mobility field: a few units of sheltered housing for elderly guide dog owners; a holiday centre where owners know their dogs will be welcome and well cared for; and an adventure group. The Association is also sponsoring a number of research projects, mainly in the veterinary and ophthalmic fields.

None of this new work implies any reduction in the provision of guide dogs. It is no more than a recognition that there are now the resources to pay some attention to the long-neglected passage in the memorandum which specifies that one of the purposes for which the Association exists is to provide 'other services and facilities' to help blind people. In fact, the resources devoted to these additional services is a very small proportion of the funds allocated to guide dog training, a situation that is unlikely to change much in the near future. But even these relatively small sums, applied in fields that have not attracted funds from elsewhere, could make a major contribution to blind welfare. Ophthalmic research, for example, is expected to advance significantly as a result of the Association's funding.

Output of guide dogs may have marked time for a few years in the latter part of the 1980s while advances were taking place on other fronts, but there was no halt to the investment in training centres that had been going on for some years. With a seventh regional centre emerging at Redbridge, in north-east London, during 1984 it was felt that there were now enough major training schools covering the country. But that still left many existing or potential guide dog owners a good distance from a centre. It was therefore decided that future expansion would take the form of very much smaller establishments which would draw trained dogs from one of the major units and offer a more local service, training no more than two or three people at a time, sometimes at home, and bringing the aftercare service closer to the client. The first of the new mini-centres opened in Belfast at the end of 1984, since when others have opened in Cardiff, Maidstone and Glasgow. Development of this type of centre will almost certainly continue.

There has also been a huge modernisation programme at all the older centres in recent years, resulting in much improved facilities for clients and dogs in training. One establishment that remained relatively unchanged was the office at Park Street in Windsor to which the headquarters moved from Ealing in 1978; but by the end of the '80s it had been stretched to its limit and in 1989 Hillfields, a large Victorian house in the country near Reading, was bought to convert into a new headquarters and staff training school. The move from Windsor is expected to take place at the end of 1991.

The developments of the 1980s have inevitably resulted in a big increase in staff and running costs. At the end of 1989 the Association employed the full-time equivalent of 635 staff, compared with 403 in 1983. Expenditure for 1990 was expected to be nearly 80 per cent higher than the 1988 figure, which meant that for the first time in about 40 years it would not greatly exceed income (including legacies). The days of large surpluses of income over expenditure are therefore over, at least in the short to medium term. No-one is banking on a continuing boom in legacies, much of which has been accounted for by the huge rise in property prices in recent years. Equally, no-one is anticipating another burst of activity to equal the middle and late '80s.

The re-structuring and strengthening of the management that was one of Groom's early actions paved the way for a formal reappraisal of the role of the council. Its concern with day-to-day matters had been much reduced after 1983 and this was followed by a reorganisation of its sub-committees. It is now a more 'senatorial' body than before with a membership of 20 drawn from 'the great and the good' (former Government minister Lord Jenkin and chairman of the Stock Exchange Andrew Hugh Smith), the City, the law, the veterinary profession, dog breeding, ophthalmology, architecture and blind welfare, together with the chairman of the Scottish Committee and two guide dog owners elected in their own right and not as representatives of organisations for the blind. After Kenneth Butler's retirement in1981 the chairmanship was taken over by Ian Findlay, a former chairman of Lloyds of London. His successor in1987 was Colin Macpherson, a senior partner in Smith & Williamson Securities, who had been a member of the council since 1964, vice-chairman since 1975 and chairman of the investment committee for many years. Sadly, he died of cancer only eight months after taking office. His place was then taken by the current chairman, Dennis Armstrong, who had previously been vice-chairman and hon. treasurer and also has a City background.

By 1989 John Groom had been director general for six years. During that time he poured out a bewildering assortment of challenges, exhortations and impulsive ideas that often confused and exasperated the Association's staff. He could be extremely charming and persuasive when he chose, and in moments of relaxation was as genial a companion as you could wish for, but his restless mind and mercurial temperament were unsettling, and people never knew quite where they stood with him. He trod more carefully with members of the council, but some of them grew increasingly concerned about his style and in late 1988 they declined his offer to carry on beyond his normal retirement age. He was succeeded in 1989 by Julian Oxley, who had been director of administration since July 1984.

The challenge that the Association faces in the 1990s is to live up to the expectations that it has now generated by the growth of its work and the widening of its horizons. Greater emphasis is already being given to ensuring that all centres work to a common standard of excellence in training guide dogs, and there are ambitious targets for the aftercare service. If, sometime between now and the turn of the century, the increase in guide dog ownership should slow down or reach a plateau, the Association will still have a huge long-term commitment. Young people being trained with their first guide dog in 1991 may well be returning for their seventh or eighth dog in 50 years' time, and there is little prospect, unfortunately, that medical science will overcome all the causes of blindness. The Association's fund-raisers have always been successful in providing it with financial security and there is no reason why this should not continue, despite the very much larger commitments that there are now. There is every likelihood, therefore, that the Association will be playing as important a part in blind welfare in the years ahead as it is today.

*   *   *

When the first British guide dogs were trained in Wallasey 60 years ago it was with the help of a generous American woman and the staff of her schools in Switzerland and the United States. Now, it is to Britain that emerging guide dog movements in many countries look for help. There is widespread recognition of the high standards achieved by the British breeding, puppy-walking and training programmes and the numerous requests for advice or support have been responded to as generously as possible. In some cases breeding stock or puppies have been provided, in others experienced training staff seconded while local expertise is acquired. The outstanding example of aid to another country is the commitment that was undertaken in the late 1980s to train Spanish apprentices at the Association's training centres for a guide dog school being built in Madrid. By the middle of 1991 nine instructors will have completed the two-and-a-half-year apprenticeship. Five other Spaniards have already completed a 10-month course to become trainers.

There are now guide dog schools in over two dozen countries around the world. Most are small and many of recent origin, although organisations such as The Seeing Eye have a long history and a substantial output. Even The Seeing Eye, however, has not grown to the size of the British Association, and in the United States there are more than a dozen separate guide dog schools covering the country. There are arguments for and against large organisations, but one indisputable advantage that the British Association has derived from its size is a breeding and puppy-walking programme that would be nothing like as effective on a smaller scale. Without a substantial breeding stock it is not possible to provide a variety of physical and temperamental characteristics to match the needs of a wide range of clients.

A natural outcome of the growth of guide dog movements around the world has been the emergence of a forum in which ideas can be exchanged. International guide dog conferences were held in France in 1973, Britain in 1976, Austria in 1983 and Britain again in 1986 and 1988. As a result of this continuing interest in international co-operation The International Federation of Guide Dog Schools for the Blind has now been formed, with five specialist committees and a set of general guidelines for the conduct of guide dog work.

It is a measure of its standing in the world that The Guide Dogs for the Blind Association has played a leading part in helping overseas schools and setting up an international body. But it is on the domestic scene that it will continue to make its most important contribution. No-one who knows the organisation and the commitment of its staff can doubt that it will go on to extend its reach in blind mobility and welfare and to achieve even higher standards in providing the blind with 'another pair of eyes'.

Chronology

1916 .... Start of the modern guide dog movement in Germany.

1927 .... Mrs Dorothy Eustis impressed by visit to guide dog school in Potsdam and describes the work in the American magazine *Saturday Evening Post*.

1928 .... Morris Frank persuades Mrs Eustis to train a guide dog for him at her Swiss kennels and returns to America with Buddy.

After attending German championships, British alsatian breeders visit Potsdam school and Lady Kitty Ritson is given Lona, a former guide dog.

1929 .... Morris Frank and Mrs Eustis start The Seeing Eye in America.

1930 .... Letters in the press lead to Miss Muriel Crooke's interest in guide dogs. Mrs Eustis offers encouragement and help. NIB interested but cautious.

Miss Crooke acquires makeshift facilities for running a trial training course in Wallasey.

1931 .... First organising committee formed and affiliated to NIB.

Mrs Eustis lends William Debetaz from The Seeing Eye in America to run the trial course in Wallasey.

October: Four guide dogs and their blind owners complete the first trial course.

1932 .... Mrs Eustis lends Georges Gabriel from Switzerland for a second course and he stays on to run a third in 1933.

The Tail-Waggers' Club adopts guide dogs as its 'official charity'.

1933 .... Committee agree to NIB and St Dunstan's memorandum restricting guide dog appeals to doggy circles.

NIB rejects informal approach to take over fund-raising for guide dogs and committee ask the Tail-Waggers' Club to assume financial responsibility.

Captain Nikolai Liakhoff arrives, initially for one year, but stays on as first permanent trainer.

1934............................ The Guide Dogs for the Blind Association formed, backed financially and administratively by the Tail-Waggers' Club. The club's founder, Captain Hobbs, becomes treasurer and A. Croxton-Smith chairman.

1935............................ Wallasey Corporation offers the Association a large old house, The Cliff, at a nominal rent as a training centre.

Mr (later Sir) Victor Schuster becomes treasurer, following the death of Captain Hobbs.

1937............................ Discussions about a possible takeover by the NIB come to nothing.

Sir Victor Schuster succeeds A. Croxton-Smith as chairman.

Lady Freda Valentine joins executive committee and council.

1938............................ An early (unsupervised) puppy-walking scheme gets poor results and does not last.

In crisis atmosphere following German invasion of Sudetenland, alsatian breeding drops off and Association turns its attention to border collies.

The Earl of Athlone becomes first Royal patron. The Earl of Derby becomes president.

1939............................ Outbreak of war. The Cliff taken over by anti-aircraft battery. Number of working guide dogs reaches 76.

Further talk of NIB takeover.

Lady Freda Valentine becomes hon. treasurer (and holds post for another 39 years).

1940............................ Deteriorating relationships with Captain and Mrs Liakhoff lead to Miss Crooke's resignation.

Edmondscote Manor in Leamington Spa purchased and becomes first permanent training centre.

1942............................ Work continues after difficulties of early war years with three female apprentices and an annual output of 22 guide dogs.

1944............................ Captain V.M. Deane succeeds Sir Victor Schuster as chairman.

1945 .... War in Europe ends with the Association expanding and in a satisfactory financial position.

1947 .... Council considers asking St Dunstan's to take over the Association.

1948 .... Tail-Waggers decide they can no longer continue sponsorship and administrative support and the Association establishes its own office in London at 81 Piccadilly.

Sir Victor Schuster resumes chairmanship on Captain Deane's resignation due to ill health.

Captain Sington, one of the original 'nucleus', becomes president on the death of the Earl of Derby, but dies later in the year.

1949 .... Council considers setting up a second training centre, but deterred by cost.

In December all four training staff and one kennel maid resign after a crisis in relationships with Captain Liakhoff.

1950 .... Rebel staff persuaded to return and run a second centre outside of Captain Liakhoff's control. Cleve House, Exeter, purchased.

Liakhoff rebuilds staff at Leamington.

Roger Eckersley appointed as first general manager.

1952 .... The Earl of Lanesborough succeeds Sir Victor Schuster as chairman.

1953 .... Guide dog harnesses change from brown to white.

1954 .... Princess Alexandra becomes president.

First steps towards a systematic aftercare service.

Circle of Guide Dog Owners formed.

1955 .... Roger Eckersley dies and is succeeded as general manager by Charles Maton.

1956 .... Inspired and led by Callum McLean, a member of the council, puppy-walking starts in earnest.

1957 .... Princess Alexandra becomes patron on the death of the Earl of Athlone.

1958 .... After a long-running dispute the Association tells the RNIB it no longer feels bound by the 1932 fund-raising agreement.

Failing health forces Captain Liakhoff to give up post of director of training to become consultant.

Decision to spay all bitches in future. (Castration of dogs follows in mid-1960s.)

Number of working guide dogs reaches 500.

Annual output of trained dogs: 89.

1960......................... 'Flourishing' financial position reported at AGM.

Puppy-walking scheme achieves 40 per cent success rate.

Breeding programme begins to develop.

1961......................... A third training centre opens at Bolton.

Charles Maton dies and Sir Michael Nall appointed general secretary, becoming general manager in 1962.

1962......................... Captain Liakhoff dies two weeks after retiring at the age of 65.

Head office moves to Ealing.

1963......................... Aftercare service now well established, with 769 visits to guide dog owners during the year.

1964......................... The Earl of Lanesborough becomes president after handing over chairmanship to Sir Joseph Napier.

Paul McConnell succeeds Sir Michael Nall as general manager.

1965......................... Forfar training centre opens.

Number of working dogs passes 1,000 and annual output reaches 199.

Aftercare visits: 948.

1966......................... Derek Freeman becomes first breeding and puppy-walking manager.

1967......................... Paul McConnell leaves and Dick Forrester becomes general manager.

1970......................... Tollgate House, near Warwick, opens as a specialised breeding and puppy-walking centre.

Head office moves to better premises in Ealing.

1972......................... Dick Forrester resigns and Tony Clark becomes general manager.

Healthy financial position leads to introduction of maintenance allowance to help owners with feeding costs of their guide dogs.

Standard 50p nominal charge replaces voluntary contribution by students for their guide dogs.

1974.......................... General manager's title changed to director general.

1975.......................... Kenneth Butler succeeds Sir Joseph Napier as chairman.

First meeting of the Guide Dog Owner Liaison Committee.

Number of working dogs: 2,122.

Guide dogs trained: 401.

Aftercare visits: 2,107.

1977.......................... Fifth training centre opens at Wokingham.

1978.......................... Staff Consultative Committee formed.

Lady Freda Valentine relinquishes the post of hon. treasurer.

Head office moves to Windsor.

1980.......................... Council sets age limit of 75 for its members and 70 for its chairman.

Ian Findlay succeeds Kenneth Butler as chairman.

1981.......................... Golden Jubilee celebrations.

1982.......................... Guide dog ownership reaches 3,000.

Output: 575. Aftercare visits: 3,763.

1983.......................... Sixth training centre opens at Middlesbrough.

Major General John Groom succeeds Tony Clark as director general.

1984.......................... Management restructuring creates seven operational regions based on the major training centres.

Start of programme to give guide dog instructors additional skills in orientation and mobility training.

First mini-centre opens in Belfast.

1986.......................... The Earl of Lanesborough retires from the presidency.

Seventh training centre opens at Redbridge.

Second mini-centre opens in Cardiff.

1987.......................... Colin Macpherson succeeds Ian Findlay as chairman.

1988.......................... After Colin Macpherson's resignation due to ill health, and subsequent death, Dennis Armstrong becomes chairman.

1989 .... Julian Oxley succeeds John Groom as director general.

Hillfields, near Reading, purchased for head office move in 1991/2.

Third mini-centre opens in Maidstone.

Number of working guide dogs: 3,946.

Guide dogs trained: 674.

Aftercare visits: 7,669.

1990 .... Fourth mini-centre opens in Glasgow.

Sources

Among the documentary sources on which I have drawn the most important are:

1. The Association's minute books, annual reports, training reports and numerous other records, including its journal *Forward*.
2. Correspondence, notes and records left by Miss Crooke and now in the Association's archives.
3. Correspondence and minutes from the archives of the RNIB and St Dunstan's.

Interviews, transcripts of which are now in the Association's archives, have been valuable in providing memories and anecdotes to fill out the documentary record. Many of the past and present members of the staff and general council of the Association, guide dog owners and others who have talked to me are identified in the text.

Other sources (for chapter 1 except where shown otherwise) are as follows:

A Brief History of Dog Guides for the Blind, a well-documented and scholarly account by Nelson Coon, published by The Seeing Eye in the United States in 1959, has provided much of the information about the association between dogs and blind people before the 20th century. Mr Coon compiled his book from the resources available at the Blindiana Reference Library of the Perkins School for the Blind in Watertown, Massachusetts, where he was head librarian. Another authority is Dr Hans Haupt, who wrote a history of the origins of guide dogs in *Kriegs-Blinden Yahr-Buch* (Year Book for the War-Blinded) in 1951. An article in *Forward* 1958 is based on this account. Haupt also outlines the early history of guide dogs in an article in *World Veteran* of May 1958.

Thomas Bewick's reference to dogs leading the blind, from his book *A General History of Quadrupeds* (1807), is taken from Nelson Coon's history.

Johann Wilhelm Klein described his method of training dogs to lead the blind in *Lehrbuch zum Unterrichte der Blinden* (Textbook for Teaching the Blind), which was published in Vienna in 1819. The passage quoted in chapter 1 is a translation taken from Nelson Coon's history.

Leon Whitney's account of blind men being led by American fox terriers on the end of a rigid cane is contained in a letter dated 11 December 1967 to Mike Csernovits, a member of the Association's staff.

The account of the origins of guide dog training in Germany is based mainly on a thesis and paper delivered in September 1986, on the occasion of the 70th anniversary of the start of the modern guide dog movement, by Giselher Mueller, senior instructor of the Johann August Zeune School for the Blind, Berlin-Steglitz.

The number of guide dogs in Germany in the early 1930s is taken from a Report to the World Conference on Work for the Blind, May 1931, given by Mrs Eustis, and a letter from her to Richard O'Farrell dated 2 February 1932.

Sir Arthur Pearson's doubts about guide dogs in 1919 were expressed in his book *Victory Over Blindness.*

Details of the early days of Fortunate Fields are taken from *Dogs Against Darkness* by Dickson Hartwell.

Morris Frank's experiences are taken from his book *First Lady of the Seeing Eye* (1957).

The book in which Lieutenant Colonel E.H. Richardson made his chauvinistic comments about the popularity of alsatians after the First World War (chapter 2) is *Watch Dogs, their Training and Management* (Hutchinson, 1923).

Alfred Morgan's tribute, in chapter 6, to the way his 'war dog' Fly coped with the effects of the blitz is taken from an article in *The "Tail-Wagger" Magazine* of February 1942.

Lord Fraser's tribute to W.G. Askew (chapter 7) is contained in *My Story of St Dunstan's* (1961) and John Colligan's comment was made in an interview with the author.

Index

Numbers in italics refer to illustrations